THE FAMILY OUTING

THE FAMILY OUTING

A Memoir

Jessi Hempel

HarperOne
An Imprint of HarperCollinsPublishers

The names and identifying characteristics of some individuals in this book have been changed to protect their privacy.

HarperCollins books may be purchased for educational, business, or sales promotional use. For information, please email the Special Markets Department at SPsales@harpercollins.com.

FIRST EDITION

Designed by Kyle O'Brien

Library of Congress Cataloging-in-Publication Data is available upon request.

ISBN 978-0-06-307901-4
ISBN 978-0-06-328197-4 (Intl)

22 23 24 25 26 LSC 10 9 8 7 6 5 4 3 2 1

For Felix, Alexandra, Jude, Sebastian, August, and Alice Camille

Table of Contents

PART FOUR *Heal*

THE FAMILY OUTING

Prologue

Everyone has secrets. I exist because of two secrets—one acute and un-usual, belonging to my mother, and one common and culturally con-demned, belonging to my father. These hidden truths worked their way into the fabric of my being, coming up through me. My parents' shame became my shame. Without ever being told, I learned what I could share about myself and what I had to hide. I didn't have a name for this, only a fear that I was in danger.

I dreamed about this before I had language for it. It's my earliest memory that I know to be all my own. I must be almost three, because I don't remember being in my crib. I already sleep in a big-girl bed, with a mesh safety net attached to it. This bed is nestled against one pink-patterned wall of a room where my dad, a law student, studies. Our fam-ily lives in a duplex in Acton, Massachusetts, with train tracks that cut a line through the backyard. In a house nearby are Raina and Bill Rice, the landlords. They are retirees who have shells and sea artifacts all over their home from Bill's scuba-diving hobby. Raina is a mousy woman with tightly curled white hair. Bill is good-natured, grandfatherly. He gives me orange soda when I visit. But in the dream, I awake to noise outside my window. This is the confusing part, when I am awaking but still asleep in a dream—the reason that, later, I will be so certain that these events actually happened. Dream-me pulls back the curtain and peeks out the window, and there are Raina and Bill coming toward me, flanked by a fireman and a police officer. The sky behind them is orange and red, dusky, opening up as if it will swallow all of us. Raina has a black pistol. Bill is pointing a green water gun at me. They know what I have done, who I am. If they reach me, they will shoot me. I'm sure of it. I'm screaming. I'm screaming in my sleep so loud that I have screamed myself awake.

Then my mother is there. She's lifting me up out of my bed, and she sits down in the mahogany rocker that my grandparents in Ypsilanti bought my parents for their first Christmas together. Adrenaline runs through my body as I try to explain the danger. But I don't have enough language yet. I can only express that there is someone outside the window. My mother reaches forward and pulls the curtains open, says there is nothing. I don't believe her.

For a while, this happens most nights. We sit there in the chair. My mother is trying to help me, but she can't understand the danger. I can't communicate it to her. When I think about it then, and even when I think about it now, my arms freeze up so that I cannot lift them. Eventually my mother carries me back to my parents' room, to the large waterbed they share. It's one of those mid-1970s mainstays, one big bag of water that sloshes anytime anyone moves. I'm sandwiched between my parents. I know that I must lie very still if I'm going to be permitted to stay, that I must try to sleep. And there, right there in between their bodies, my mom's elbow draped over me, I relax. I'm safe. But I can never sleep. I can't stay still, and the waterbed roils like the ocean every time I move. No one is sleeping. Now my parents are annoyed with me. Dad lifts me up to return me to my bed. "No," I cry. *No. I'll be killed, the landlords are coming for me.* Dad carries me through the kitchen and back into our shared bedroom-study. He tucks me into bed and then plops into the rocker, waiting and waiting for me to sleep.

THIS DREAM STAYS WITH ME in the years that follow. I have it when I am six and seven, and I wake up in a cold sweat. By now, I've learned not to call for my parents when dreams scare me. They cannot make it better. And anyhow, now we live in a four-bedroom split-level on a cul-de-sac in

Greenville, South Carolina, and Raina and Bill are still back in Massachusetts. I know as soon as the adrenaline shoots my body into waking that there is no one outside my window. I pad down the hall to the bathroom and pour a glass of water that I drink slowly. This is the first time I remember thinking I'm a bad person.

I have the dream at nine, as we move to another new house. We are back in Massachusetts, staying with my aunt while we get settled. Katje, Evan, and I sleep on the floor of my aunt's study like a pile of puppies. Katje is five and Evan is three, and as I watch them sleep, I'm angry at them for their relative youth and innocence. It doesn't occur to me that they may already have fear and shame, too.

For a little while, the dream comes frequently again. I'm nervous about starting another new school. Then I make some friends and get to know my teacher. The dream recedes.

At sixteen, when I've figured out that (maybe possibly but not for sure) I am gay, the dream comes back. I'm old enough to notice how the emotions it conjures are filtered through a younger me, toddler-sized, amorphous and physically grounded in my body. Raina and Bill are there, more muted, with their guns. Now they feel more distant. As scared as I am, I'm also curious. In the dream, I know that I'm in the dream. I can pause it in still frames, but I can't figure out how to move closer to the figures who are pursuing me. I wake up panicked and sweaty.

The last time I have the dream is when I'm twenty-four. I live in the Bay Area, and I've just started therapy with a therapist I don't perceive to be helpful because I don't feel better after I speak to her. I tell this woman everything I know about myself. She's like the garbage barge that runs along the bottom of the river dredging up sediment so that the water becomes cloudy, leaving it for something else to clean. Only what I don't realize then is that the work is the dredging. Cloudy waters come clean on their own.

I tell her about the dream, about how it makes me feel. And then I never have it again.

———

WHAT HAPPENED TO ME? I used to think this question was important, that in its answer was the reason I didn't have the things I thought I wanted in my adulthood—namely, love, partnership, a relationship whose bottom wouldn't fall out. The security of knowing that the bottom of my own life wouldn't fall out. So starting in my late twenties, I'd sit in a therapist's office every Thursday morning and explore my memory: Did Bill abuse me? Did someone hurt me? Did the twin secrets of my family doom me?

I thought I was the expert on my messy, overwhelming family then. I thought I understood my parents, that their missteps were both unusual and unfortunate. I thought I understood my brother and my sister, that their indignities were somehow undeserved compared with my own. I've always been an effective storyteller, I think. If you had asked me about my family back then, I would have held you in an uncomfortable mix of horror and pity with stories about my adolescence, about Mom's depression and Dad's absence, and then left you laughing with the punch line: "We all came out of the closet, and now we're okay!"

You would feel satisfied with this ending. You would feel better.

I would not.

That was when I believed that pain was earned instead of felt, and I hadn't earned the right to claim it yet. When the feelings came, rising like a tsunami threatening to take me under, I pushed them back. I worked out or went out partying. I drank enough to forget for a few minutes, or I threw myself into an article I was researching. I was thirty by then, a grown woman with a media career and a big hole where I felt a family should be. I wrote cover stories for magazines and had a regular spot on the ABC News's morning program as a technology expert. And sometimes, because of circumstances that felt largely out of my control and that I couldn't predict, the feelings would overpower me. I had a name for this. I called it the emotional flu. I'd sit in the bathroom of my apartment, under the sink, holding my head between my elbows, rocking. Silent screams emerged in heavy gasps. Time collapsed and turned in on itself. I missed deadlines, flaked on email. Once I arrived unprepared for a live spot on CNN. I was booked to comment on the 2012 Olympics, which would be held in London. "What do you think of the surprise city choice?" the anchor asked me, because evidently everyone thought the location would be Paris. And reflecting back now, I can imagine any number of things I might have been able to say. But at the time, I looked dead-eyed at the anchor and said nothing.

Five seconds of nothing on live TV is terrifying. It's a break in reality. It's a crisis. It's what drove me to therapy.

"How do you feel?" the therapist would ask me. How am I supposed to know how I feel until I know what prompted how I felt?

"I'm trying to remember what happened," I'd answer. There's what I think happened. There are the made-up bits I've told people along the way, exaggerated for the sake of the story or withheld for fear of the same. There's my dad's version of the story. There's what my mom believes. There's our childhood according to my brother and my sister, neither of whom understood the other in our youth. I'd fall silent until my brain hurt and I zoned out, and then I'd ask the therapist, "What happened to me?"

I spent a decade trying to answer this question. Now I know that the answer is as irrelevant as it is unknowable. Our memories are imperfect. In every retelling, we expand them. We change details, and then we tell the important stories so many times that those details become truer than the original details. What matters is the emotional seat of an experience, and this can change with time. The terror I felt in my childhood nightmare about Bill and Raina is true. So is the freedom that came from speaking it.

WE ALL CAME OUT OF THE CLOSET, and now we're okay. These things are correlated, but they are not causal. Coming out was an inevitability. For close to two decades, my family lived in the shadow of our closets. We lived with the pain that comes from hiding one's most authentic self and the pain that comes from being raised by people who are hiding their most authentic selves. It was a shame that began on the inside and spilled out of us. Disguising this shame took effort. It took thinking and planning and always being on the verge of being found out. It took lying, and lying about the lies. It took our life force. Collectively, we reached a point where the hiding had robbed us of our oxygen. Something had to change, or we would die.

Then, in the space of five years, like a chain reaction that couldn't be stopped once it had been set in motion, we each revealed our secrets, first to ourselves and then to everyone: I came out as lesbian. Dad announced he was gay. Katje told us she was bisexual. Evan found the courage to say he was transgender. And Mom found the voice to call herself a survivor of a series of crimes so reprehensible that I could only allow myself to learn about them in small doses over many years.

But revealing our secrets is not the same as living our truths. We came out of the closet. Also, now we're okay. I'd go so far as to say we are thriving. As a family, we're close. My dad takes yoga over Zoom and cooks luscious meals of food he grows. My mom just finished another continuing education class for her counseling practice. My sister and her wife have just had their second child, a pandemic baby. My brother's second child arrived a month later. It was early in the pandemic and COVID was raging, so he chose to deliver at home, his wife counting the seconds between his contractions. My newest nephew arrived less than an hour after the first contraction.

And me. Somehow I've come through it. I have the things I never believed I'd be able to have: My own family. A wife. Children. A gentle confidence that I'm not about to fall out of the bottom of my life. But all of that is a proxy for the way that I am able to feel. I love, and a lot of the time, I feel loved.

MY SON IS NEARLY THE same age as I was when I first had the shame dream. I can hear him upstairs, talking with his other mother. His language is coming in phrases. He repeats things. "I go the whole wide world, go the whole wide world just to find her," the radio plays softly. My wife sings along to the end of the song as she moves around the living room: "Just to find her." And then there's Jude: "Jutht to find er."

He's just starting to pick up words. But even now, his memories are taking shape. They live within his body. And already, he has a strong sense of what is unjust. He falls constantly in the way that new walkers do, and he brings his scrapes to us to witness. "Boom," he tells us, and shows us with a hand motion where he has fallen, what table edge has bonked him. So many bonks. He still has perfect faith that telling us will release the pain.

He isn't wrong.

This pattern of correspondence is something we all eventually forget. Not how to name what has hurt us, but how to listen to those we love who have been hurt. How to listen to ourselves, to take our own pain seriously. Right now, I listen for Jude's cries and attend to his bonks. "Explain what happened," I tell him. He goes through the details maybe eight times. The table edge. The floorboard. The stumble. He uses grand hand motions, and I nod and reassure him: "I hear you. And look, you are okay."

This will change, slowly. Before he forgets how to tell me what hurts, I will forget how to listen well. This is almost a guarantee. So he'll start to edit his fears, to share with me only what he believes I'll deem worthy of sympathy. He'll take the rest to someone else who may listen better, or he'll tuck it inside to let it fester. This is how a secret is made.

WHAT HAPPENED TO US? This is the question I asked my family. I wanted to find out what would happen if I really listened to their answers. What did our individual closets do to us? And where did our liberation take root? At the start of 2020, I called everyone to see if I could interview them about coming out. There were so many things that none of us had ever spoken about. Up until then, I would sooner talk to strangers about what transpired in my home than talk to the people who had lived through it alongside me. There was too much of a threat that our stories wouldn't align, that this misalignment would be painful. I feared these conversations would shake my own fragile confidence in the peace I'd found in my adulthood.

The gift of the pandemic was a shift in perspective. In 2020, we had time—hours that accumulated into days that rolled on and on with little structure. Our goals dissolved. Our social lives disappeared. After an early frenetic month of Zoom socializing, we fell out of touch with the people around us. But the five of us—my father, my mother, my sister and brother—leaned in to one another. Quarantining in five separate houses in four different states, we called and texted and Zoomed. With COVID-19 raging, we were aware of our mortality, conscious of the fact that we had to work for our connectedness. So I asked whether I could try, at least, to synthesize our disparate narratives. Could I deliver a story that felt like truth to all of us?

The first person to bless this book was my mom, the person with whom I struggled the most. Dad and Evan signed on shortly after. "It scares me," Evan told me. "Which is why I think we should do it." Katje let the idea sit for a few weeks, taking the time to fully consider the implications of sharing her thoughts, filtered through my words, with you. But then she agreed, too, because that is what we have become: a group of people who are willing to trust one another. We all understand that there is no one story of a family, but instead competing stories that contain overlapping truths, some of which are contradictory.

Independent of the details, we can all agree on this: We were broken. We broke one another. We hurt one another. Things seemed irreparable. And then we let go. That is when we grew. We became people who knew how to love and feel loved, people who loved themselves. And, improbably, we grew into a family again—a different kind of family, reflecting a new set of values. Every version of ourselves is okay in this family. Every mistake is embraced. Missteps are tolerated. We turn to one another in difficult moments. We delight in one another. What happened to us?

In talking about the hero's path, Joseph Campbell wrote, "We must be willing to let go of the life we planned so as to have the life that is waiting for us." The life we planned is always mapped outside of us, born of a value system inscribed by our culture, our religious institutions, our television shows, our parents' fears and perceived failures. The life that awaits us is mapped entirely within. It is expansive, a waterfall of liquid love. Coming out is the act of letting go of our planned lives in pursuit of the lives that wait for all of us. It requires us to listen well to each other, to make room for the people we love most to reveal the secrets that change who they are to us. It requires us to make peace with our own secrets. This is a story about how my family made that peace.

PART ONE

Origin

ONE

The Stakeout

Of all the details my mom has told me about the Michigan murders, one evening remains lodged in my imagination. It's one of those stormy July nights, that midwestern summer storm weather that hangs thick in the air, thunder tumbling across the top of the clouds, until the sky breaks open, spewing wind and water everywhere. That summer, Mom is eighteen. She's already in bed, finally drifting into a preoccupied sleep, when the phone rings. Her father, Kermit Berry, gets to the receiver by the second ring. I can imagine her straining to pick up his words. The water pelt-pelts so that she cannot hear the conversation happening just outside her bedroom door. She can only tell that Kermit is mostly listening, as though he is taking instructions.

She knows without being told. Karen Beineman has been found.

The call is brief—a few affirmative grunts, and then Kermit drops the receiver into its cradle. In the slit of light beneath her bedroom door, Mom sees his stocking feet, motionless as he takes the news in. She flips on her nightstand light to signal to Kermit that she's awake. She hopes he'll come talk to her, reassure her. These nights, when she sits in her bed and worries, have become increasingly frequent. Her questions are always the same.

Why are girls still disappearing? It has been two years since the first woman turned up. A year after that, almost to the day, a twenty-year-old art student appeared nearby, her body stabbed twenty-five times and raped. Things go quiet for a few months. Then, in the spring, the killer begins to pick up momentum. The murders come more often, every couple weeks. A law student. A teenage runaway. A middle schooler. The victims range in age, but they all have dark brown hair with a bit of a wave. They have pierced ears. They're around the same height—my mom's height. Their bodies have all turned up within five miles of Mom's home.

Who is the killer? Mom perseverates on this question. Surely she can figure it out. All of the victims have disappeared from Ypsilanti. They're women Mom mostly knows, or knows of. The student art teacher at the high school. The deacon's secretary at Mom's church, First Baptist. Many are students at the local college, Eastern Michigan University. These are smart women, women who read the newspapers, who know better than to get in a car with strangers—especially when the university is giving out mace keychains as warnings and the city has established a curfew. He, or they, must be someone everyone knows.

Now it seems a woman disappears every couple weeks, and Ypsilanti—all of Michigan—has become obsessed with finding the killer. Kermit is among the volunteers who support the police in their search. Special reports break into Mom's favorite television shows when victims turn up. A middling Hollywood psychic has checked himself into a nearby hotel to attempt to relaunch his career by solving these crimes. Newspapers as far away as London have picked up the story of these killings, of this town, giving the murderer a name: the Ypsilanti Slayer.

WHAT MIGHT IT BE LIKE for a young girl to grow up in 1960s Ypsilanti? When Mom tries to describe her childhood to me, there's an idyllic quality to her stories. It's an auto city, an hour outside of Detroit. Economically, it has already started a gentle decline, its largest factory having been shuttered a decade earlier as a result of a corporate merger. But many of her friends' fathers work at the smaller factories. The country is changing by the second half of the decade. There are race riots in Detroit. On the campus of nearby Eastern Michigan University, students are protesting US involvement in Vietnam. But Ypsi is a town with wide sidewalks where children ride their bikes between homes without supervision.

Until the murders, the worst day of my mom's life was the day John F. Kennedy was shot. She was in Mrs. Dalton's seventh grade class when the principal's voice came over the intercom. "He just turned on the radio," Mom remembers, "and everybody heard it at the same time." The president had been shot. "Some of the kids were laughing," she said. "And the teacher, she said in a very stern voice, 'Quiet, this is going to be a moment you will remember the rest of your lives.'" Then school was dismissed, and Mom walked home with her best friend, crying the entire way.

There is something cathartic to this communal grief, the way everyone leaned in together to express their sadness. It's out in the open. Everyone acknowledged it. Even now that we understand that JFK was a flawed human, a womanizer, and that his presidency was imperfect, we can look back and tap into that sadness. The iconic image of his two small children dressed in their funeral attire, little John-John saluting the president's casket. Can you feel it in your chest right now? This is permissible sadness. It's sadness without shame. There's nothing secret about it.

MOM IS THE BABY OF THE FAMILY, adored by her parents and both of her sisters. They are much older; by the time she is ten, they are out of the house. She loves the singer Andy Williams; JFK, may he rest in peace; and her guitar, which was a present for her fourteenth birthday. She has a face as round as those of the Campbell's Kids, from the soup ads, and chestnut hair that she rolls into curlers every evening to create the flip style that is popular at the time. Although she's very pretty, Mom thinks of herself as average—lovely but able to escape notice, not to be vain.

The family's house is a 1955 ranch with white aluminum siding and three tiny bedrooms. In the basement, Kermit has a study where he lifts weights and grades his papers. Later, in a sign that times are good economically, they finish off part of the basement as a den. There, in a wood-paneled walk-in closet, Kermit collects every issue of *LIFE* magazine, cataloged by date.

Mom adores her dad. Many of the local fathers still work in the smaller factories, but Kermit is a high school history teacher. He's five feet six on a good day, with a wide barrel chest, and he coaches the wrestling team. His students rarely win their matches, but this doesn't concern him. He's the kind of coach—and father—who cares more about strengthening the skills and self-esteem of his weakest players than honing the ambitions of his strongest. Kermit is also a prankster, and his favorite person to prank is his wife. I can still hear my grandma's voice, exasperated, calling down the hall, "Keeer-miiitttttt!" I can hear the eye roll in it.

Alice is a pianist with a dark curly bob and a nose tip that spreads out from her face like a mushroom cap. As a young woman, she studied with Ada Eddy, a pianist who learned from the great Polish musician Ignacy Jan Paderewski, and Alice would expect you to know who these people were. She teaches the Dunning Conservatory Method of piano to all the children in the neighborhood, as well as many of their mothers. By the time I know Alice, arthritis has encrusted her finger joints, making them cartoonishly large and painful. But Mom grows up to the sounds of "Für Elise" being plucked out on repeat every afternoon and often late into the evenings.

Starting in the first grade, Mom takes piano lessons from Alice, practicing during the only time the house is silent: before school. Mom has to work at it. Alice makes her work at it. For years, Mom's pretty good, and that is its own reward. By high school, she realizes Alice teaches children who have more natural talent, kids for whom the piano comes more easily. During a spring recital, Mom is two-thirds of the way through Rachmaninoff's Piano Concerto no. 2 when she forgets the ending. She remembers sitting on that bench on the small stage at the First Baptist Church, running through that penultimate chord progression on a loop, circling back to what she did remember so many times that it becomes obvious to everyone she has forgotten. The blood rushes to her face. Alice is watching from the wings. Mom stands and then storms offstage to the other side.

Everything I come to understand about what kind of mom Alice might have been is embodied by what happens next. She has watched her own daughter grow frustrated with the instrument Alice loves most. She has lived enough life to know that being the best at piano doesn't matter nearly as much as loving it. You can be the best at it and still just spend a lifetime teaching scales in your living room. It has never mattered to her whether her daughter has talent. Alice wants Mom to enjoy the playing. At home, after the recital, Mom strides into the kitchen to announce she's quitting. She doesn't want to practice, and she says she doesn't want to sit beside Alice on the bench any longer. She doesn't *like* the piano.

There is no power struggle here. However Alice feels about this, she is playing the long game. Her daughter will never love music if she doesn't come to it on her own. Alice lets Mom quit.

THE CENTER OF THE BERRY family's life is the First Baptist Church. Faith isn't so much a doctrine for them as it is a condition of their existence. Like oxygen in the air, they don't notice it, but they subsist because of it. Mom's best friend is the pastor's daughter, and the adults at the church are family, a couple dozen stand-in aunts and uncles who tend to her upbringing alongside her parents. That's probably the only reason Mom remembers that first murder, which happened when she had just finished tenth grade. The victim was a nineteen-year-old accounting student at Eastern Michigan University named Mary Fleszar. She'd been working as Earl Studt's secretary; he was a deacon at the church, and all of the adults were talking about the murder.

Two teens discovered Mary's body in a decrepit farmhouse near a cornfield. They were putting gas into a tractor when they heard a car door slam and voices in a deserted spot that had a reputation as a lover's lane. After the car pulled away, the boys went down to investigate. As they approached, they were overwhelmed by a putrid smell. Mary's corpse was so thoroughly decomposed that police relied on dental records to identify her remains. An autopsy later revealed that she had been stabbed at least thirty times in the chest and abdomen. One forearm and hand were missing. The fingers of her other hand had been removed. Her feet had been severed at the ankles.

To the people at First Baptist, it seemed to be a one-off tragedy. Apart from the murmuring at church, Mom barely remembers the murder. But not everyone dismissed the incident. At the time, a police investigator told the victim's family, "If we don't catch the perpetrator within thirty days, he will kill again, with increasing frequency within the next year or so."

THE STORMY NIGHT THAT KAREN'S body turned up is two years later. By now, the killer has picked up his pace. An informal curfew is in place for teenagers, and Kermit is one of many Ypsi men who have volunteered for searches, stakeouts, and the more banal nightly neighborhood watches. From her bedroom, Mom hears Kermit shuffle into the bathroom and close the door, hears the sound of his belt buckle, the clink of the metal clip that holds his billy club to his belt. He's going somewhere.

Mom really wants to get up and make her dad a coffee, but she can't bring herself to move from her bed. You know how sometimes anxiety washes over you irrationally, like a panic attack, and your arms seize up and your heart starts a sprint in your chest? That's how Mom explains it to me. You're lying in your bed, and you don't want to breathe. You're in the same house as the people who have reared you and exist to protect you, but they exist in a different dimension. The rain has picked up, disguising any outside noise apart from the heavy pounding of the storm. Mom clutches a pillow and looks at the lock on the one window in her room—she's fine, she's okay. She starts counting her breaths and then the door cracks open. Kermit pokes his head in. "Still up, pal?" he says. He always calls her "pal."

"Yeah." Mom sits up in bed, pushing the covers back. She feels instantly herself again. "Where're you going?"

"They found the body," Kermit says. So Karen is dead.

Rather than alert the media, police are gathering volunteers to stake out the woodsy area where Karen's body has turned up in hopes the killer might return. Mom turns this around in her mind. She wants to know a lot, but also nothing.

"The weather is awful, Dad," she says. It isn't a statement so much as an attempt at a question. Why does he think it will do any good to search in the rain?

"I know," he replies. When Mom tells me this part, she doesn't say that her father lingered there, watching her, not wanting to set out into the night and leave her. She doesn't mention that Kermit noticed the way she still sat with her legs crossed as she had as a little girl. It's not something that registered for Mom. But this is how I imagine it now that I have traveled to the middle of my own life and know exactly how much of it there is to lose.

BEFORE THIS NIGHT, THE ONLY time Kermit spoke to Mom about the murders was the evening he returned from his first volunteer police force meeting. Mom was on the front porch, just out of Alice's earshot, and he put a hand on Mom's shoulder to stop her from going in. The police had shared details of the murderers' approach that hadn't made it into the media: Kermit had learned that with every body, the killer had become more brutal. Kermit was usually a jokester, always starting something, but that night his face was drawn, giving away his own anxiety even as he tried to suppress it. He handed Mom a small bottle of pepper spray. "Here, keep this in your purse."

"What happened tonight?" she asked.

Kermit didn't answer her question. "I know you don't do this," he said, "but no hitching a ride with anyone you don't know well."

"Did they say anything about the suspects?" she tried again.

"Your mom would prefer it if you were home by dark."

Mom remembers this as The Talk, one of the only talks they ever had about the Ypsilanti Slayer. She learned most of what she knew from the news. Or from her girlfriends, who'd pass around unreported details and unsubstantiated rumors in equal measure. *Did you hear the murderer is dressing up as a police officer? Did you see he returned to that old abandoned house and left an earlier victim's earring?* She collected these pieces of fact and fiction, doused them in time, and then attempted to forget them for several decades. When she finally tried to put the whole story together, like a vase that shatters and is glued back together, it was almost unrecognizable. But the story of a memory—the way that it shapes you—doesn't rely on a time line of events for its meaning. It's made up of the feelings beneath. The facts, and their order, exist only to propel us to the truth of the experience.

Fifty-one years later, I ask Mom to tell me everything she remembers about that summer. It's the first of a dozen conversations we'll have for The Project. It's a summer day, three months into the global pandemic, and both of us have time. We're home, in separate places, just as we've each been for months. She lives with her two elderly dogs in a house full of windows in central Massachusetts. She's an artist, now, and a therapist, and her practice is booming as her clients grapple with the impact of the COVID-19 pandemic and its accompanying quarantine. For Mom, some good things have emerged: She can work over Zoom now, seeing clients from her easy chair. And her kids—Katje, Evan, and I—call even more often. I speak to her briefly almost every day in 2020. But these calls for The Project are different, more formal, a collective investigation of our past. First we FaceTime, and I can see her brown hair, gray barely visible around her temples, her pronounced cheekbones. I realize I want to record the chat, so we switch away from FaceTime. I don't realize it at first, but the audio-only phone is better. Without the distraction of our faces, we are each free to listen more fully.

Mom's slow to speak. She's reaching, as if her memory is a chest that can be opened and explored—as if we're both sitting by that chest, taking turns peering inside, trying to make sense of its contents. In our conversations about the evening of the stakeout, she's the one to point out her memories' discrepancies. "Well, see now, that's where things don't add up," she muses.

I pause, trying not to fill in her details.

She continues. "I have it in my head that Dad went to a cemetery." She falls silent for so long I think our connection has cut out. "I thought Karen's body was found propped against a tombstone, that that's where the stakeout was," she said. "But it couldn't have been."

She's right.

Karen's body was dumped in a gully off Riverside near the Huron River in neighboring Ann Arbor. I know this because my mom wasn't the only one haunted by the events of 1969. Most of what I learned about the Michigan murders did not come from her. It was recorded in the archives of the *Ypsilanti Press* and the *Detroit News*, where by 1969 local reporters published updates nearly every day. Or it was documented in a multipart special report that ran in the *Detroit Free Press* on the fiftieth anniversary of the murders. Or it came from the retired high school teacher who was an EMU student at the same time as the killer and looked just enough like him to be haunted by the event for an entire lifetime. The teacher had made it his business to report and capture as much of the story as he could and self-publish a true crime book called *Terror in Ypsilanti*.

That's how I know that on the night the phone startles Mom awake, Kermit joins a group of men who squat in the stormy woods, waiting for the killer's return. By then, they know their suspect often returns to visit his victims. The police have removed Karen's body, which was covered in tiny blond hair clippings and brutalized beyond recognition. They've replaced it with a mannequin. No one has called Karen's family yet. It's part of the media blackout intended to lure the suspect back. The rain falls in sheets, clouding the men's view. Sometime after one a.m., there's a rustle. A man creeps through the woods toward the body. As Kermit and his crew watch, the suspect draws close enough that he can touch Karen's hand. Close enough to see that the victim is plaster, fake. Then he flees, showing a comfort with the woods that his pursuers lack. The men rush through the muck and the rain, tripping over themselves until they realize he's gone. He has escaped capture again.

TWO

Crush

The next morning, Mom doesn't ask about what happened, and Kermit doesn't volunteer any information. I imagine her waking up late, her stomach in knots, realizing she's supposed to be at work. She breezes past her dad at the kitchen table to the counter where Alice stirs oatmeal. Kermit scans the paper, brooding, drinking his coffee black because they're out of cream. That's how she knows the stakeout has failed. Mom doesn't usually drink coffee, but Alice pours her a cup. Mom slugs it down. She leans into Alice for a side hug and then clatters out to the driveway, the screen door banging behind her.

Mom is a clerk at the Montgomery Ward at Arborland, the outdoor mall. "Monkey Ward" is what her friends call it. It has everything. Watches. Winter coats. Women's shoes, and men's too. She's worked summers there since her sophomore year and plans to keep the job when she starts a nursing program at EMU in the fall. She's a floater, which means that she moves from department to department to fill in where people need help. She usually opts for the shoe department, if given a choice, because then she makes a small commission on her sales. Also, Arnie works there, a fact that has come to matter more and more in recent weeks. As she pulls the car into the lot, she says a quick prayer— she really does believe God listens to her prayers—that she's assigned to shoes, that he is working.

The TV is blaring in the break room by the time she punches in. Her colleagues are gathered around it, watching the newscaster's special report as the cameras pass over the woods, which are threaded with yellow crime scene tape. Mom checks the clipboard, and God has delivered! She's in shoes for her entire shift.

The TVs are so annoying. Just for a little bit, Mom doesn't want to think about the news, the murders. She doesn't know it, but this is the day that will change her.

WHEN MOM THINKS ABOUT KAREN'S disappearance, it almost seems to be the girl's fault. Mom doesn't really believe this, but it's hard for her not to think about it this way, even now. Everyone knew about the Ypsilanti Slayer by then. Young women avoided strangers. They didn't go places alone. And there was Karen, exactly the same age as Mom. Like Mom, Karen had long dark brown hair and pierced ears—just the killer's type. She'd planned to study special education in the fall, enrolling early to take some summer classes. Also like Mom, Karen had been scared. She'd requested a room on a higher floor specifically so no one could climb into her window in the night. In a letter to her parents, mailed one day earlier, she insisted she was being careful.

When I ask Mom what she remembers about Karen, or any of the victims, she has an encyclopedic capacity to produce the details. She's sitting in her leather recliner again, the FaceTime feature on her phone angled so that I can see only her forehead and hair. This is also the place where she still googles regularly to see whether any new details on the murders have cropped up.

Here's what she has learned: On July 23, Karen finished up lunch with her dormmates around twelve fifteen p.m. It was a warm, humid day, and she asked whether anyone wanted to walk downtown with her to pick up a hairpiece at Wigs by Joan. She had no takers, so she set off for the mile walk down wide, well-lit streets. The next person to see Karen was Joan, the wig store proprietor, who noticed the girl hop off the back of a motorcycle. The women chatted as Joan wrapped up Karen's hairpiece. Karen joked that she'd made two foolish errors in her life, buying a wig and jumping on a stranger's bike. "I've got to be either the bravest or the dumbest girl alive, because I've just accepted a ride from this guy," Karen said. As she left, Joan stepped out onto the sidewalk to have a look at him. She described him as white with defined cheekbones and a green-and-yellow striped shirt, riding a Triumph motorcycle.

Joan watched Karen attempt to decline a ride home and then change her mind and climb up behind him. When Karen didn't turn up before her eleven p.m. curfew, her roommate told the dorm adviser, who called the police.

Mom is aware of the myriad choices a young woman makes in a day, the people you trust for little things here and there. You stop to fill the car with gas. Or you follow a salesman into a quiet part of a store. You trust a policeman to drive you home after curfew. It takes only one slip, one miscalculation. What was Karen thinking? Mom is still angry with her. To think of it in any other light is to admit a vulnerability, to own up to the truth that bad things happen to people and we won't always see them coming. We can't always protect ourselves.

ONE HALLMARK OF THE IMPACT of persistent danger is our ability to partition it off and live as if it doesn't exist. This is how Mom survives the summer of 1969. By the time she fastens her name tag—"ANN"—to her blouse for the day at Montgomery Ward, she's lost in the minidramas of an adolescent social life. Mostly, this involves thinking about her crush, Arnie. He's older; he's just finished up at Eastern Michigan University. And he is handsome. Arnie has a shock of dark hair that falls across his forehead and charismatic eyes.

A month ago, they'd started having lunch together in the break room. They had so much to talk about. Mom was a guitarist, and Arnie played banjo in a band. He joked with her in that flirty kind of way. "Guitars are for broken-hearted teenage girls," he'd say. She'd scowl, but inside, she was pleased by the attention. And then he asked for her phone number.

The first time Arnie calls, he offers to play her something he's been working on. Mom is a phone talker; it's her medium. The phone's base hangs on the wall at the end of the hall, and she splays out on the floor beneath it, stretching her legs up the wall the way she does when she is talking to Nina or Becky. She can hear Arnie place the phone down in front of his instrument and then the strings pick up. These calls become regular. An hour might go by, longer. I think of Alice, stepping over Mom's torso as she traipses back to bed in their tiny house, then poking fun at Mom for this in the mornings.

Arnie lives in a boardinghouse across town with a shared phone, so Mom never calls him because she never knows who might answer. She waits and hopes, and most nights, she goes to bed disappointed. But when he does call, he opens up. There is something safe and distant about the phone that allows for this. He tells her about his life; about his fraternity at EMU; about his best friend, John, who lives across the hall. Arnie talks a lot about his motorcycle. This would bore Mom if she didn't have the kind of infatuation with him that leaves her hanging on his every word.

ONCE, MOM GOES TO HEAR Arnie's band. He plays at a local bar on Wednesday nights, and most weeks, he invites her to the show. It's a passive invite, delivered in front of others and often to others as well: "You should come hear me play." When Mom finally goes, the whole thing feels Significant. She enrolls her friend as her wingwoman. They flash fake IDs, and the bouncer doesn't even look before waving them into the smoky, crowded room. They linger in the back, watching as the band assembles. It's a bluegrass group, something different from the Beatles cover bands that litter the college town's bars. As the band starts to play, the hum of the crowd settles. Arnie is good, better than the other players. The ring and pinky finger of his right hand rest against the banjo while his other three fingers dance as if the instrument is hot to the touch. He looks up, and she can feel that he is looking directly at her. She glances down and up again, and he smiles.

When the band takes a break, Arnie parks himself at the bar. "Go on," Mom's friend says, nudging her. It takes her most of the intermission to collect her courage, so that by the time she approaches him, the second set is starting. He nods at her, smiles. Is he a little nervous? She can't tell, but it seems that way. "Nice set," she says.

He sets his glass down hard on the counter. Then the announcer is introducing him. "Gonna stick around after the show?" he asks her.

Before Mom can answer, he's gone. It sounds like an invitation, right? Nina nods. *Of course* it did. But the second set drags on. Mom starts to get nervous. She'd never hung out with him after work. What if he actually had a girlfriend she didn't know about? What if he didn't respond? She looks down at her watch, and it's already nine p.m. Her parents aren't the type to bug her about curfew, but she knows they're sitting up on the davenport, watching the news until they hear the screen door bang. "Come on," she says to Nina. "Let's go."

THE MORNING AFTER THE STAKEOUT is the first time her shift has overlapped with his since the show. Arnie is late. He brushes past her to punch his time card. But then he makes a point to circle back around. "Thanks for coming," he says to her.

"I love live music," she tells him, and that's true. "I go hear stuff all the time," she says, and that is not even a little true. She says this casually, as if it's nothing, as if she wouldn't pull out a miniskirt and invest in a new sweater the next time he invited her.

"You didn't stick around," he says.

"I had something," she replies.

"Come again sometime?"

"Yeah, sure," she says. As he walks past her, his hand brushes her shoulder blade. It's so imperceptible, it might have been an accident. Mom still remembers the feel of the tingle that runs down her body.

How come that tingle feels good?

Later in the morning, Mom is stocking men's loafers in the backroom, behind the velvet curtain that separates it from the showroom. It's a Monday, a quiet day, and there aren't many people out in the store. The curtain is to Mom's back, but she hears it brush aside. Without turning her head, she knows it's Arnie. Is he going to kiss her? She remembers thinking this.

She's been hoping for this moment since she watched him play at the bar, since before that. She makes as if she has no idea he is behind her. She tries not to hold her breath even. "Just be normal," she remembers telling herself. Arnie comes up to her and turns her around. But this isn't what she thought. "He had such an odd look in his eyes," she remembers now. He grabs her arms just beneath her shoulders and squeezes so tightly that his grasp burns. Mom is caught. Her hands seize his arms and she yanks down, but his grip only tightens. Arnie is as still as a monk in deep meditation. This is weird, not fun. He drops his mouth to her ear. "Got you!" he hisses. She panics. The room begins to spin. Then, just at the point when the room is going dark, he lets go. She collapses backward, falling against a shelf. He starts to laugh, his facial features relaxing. "Got you," he says, and now he is chuckling a crazed chuckle.

"What are you doing?" she asks. She's free of him, but not safe. She knows that he can overpower her again easily, that he stands between her and the exit. She pulls herself back to standing and looks at his eyes. They're different, distant.

"It was a joke," he insists, but his words don't match his voice, which remains monotone. "Don't you ever wonder?"

Mom doesn't speak. He continues. "I mean, wonder what it'd be like to be one of the women?" She checks the room for other exits. She can hear a customer talking just on the other side of the curtain. Should she just rush out? He could seize her again. She begins to cry. It's involuntary. The emotions heave through her in waves. "You can't do that!" she says.

"What?" he responds, without attempting to comfort her. Then the curtain sweeps back, and another colleague comes in with a set of mules to put away. Mom rushes from the supply room. She considers telling someone, but who? What is the thing to tell? As soon as she is free again, her mind begins the process of chipping away at the thing that her body has just learned: this man can crush her.

MOM'S MEMORIES OF THAT WEEK spin in on themselves and then spread out like a kaleidoscope, the patterns changing even as the colors remain static. By

now, the memories have been laced with dreams and thoughts and stories. She's parsed through them with therapists and painted them onto
canvases. I've come to think about this week as the week of revelations in
Mom's life. She learns three things, each of which will change her more
than the last.

First, there's what's revealed about the Ypsilanti Slayer. Upon listening to the wig store proprietor, a rookie campus patrolman finally puts
it together. This guy sounds a lot like an EMU grad, a former fraternity
brother of his—a guy named John Norman Collins.

Across town, a Michigan patrolman comes home from a vacation at
the lake to discover that something is amiss. It looks as though someone
has been in his house. He's involved with the murder investigations, which
is how he knows that his nephew, John, is now a suspect. It doesn't make
sense to him. John is respectful, a babysitter for the patrolman's three boys.
His nephew plans to be an elementary school teacher. The patrolman goes
down to his basement, which is still littered with the fine blond clippings
from the cuts his wife had given the boys just before their vacation. There,
he finds several splotches of a dark substance on the cement floor. Large
sections of it have been painted over. Why has their basement floor been
painted?

That's when he knows that John must have killed Karen.

Later, when John is convicted of Karen's murder, the incontrovert-
ible evidence will be the hair clippings found all over her body.

AND SO ON TO THE second revelation: there's what emerges about Arnie. He is
John's best friend, and he's tinkering on a motorcycle with John when
the police show up at his house. At first, Arnie is arrested along with
John. For years, the two men have done everything together. They were
members of the ski club and fraternity brothers. They were both kicked
out of the fraternity because they burgled homes and robbed stores together, too.

Within a couple of days, Arnie is released from jail. He is given full
immunity in exchange for agreeing to testify against John. The whole

thing confuses Mom. It's as if the law isn't concerned with what exactly happened; the system wants to put *someone* in jail for Karen's murder. The trial doesn't even address the seven earlier murders that were alleged to be attributed to the Ypsilanti Slayer.

Independent of the trial, the detectives continue to look for evidence that ties John, Arnie, or anyone else to the earlier murders. Arnie often turns up in the vicinity of the victims. He was in the car that picked up the second known victim, for example. She was hitchhiking back to campus. Her red beaded burlap purse is found in Arnie's bedroom closet.

Maybe Arnie was an accomplice. Maybe he had held Karen down in that basement while John rammed a knife into her body thirty times. Or maybe Arnie hadn't played any role at all. What's clear to my mom now, what she suspected then, was that if he hadn't committed the crimes, he also hadn't helped solve them. Arnie knew John was involved. He knew by the time the second victim was murdered; Arnie had driven the car that had picked her up. If he'd turned the victim's purse over to the police, the six women who died after her might have lived.

There was something else Mom knew, something that the people around her did not, something that made her feel small and scared and alone. It became the secret that would grow to define her: Arnie himself was capable of killing someone.

FINALLY, THERE IS WHAT IS revealed to Mom about herself. She finds out that the Ypsilanti Slayer has been apprehended when Alice gives a slight rap on the door and throws the newspaper into Mom's bedroom. It thumps onto the bottom of her bed. It's a Saturday, one week after the stakeout, and the light shines bright through her windows. It must be past ten a.m. Mom picks up the paper and tries to read the news, but it's hard for her to see past the photo. There is Arnie, in cuffs. Arnie, the paper says, has been arrested, alongside John Norman Collins, for the murder of Karen Sue Beineman. Her mind flashes back to the supply room, to the incident just two days earlier when he'd pinned her tightly enough that, for a moment, she feared she wouldn't be let go.

If Mom is relieved, it soon gives way to dread. There are things we don't want to learn we are right about. Where is Arnie now? Just outside her door, she hears the phone. Alice picks it up on the first ring as if she's been lingering there. "Hello?" Mom hears Alice say and then, quickly, "She's not available."

A few seconds go by. Alice is listening. Then she interrupts the caller. "She's not here. Don't call again."

Mom brings the paper out to the kitchen table. Alice's Saturday students will begin arriving shortly, and she hurries about the kitchen, putting dishes away. Kermit stares out the back window at his raspberry patch. Mom knows it was Arnie who called—from jail. She knows her mother won't bring this up.

If I were to rescript my mother's adolescence, this is the point when things would go differently. She'd cry. She'd tell Kermit and Alice that she thought Arnie was involved. She'd explain what happened at the store. Her parents would both sit down at the table across from her, and Alice would take Mom's left hand and squeeze it gently as she coaxed the details from her daughter. Kermit might make a call down to the station to share this information with investigators. Alice might reach out to a therapist on her daughter's behalf. "Do you feel safe?" she might ask, when Mom left to go to work. "Would you like me to drive you?"

That's not what happens. Instead, the air in the kitchen hangs heavy and still. The only noise is the light screech of steel wool as Alice scrubs a pan obsessively in the sink.

"Was that Arnie on the phone?" Mom asks.

"I don't want you talking to him anymore," Alice snaps. "I don't want you to talk to anyone about this."

And so, for a very long time, Mom doesn't.

THREE

Oh Lamb of God

My father got saved the year he turned ten. It's one of the last things he tells me about his childhood, mentioned as an aside just as we're finishing up a series of Zoom calls for The Project. I'm at my desk, tucked under the stairwell of our duplex in Brooklyn, just a few miles from where Dad grew up. He leans into the screen so that his profile is captured from shoulder to forehead. He has a shaved head, a salt-and-pepper mustache that stretches down to a trimmed goatee, and a small gold ring in his left ear. He's in his study, above his husband's woodworking studio, all the way across the country, on the coast of Oregon. The town where Dad lives now, Gold Beach, sits fifty miles north of California; this spit of coast is among the farthest points west in the mainland United States.

Look out the east window of Dad's study, and you'll see his gardens, where he grows most of the fruit and vegetables he eats and which he has had to encircle with an eight-foot wire fence sunk into concrete posts to keep out the elk and deer. Turn to the northwest window, and you'll see the main house, perched right at the top of a hill that rises up over the ocean. Oregon's prodigious Douglas fir trees follow the hill's slope all the way down to the beach where, when the tide is out, Dad picks mussels from beneath the rocks to serve for dinner.

Downstairs, his husband restores the baritone pipes on an organ. Bruce is a soft-hearted former Mormon with a passion for self-playing instruments. Shortly after he and Dad were married, Dad supported Bruce in leaving his administrative job to devote himself to this passion—fixing organs and player pianos—full-time. Now that Dad is retired, he keeps the books. COVID hasn't appeared to slow the business down much. Dad and Bruce travel up and down the coast, picking up disintegrating organs from private collectors and delivering back melodious instruments, often sounding more beautiful than they did at their advent. Bruce has this quality about him—this ability to see the possibility in instruments other people have given up. He works over many months to rebuild thin wood pipes and shape keys by hand. He can coax the music out of any broken thing—like, for instance, Dad.

Before COVID, Dad and Bruce spent at least half their time traveling. They rode old trains across Australia and partied on beaches south of Barcelona. They visited beer halls in Germany with friends they'd met on the internet. They flew to Maui or hopped down to Palm Springs as often as they could. And they made dedicated trips to visit each of us—the six children they've amassed between them and whom they think of as children despite the fact that we were all well into our adulthood by the time they met. This year, however, they've stayed home because of the pandemic. Their quarantine is making Dad antsy. He has filled his schedule with nonprofit volunteering and Zoom yoga classes and trivia night get-togethers, and he is posting daily photographs on Facebook of the dinners he's making for Bruce. And, luckily for me, Dad has more time than usual to engage deeply in the questions of where he came from.

Listening to my Dad recount the stories of his childhood offers a window into how his brain works. He explains with precision the floor plans of the parsonages in which he grew up, in Brooklyn and then in Queens. He describes Hollis, the Queens neighborhood where he went to junior high, as a flat grid below Jamaica Avenue, but the streets dissolved into a tangle of twists and turns north of Jamaica as they climbed up the ridge that snakes its way down Long Island. He remembers the acreage of the private Christian boarding school to which his parents sent him, and he can still guide me from the Long Island Rail Road station to his dorm, pointing out the headmaster's house and Hegeman Hall. But ask him how he felt about events in his childhood, and his answers grow less precise. He is reaching into archives he hasn't visited since the therapy he sought more than two decades ago when he came out. Ask him how his parents might have felt back then, or his two older sisters, and his imagination fails to fill in the details. Who can blame him? As children, our points of view are so narrow—we don't know how to differentiate between our internal dialogues and the broader landscape around us. In the movie versions of our lives, we are the main characters, and we don't yet understand that the people around us are in different movies, playing the main characters in their own lives.

It's also possible that my dad's earliest experiences—the ways in which his own family failed to see him and the expectations they placed upon him—caused him too much pain to revisit. Failing to remember consciously is a skill, a mechanism we've evolved to take care of our sweet selves. But language isn't the only tool for memory. We carry everything that has ever happened to us, everything that has happened to the people who have reared us. We absorb it and act on it, until we finally find a way to heal it.

MY DAD'S SIDE OF THE family has never been all that interested in the past. I live forty-three years on the earth before Dad thinks to tell me that he'd been named for his grandfather, and that's only when I am looking for names for my own children and think to ask him.

"Paul Timothy Hempel," he says.

"Paul, like your name?"

"Yes," he says. His voice is muffled. His phone is tucked under his chin so that he keeps going in and out. "You have to stir the beans in slowly." He'd been cooking a white bean chili when I called, and he starts right in with instructions for how I can make it.

"So you were named for your grandfather?" I ask.

"Yeah, I guess I was," he says.

He's only partly correct. I discover this after a visit with my aunt. She sends me home with two plastic shoeboxes full of photos and documents that have been in her basement since her own father died. That's how I learn that my great-grandfather's actual middle name was *Hermann*, not Timothy.

I keep those shoeboxes for six months before I finally think to explore them. (I'm my father's daughter in this way.) But as I begin The Project, I start to wonder about my father's people. He spends so much of his life reexamining, and dismissing, the values they have attempted to pass down to him: Where did these values take root? One day while Jude is napping, I pull the boxes onto the couch and begin to sift through letters that haven't been opened since they were written more than a century earlier. There's a diary and a budget from 1925 (dinner out: twenty-six cents), a half dozen confirmation and wedding photos, and a child's school project that traces our family lineage back to the mid-nineteenth century.

I'm almost done when I find a typed letter proving that among my ancestors, there were also those who did not conform to expectations. It's written by my grandfather's great-uncle, August, who was born in 1833. In it, August tells his own story of coming out, not as a gay man, but as a Methodist. I love this letter so much. I feel as though it was written expressly so that I could open it, 175 years later. August is one of three Dimmlich brothers—devout Methodists from the same small German village in the eastern part of the country, Hohenleuben. He trains to be a weaver, but machines replace human weavers by the time he learns the craft, so he runs the family's pig farm instead. Hohenleuben is a town of status quo Lutherans until 1855 or so, when the Dimmlich brothers are among the early converts to the more evangelical Methodist Church. No one in Hohenleuben likes the Methodists. Even the government is run by the Lutheran Church.

My great-great-grandfather, Karl, is the first of the three brothers to be converted. He seeks God after a dream in which six or seven men wearing black see him at the county fair, a place of sinful debauchery, and attempt to come after him. Reading this account of my great-great-grandfather's interior life, the contents of his dream, captures my attention. The description—of the men, dressed in black, emerging and coming after him—reminds me of my own childhood dream. Karl doesn't sleep for a week, and then he feels the Lord come into his heart. "His sins peeled off like tons of burdens," his brother writes.

In prayer, August discovers the blissful peace that comes from living the truest expression of himself. Eventually, he marries. He and his wife baptize the first of their eight children as Lutheran because the town requires them to. By the time their second child is born, August can no longer follow the status quo. The family has their daughter baptized by the Methodist minister. The consequences are significant. The town mayor fines August five dollars, roughly the same amount as two parking tickets in my Brooklyn neighborhood today. As a pig farmer, August leads a frugal life, but it's worth the tremendous effort to save up this amount in order for him to be right with God, to be true to himself.

I think, at length, about this man. Before me, there were people in my family who realized that at any price, they had to be true to themselves. Even if it meant their community would disown them, that they might be broke, that their future prospects were uncertain. Karl, August, and their third brother, Franz, felt compelled to act according to their consciences. These are the people I came from.

I'VE COME TO THE CONCLUSION that we inherit most of our beliefs, and usually they suit us well enough to see us through contemporary lives. But as they are reproduced from generation to generation, these hard-won personal philosophies often give way to dogma. The Dimmlich brothers chose the Methodist Church as an act of rebellion, a counterculture decision. They embraced this approach to worship, to life, as the path to inner peace. To wit: they felt better, blissful, freer. Their children grew up within the church, and it suited them. They were never possessed by the need to renegotiate their circumstances in order to stay true to themselves.

Paul *Hermann* Hempel is in the last generation to be born in Hohenleuben. In 1893, his mother brings him and his brother to the US to avoid compulsory military service. His family settles among other Methodist Germans from Hohenleuben in Lawrence, Massachusetts. There, Paul completes a one-year evening course in bookkeeping and gets a job in the office of the local mill. He marries Franz's daughter, Anna, whom Paul meets in Sunday school, over at the First Methodist Episcopal Church on Vine Street. He puts seven hundred dollars down on a house, a big deal in his small social circle.

From what I can tell in reading through retirement speeches, wedding announcements, and old letters written by their children, Paul and Anna live in harmony with the expectations of their community. By all accounts, Paul appears to be a jovial, well-respected man who runs the office at the mill for his entire career. A retrospective of his life, put together on the occasion of his eightieth birthday, describes him as a hands-on father who washes the dishes after Sunday dinner, polishes all the shoes in the house, and runs into the children's bedrooms on Christmas morning dressed in a red woolly jacket and ringing a bell. In one of just two photos I've found, Paul is a young father, holding his first baby, Cornelia, on a winter day. She is four months old, so it must be January 1907. In every other photo from these years, the subjects stare flatly at the camera. But in this snapshot, Paul wears a fedora and a dark suit, his pants rolled slightly at the ankle to fend off the snow that lays thick around them. Cornelia's tiny, serious face peeks out from the nest of blankets he cradles. I swear he is smiling—an easy, prideful smile—as he looks directly into the camera. Is this the life he wanted for himself?

By the grace of God, Paul and Anna's third child is a son, born before dawn on a January Sunday in 1912, early enough that Paul can make it next door to the parsonage to share the news before Sunday services. This is my grandfather. The matter of the boy's name is a discussion cantankerous enough to be recorded for future generations. Anna wants to call him Nathanael, a name that the Reverend loves for its meaning: a disciple in whom there is nothing false (John 1:47). But she worries her son will be called Nat. She also loves the name Edward, but someone in the family knows an Edward "who is apparently not a good person." They settle on four names, calling their son Edwin Nathanael Paul Hempel. From this point on, he'll be Ed to nearly everyone who knows him—everyone except the Reverend, who will always call him Nathanael. Maybe the Reverend knows that Ed will grow up to become a preacher.

AS A CHILD, I SOMETIMES stayed with my Hempel grandparents, Ed and Betty, in the summers. Grandma taught me to fold hospital corners; Grandpa told me bedtime stories about missionaries. Inevitably these stories involved Africa, bad things, and God. This is how the stories would go: "Tonight I'm going to tell you a story about Michael and Shirley Groener. They were doing the Lord's work in Africa. One night Michael awoke, and he did not know why. He reached over and was about to turn on his bedside lamp. But then God spoke to him and told him to reach for his flashlight instead. He flipped it on and there, wrapped around his bedside lamp, was a boa constrictor. Michael gave thanks to God for sparing his life!"

The story would go on, all about how the Groeners got rid of the snake, but I don't remember it from there. I became obsessed with the moment of danger, the snake in the dark, and the vengeful God. I pictured Him—it was always a "Him"—as a man with a book, keeping track of the nights that I remembered my prayers, noting my sins even when I did not confess them. Even then, I knew I did not have a direct line to Him, that I did not hear Him speaking just to me. If there were a snake curled around my lamp, I would be a goner. I have been terrified of snakes my entire life. And the trouble with my grandfather's vision of the world is that there are always snakes, everywhere.

This is the culture in which my father was raised. The Methodist Church moved Ed to new posts every few years, and while he had grown up in this church, he worried that it had become less evangelical. Services were in English instead of German, and they had become limited to Sundays. He brought his own family—Dad and his two older sisters—down to First Baptist for a little extra churching on Wednesdays. During the times that they were based in New York, they often hosted missionaries in between teaching posts in India or Africa. "One of them brought a monkey back," Dad says. This is during our Zoom conversation, and he's laughing now, so hard that he's coughing. "He lived in a cage in our backyard the whole summer," Dad says, "and he bit me!"

It takes several more conversations for Dad to get around to the story of how Billy Graham saved him. This isn't because this event is particularly significant for Dad—in fact, the opposite. Faith wasn't a thing that my father had as much as it was a condition of his life, like being born with brown hair. It was immutable. God had chosen his family; he understood this. Both Ed and his mom, Betty, had known Billy Graham since they'd graduated just a few years before him from Wheaton, the Bible college in Illinois. So in 1957, when the youthful preacher came to flush the sinners—the Jews, the Catholics, the unchurched—out of the Big Apple, Ed was among the first preachers to gather his flock. For sixteen weeks, the evangelist preached every night at Madison Square Garden. Ed and Betty brought Dad many times.

I've watched YouTube videos of Graham's Crusade sermons. I've read testimonials from some of the 742 people who were saved on the opening night alone. I've gotten to know Ed and Betty—the kind of parents they might have been, the values they held—through the letters they wrote to each other, which are tucked into my shoeboxes. From all of this and my conversations with my dad, I can guess at how that night unfolds: At almost ten, Paul holds his parents' hands as they come up from the subway in midtown. The first thing he notices is that there are so many people who love Jesus, crammed into the stadium as if it is the Knicks playoff. The great Crusade choir alone has more than fifteen hundred singers. Billy Graham opens his sermon by asking all twenty thousand attendees to "listen with your soul, tonight," telling them, "your heart also has ears."

Does Dad take Billy's words literally? Does he picture a heart with two large ears?

Dad's parents sit in the first mezzanine, close enough that he can make out the preacher's silhouette. But Dad spends more time looking up at Ed and Betty. Ed's face, as usual, gives no clue as to his feelings, but he places a hand on his son's shoulder. Betty has to sit for part of the time because of her heart condition. This brings her face even with Dad's, so that he can see tears settling into the bottom of her eyes. She takes his hand and squeezes it. This expression of warmth catches young Paul off guard.

He doesn't look at her, but instead stares forward, trying to listen with his soul as he's been instructed. Billy's arms move as he speaks, his right hand coming down and chopping his left palm as he tells the crowd: "A barrier has been built between God and Man!" and "The Bible says that man is born into trouble as the sparks fly upward!" Each time he raises his hand, Dad can feel Billy pulling his own collar up by an invisible string. Is this the hand of God? As Billy wraps up, the choir's voices fill the stadium with a slow rising chorus: "Just as I am, without one plea." Billy looks out over the crowd, asking those who felt moved to come forward to surrender their lives to Jesus. "And that Thou bidst me come to Thee." People step out into the aisles, and then Dad's own feet are propelling him forward. "Oh Lamb of God, I come! I come!"

And then a volunteer counselor with a yellow name tag sweeps in, placing his hand on Dad's back, which is so slight that the skeletal knobs of his spine are visible through his dress shirt. Dad looks at the man, reconsidering whether he should follow a stranger away from his parents in such a crowd. But the man has soft eyes and fleshy jowls, and he tells Dad they will come right back. Dad glances behind him. Now his mother is weeping, her shoulders shaking. His father's eyes are wet. But Billy Graham isn't crying, so Dad doesn't cry. He is being saved! The volunteer steers him by the shoulders away from his parents and back into a breakout room where other counselors kneel on prayer stools in front of other people stepping forward to be saved. Dad drops down on his knees.

This older man, whom he will never see again, places calloused paws over Dad's soft child hands. "Do you accept Jesus Christ as your Lord and Savior?" the man asks. Dad nods, mumbles yes, and the man asks him to sign the card. Dad scrawls his name in loopy little-boy cursive. The choir is on the final verse of the hymn when Dad returns to his parents: "Because Thy promise I believe, O Lamb of God, I come, I come!"

I try to ask Dad more about this event, but he's lost interest—or maybe he doesn't want to talk about it. "It's pretty intense for a young kid," he says. "But then that's sort of how they keep you, you know?"

FOUR

Therapists

Shame gets the better of my dad the first time he's sent to see a therapist and learns that he is capable of lying. He's less than a month into his first semester at boarding school. The Stony Brook School is a cluster of brick buildings set around a chapel on a leafy campus on the bay side of Long Island. Boys can start there in seventh grade. It's a Christian school founded by the evangelist Frank Gaebelein, and I'm pretty sure Ed and Betty send Dad there because they want him to be Not Gay. "They were worried about me by that time, because I was already showing signs," Dad says. We're on Zoom again, and Dad has leaned forward into the screen so that his face feels closer to mine, but he's actually looking out past me. He's remembering how Betty caught him parading in front of his sister's mirror in one of her petticoats. He tells me that Ed found his muscle magazines, the penny-store purchases that passed as gay porn in the 1960s. This was the only sex talk they ever had. The language was awkward. Ed told Dad to be careful because he would become addicted and then he wouldn't be able to please his wife.

By then, Dad had had sexual experiences with his friends. These were innocent experiences. They arose out of a natural desire expressed through play. And if he didn't share these things with his parents, it wasn't because of *homosexuality*. That wasn't even a word he knew. It was because Dad knew by then that anything he did when he wasn't with his

parents was probably a sin. This list of transgressions was long and specific: dancing (vertical expression of horizontal desire), eating spaghetti
(too Catholic), going to the movies (bad influences). By the time Dad is
twelve, he applies a need-to-know policy with Ed and Betty.

He arrives at Stonybrook in the fall of 1961. He's one of fifty boys
in the freshmen class. They live on the first floor of an older Victorian
wooden structure toward the back of campus. Right from the start, he
can't stand his roommate. "I don't remember his name, to be honest,"
Dad says. One evening this nameless older bully boy climbs down into
Dad's bed and touches him in ways that make him feel uncomfortable.
And this, in itself, isn't traumatic to young Paul. He's had experiences like
this before. But he doesn't like this experience, or this boy. He knows
this attention is uninvited and wrong.

The next day, even before the breakfast bell rings, Dad approaches
his dorm mother. It doesn't occur to him that he should weigh telling her,
that she might do anything other than enforce justice. But the woman
doesn't react as Dad expects. I wonder now if she saw Dad as queer when
he arrived on campus, if he was the kind of kid who ironed his shirts and
combed his hair without being asked. Regardless, the woman doesn't
automatically defend him. Instead, she calls in the perpetrator to get the
other side of the story.

From this point, things happen quickly. First, there is a lengthy inquisi-
tion. Dad and his roommate are each called in to the headmaster's office for
questions. Then, to the school chaplain. Then, to the school nurse. After a
week, the headmaster calls Ed, who drives the Buick up to campus and does
not make eye contact with his son once he arrives. No one can decide what
has really happened. It's determined that both boys should be deposed by a
Christian psychologist in Syosset. A few days later, Ed returns to take Dad
to this appointment. They do not speak during the forty-five-minute drive
to his office or on the return trip. "I remember spending an hour or two
hours with the guy," Dad says. "Then a week later, he delivered his opinion
to the school, and the other boy was asked to withdraw. I was allowed to
stay. No discussion. No explanation to me, just, 'You're allowed to stay.'"

"Did any adult ever talk to you about it?" I ask. Dad has gone silent. He's a seventy-two-year-old man gazing beyond and above me with all the vulnerability of young Paul.

"Nope, no," he says.

"Oh, God," I say, because I don't know what to say. And then Dad starts talking again, and this time his voice is faster, the color rising a bit in his face. "I knew I'd had some sexual experience with boys before," he says. He explains that the therapist asks him, "Do you like boys?" Well, what's the right answer to that? Because *yes*. But it seems that what this therapist wants to know is, *Did you want this boy to touch you?* No—no, he did not. So there was no truthful answer to this question. The test was rigged. Did he like boys? He had to say no, but it was a lie. When the verdict comes back, he understands. "I was kind of sitting there thinking I must have fooled the psychiatrist. So I know what you have to do now. You can do whatever you want, but you can't ever get caught. And you can't ever actually admit that."

From this point, Dad is tormented by his classmates. It doesn't matter that his roommate has left, or maybe it makes everything worse. Other boys ignore him or make fun of him. His only friend is the other weird kid. "I mean, he collected yogurt cups," Dad says. "You know, those big old Dannon yogurt cups? He had hundreds of them in his room." These boys are only sort of friends, because sometimes they also ignore each other. This is the point when Dad's consciousness splits in two. There is Stony Brook Paul, who will manage the tennis team and attend devotions every day and graduate as valedictorian of his class. There is Secret Paul, encased in shame, who behaves in ways that are ungodly. Secret Paul is unlovable. Secret Paul must remain unknown—increasingly even to Paul.

School for my dad is a collection of accolades. He's intellectually minded, and he also applies himself. He attends college on the full scholarship that Middlebury provides its top student, and his spare time is taken up with religious gatherings. He has a girlfriend, but the relationship is fairly platonic. One summer he doesn't hear much from her, and when he returns to campus, she has moved in with a guy she's just met. "She didn't even tell me!" he says now, but it doesn't matter much to him. He just feels generally confused about how that dimension of a life is supposed to work.

After his junior year, Dad takes time off to join his sister Mary on a Methodist mission in a jungle in Zaire. This is a somewhat ill-considered decision—he loses his educational draft deferral from Vietnam. But my father deals with this specter of uncertainty the way he deals with all challenges then. "I just kind of prayed about it," he says. For his birth year, the drawing reaches 195. His draft number is 196. He takes this as a sign that God has come through for him.

Because he's been away in Africa, Dad graduates from college off cycle, in January. This is when his life goes sideways. He decides to apply for a mission. He doesn't feel called by God as much as he feels no calling by anything at all. The ambivalence with which he approaches this decision is poisonous to anyone within his orbit—anyone except his parents. Ed and Betty are thrilled. A second missionary in the family! Ed wanted to be a missionary earlier in his own career, but he was disqualified because he'd had polio as a child and walked with a limp. Now they'll have a daughter *and* a son in the field, soldiering on behalf of Christ!

The Mission Board, from what Dad remembers now, is less clear on Dad's aspirations. From the start, board members question his motives for joining. Sure, he's qualified—he's fluent in German, which was his college major, and he speaks passable French. But unlike the other new sign-ups, his commitment to Christianity is less clear. Reluctantly, as a favor to Ed, the board members admit Dad to the training program. After a two-month French-language intensive in Belgium, Dad arrives at a retreat center in the Hudson Valley for eight weeks of collective devotions, field instruction, and psychological examination.

His primary memory of the training is the T-groups, a corporate leadership training fad that dies out by the mid-1970s. Participants learn how their own words and actions trigger emotional responses in others. "They have a moderator, a psychotherapist, and they kind of want you to talk about who you are and why you're going and what you're doing," Dad says. It's easy to see how this could be valuable for someone on the eve of moving to a continent and a country they haven't visited with the purpose of bringing its inhabitants to God. But what if you're a closeted gay man with no authentic desire to soldier on for Christ and an unrealized concern that someone will out you to yourself? Dad is taciturn and argumentative. After just a couple weeks of daily T-grouping, both the Mission Board and Dad realize that he should not spend his career evangelizing to the unsaved on a station in the African jungle.

Here, the Mission Board affords Dad a kindness I don't understand. I wish I could go back and speak to the adults who sat with him through the hours and hours of his unraveling. I wish I could see what they saw. Do they take pity on him? Do they see their younger selves in him? What spurs their compassion? Rather than expel him, they give him a leave of absence and don't require him to reimburse them for his language training. They agree to help him find a therapist, and they offer to pay for two months of psychoanalytic treatment. On an unseasonably warm May morning, a trainer drops him at the Metro-North station with one small suitcase and a piece of paper folded in his wallet: on it is a phone number for the office administrator. He should get in touch when he arrives.

But where is he going?

Dad returns to Queens, but the Methodist Church has assigned his father to a new congregation. Dad buys a used car for four hundred dollars and drives up to the town that houses their new church in upstate New York. He wants to tell Ed and Betty what happened in person. Dad imagines it will be tough, and things go worse than he expects. Betty weeps. Ed leaves, announcing he has a pastoral visit to make. And then Dad is sitting on the davenport in a house where he doesn't feel welcome, and he has nowhere to go. So he calls his other sister, Martha.

"Just come," Martha tells him. Martha is the family's black sheep, the eldest daughter. She is six years older than her brother—born on the exact same day, August 14—and because it was the only option her parents gave her, she went to a religious college and has become a church organist. A few years after this, she'll quit the organ, quit church, and go to medical school. But in the summer of 1971, she and her husband live in Michigan.

"I don't know what to do," Dad tells her. He has called collect.

"Really, just come."

"I can't even afford this call."

"Really come."

The next day, Dad drives nine hours across New York, through Ohio, and into Michigan. He spends the summer painting Martha's house and drinking beer. At first, he drinks a lot and paints a little, and gradually the ratio changes. He knows he needs to get a job, so he opens the help wanted section of the paper. By the time Martha's house is painted, he has become a suit salesman at Montgomery Ward at the Arborland Mall. For the moment, he's settled. That's when he calls the Mission Board to get the psychiatric referral.

DR. THOMPKINS IS BOTH A psychiatrist and a psychoanalyst, and he works out of an office with no air-conditioning on the campus of the University of Michigan in Ann Arbor. Three times each week, Dad drives seven miles to meet with Dr. Thompkins. If Dad were in New York or New England, he might be a little sheepish in the waiting room. He might keep his face tucked behind a magazine. But this is a town in Michigan where he knows no one except Martha and her family and where he probably won't live for long. And besides, at this point, he is too tired to pay attention to who might be looking at him.

Invariably, on the exact hour of his appointment, Dr. Thompkins appears at the door, glancing lightly over his spectacles, and beckons Dad in. The man has kind eyes and reminds Dad of his high school tennis coach. But Dad doesn't look at the doctor during the session. Instead, Dad sinks into the large recliner in the doctor's office and stares at the tiles on the ceiling as he speaks. Dad tells Dr. Thompkins everything. He has just lost his grip on what he thought to be true—the love and support of his parents, his career aspirations, his home, his God—and he's no longer trying to hide any part of himself. The burden of figuring out who he is has become too much. He's lost. He's unhappy. He doesn't understand anything about his life. "And also, I think I might be gay," he tells the doctor.

This is the first time Dad has said these words. He's twenty-three, and he says them not as though it's the cause of his unhappiness, but more as though it's one extra thing to know about his pathetic and poorly faring self. He can't tell if this fact is why he's suffering. How could he know? The truth is that by the time he arrives in Michigan, he really doesn't know why he's miserable.

Dr. Thompkins is a traditionalist in a moment when traditions haven't yet been reexamined. It's the early 1970s. The American Psychiatric Association will not remove the diagnosis of "homosexuality" from the second edition of its *Diagnostic and Statistical Manual of Mental Disorders* for another year. Psychoanalysts won't follow suit for nearly two more decades. Most psychoanalysts consider homosexuality a normal phase in the early development of young boys. But if it doesn't resolve, it becomes an illness. Homosexuality in adults is pathological.

Dad takes a long time to get around to this subject. In the beginning, just the prospect of talking to someone helps him a lot. Pretty soon he is feeling better. His job is easy. He meets another guy at Montgomery Ward who needs a place to live, and they get their own apartment. His boss leaves, and Dad is given a promotion. He has started to have friends, easy friends who think he is interesting because he has been to Africa. This isn't any recognizable version of his life, but it also isn't nothing anymore.

MY PARENTS' MEET-CUTE OCCURS IN the men's apparel department at Montgomery Ward. Mom still works there between nursing classes at Eastern Michigan University. In late August, after Dad has worked at the store for six weeks, he gets up the courage to approach her. He's probably wearing his green paisley button-down and definitely wearing a pair of double knit bell-bottoms. I learn this story when I'm a little kid, maybe eight, and

I have a movie in my head of exactly how it happens: Mom is folding socks in the men's department. She's pretty. I know this even when I am very young. She has that long shock of chestnut brown hair that flips up at the end like those women in magazines. She has round cheeks and a round face, and her body is curvy. She's probably wearing jeans, because they are fashionable and she is fashionable. She is standing there folding socks when a ball of socks hits her in the arm. She looks up to see who has tossed them, and there is Dad. It's his version of flirting. He has an easy confidence, and she is smitten. The child me doesn't really think to ask any more questions after this.

Now, as I work on The Project, I have a fuller sense of who they are. I can see Mom, still living in her childhood bedroom. Her sisters have both moved to different states. Even her parents are in the house less often; they spend their weekends caring for her grandmother in Ohio. Only Mom is still on Evelyn Street. Things haven't gone her way. She has applied to the University of Michigan to study physical therapy twice and has been rejected twice. She's working her way through EMU's nursing program even though she doesn't want to be a nurse; she hates giving shots. And then there are the events of two years ago. Mom has run into Arnie just once, at Ted's, the soda fountain shop near campus. Presumably, he was in town for the trial. They do not acknowledge each other. But for years afterward, she'll scan the corners of public places before entering—nervous. In the summer of 1971, as she lobs the socks back at Dad, she's not looking for a husband as much as seeking a one-way ticket out of Ypsi. Out of her boring life. Out of high school boys who don't age well. She is drawn to people who didn't grow up in Ypsilanti and don't plan to stay. People like my dad. He remembers how it felt to be the subject of her attention. "I was certainly very, very excited that she was fascinated with me," he says.

I can see him, a chatty outsider. He is worldly and awkward at the same time. He knows the stories other people will find compelling about his life—stories about his time in Africa. They're so unique that Mom can still conjure them. "I remember him saying how he went in for the delivery of a baby," Mom says. "The mother, instead of screaming out, she clicked her fingers: *click, click, click click*. Your dad had to hold the light for whoever was helping, and they birthed the baby all together as a team."

They make arrangements to get pizza after work, and they talk. They discover an ease of conversation. This talking is different, echoing of adolescent discovery. Dad, the son of a minister, a failed missionary, a man who finds Mom graceful and receptive. Mom, a beautiful woman, easy in her skin, a woman who finds Dad lovable and attractive. That first night, she leaves her umbrella at his place. This is almost certainly on purpose. The very next day, they get together again. Their courtship is freedom. It's a chance for each of them to be something they are not and to leave behind the things that they are, the things they do not speak about yet.

Dad continues to visit Dr. Thompkins, and right away, he tells his therapist about Mom. The doctor does not respond, which is what he is paid to do. Now that Dad is in love, which is certainly what he believes this must be, the taboo subjects begin to feel safer. This is why he finally tells Dr. Thompkins that he still worries he is gay. It takes him several sessions to work up the courage to broach the topic, and he waits until the final eight minutes of their hour together, when he should be reaching for conclusions, not beginnings. The words hang in the air, without judgment. Empowered by his revelation, Dad returns two days later, and this time, he confesses all of his many gay experiences. He tells the therapist about Freddy back in middle school and about Stony Brook. And finally, Dad asks the doctor, "Do you think I am a homosexual?"

"And he was like, 'Oh, no, no, no, no,'" Dad remembers. This man who never speaks is verbose in his denial. These experiences have been natural because Dad was young. The assumption is obvious: this will resolve itself when Dad gets married.

Dad has not felt this degree of absolution from an authority figure since he gave himself to God at ten years old. He floats out of the office. He calls Mom to see whether he can come over, and he notices, with a certain pride, that he's genuinely excited to see her.

A few days later, they're walking through downtown Ann Arbor. "I remember we passed a jewelry store and she was pointing out how much she liked the rings in there," Dad says. "It just came to me . . . here's somebody who apparently wants to be married. She's a nice person. She goes to a good church. It ticked all the boxes."

How are you supposed to feel when you decide to get married? Even now, I think this question is a trap. For our entire lives, we are inculcated in the mistaken belief that we will meet The One. It will be clear. A marriage is waiting for us, a natural completion to our aspirations, whether male or female. This is what we are taught to look for, to want. This is a want that is manufactured outside of us, which is why it can be hard to isolate and name the feelings it engenders.

When Dad asks Mom to marry him, they're in her living room, sitting on the davenport. Kermit and Alice have gone to bed already. He does not drop on a knee, and he hasn't bought the ring yet, but he does turn to face her with the most serious look. She can tell he's nervous. She has hoped for this moment, but also, it has come sooner than she expects. Mom, who cries easily, is momentarily without tears. It's all too significant for a reaction. Warmness rushes over her as she dreams forward into her future, their future.

Thinking back on the evening, Mom mostly remembers Alice's voice: "After he left, Mom called out what she often did, 'How did things go, honey?'"

Mom sits there on the couch, turning the prospects of her future over in her mind. "Oh, fine," she remembers responding. She can re-create this conversation exactly. "He asked me to marry him."

She hears her dad cough and mumble to her mom: "She said what?" Their voices talk low, and then her dad calls out, "What did you say?"

Mom knows her answer will be yes, but she's not ready to share that just yet. Instead, she calls back and says, "I told him I'd think about it." This is where our family started.

PART TWO

The Closet

FIVE

Infinity

I'm five and a half when I realize I can't find the end of numbers. This realization will change me. Up until this point, I believe there's a consistent order to things. Everything can be known if we ask the right questions of the right people.

Two months before this incident, in September, I meet my kindergarten teacher, Ms. West, for the first time. "You're smart!" she says. She's tall and thin with leathery skin and black hair that falls straight down her back, and I want her to like me. I've just recited the alphabet.

"I can spell, too," I say.

Behind her, the other children are seated in clusters of four, coloring. I peer into the room and then turn back to my family, gathered at the door. It's already mid-September, and we've just moved to this small town outside Greenville, South Carolina, where school starts earlier than back in Massachusetts. Mom puts me and Katje, who is not quite two, in matching dresses, and pulls our hair back tight into pigtails—mine blonde, Katje's a light brown—that she fastens with pink plastic butterfly hair ties. The entire family drives over to Taylors Elementary to enroll me. It's far enough into the year that the kids don't have name tags on their desks anymore, but I'm not nervous. Adults like me. I'm outgoing and make friends easily, and also, I know I'm smart. My parents tell me so all the time.

Ms. West beams down at me and my little sister. Mom is seven months pregnant, and Katje's head is the perfect height to lean against the protruding baby bump. "Who's this, Jessi?" Ms. West asks.

Why is she asking about Katje? This is *my* day. I want her attention, so I claim it again by answering: "That's Katje!" I'm a motormouth. People always tell me this, and I don't know yet that it isn't a compliment. I continue: "You spell it *K-a-t-j-e*, but you say it KAY-tee." (Mom had taken the spelling from a newspaper comic strip, *Dondi*, about a wide-eyed war orphan adopted by an American mother, Katje Wills.) "She's really smart, too. She knows her colors."

"Oh, does she?" says Ms. West. I look up at Dad, and he winks at me. For weeks, Katje has been both my only playmate and the one subject of my kingdom. Dad's new job has put us up in a hotel with a little kitchenette and a pullout sofa while my parents house-shop. Every day, we've been touring houses, imagining the placement of a kitchen table, deciding what might make a good playroom. Then we return to the hotel and play in the stairwell or make art projects at the table.

Katje doesn't know her colors at all. She knows only one word, which happens to be a color: "yellow." But Ms. West doesn't know this.

"Here, look, I can prove that she knows them," I tell her. "Do you have any crayons?" Ms. West hands me an art box from the shelf above the cubbies where I'll hang my coat. I can tell my parents are amused by my performance, but they don't blow my cover. I hold up a yellow crayon and prompt Katje: "What color is this?"

"Ye-yow!" she responds.

BY EARLY NOVEMBER, I'VE FOUND my rhythm in the classroom. Then one day it happens. When it's time for recess, Ms. West asks us to fold our arms—crisscross—and put our heads down. She calls us individually to line up: "Rico." "Amy." She calls us according to how still we are sitting, and I want to do everything perfectly. Both my feet are firmly on the floor. My hair is woven into two French braids that flop down onto the table as I rest my forehead on my elbows. To remain still, I start to count: *1, 2, 3 . . .*

Usually I'm one of the first to be called because I'm very good at following directions. It's one of my chief strengths. But today, Ms. West calls most of the other kids first. I'm still counting: *42, 43, 44 . . .* I remember thinking, first, I am proud of the fact that I can count so high. I can really count so high. In school, we have learned our numbers only up to ten. But I can count to one hundred. *78, 79, 80 . . .* I can count higher than that. I work the numbers around in my mind. I can see them, and I'm following them all the way to the end. The end, which is . . . where exactly? Well, when I get to one hundred, I can keep going ten more times and get to one thousand. And when I get to one thousand, then I can keep going. Where is the end?

This question is disconcerting. My eyes begin to smart. My head is still facedown on my elbows, only I've stopped listening. All the other kids have lined up now. Ms. West has called on me, but I haven't heard her. She has kept going, and now the children are in line and she is saying my name: "Jessi, Jessi, are you okay?"

I lift up my head, and my face is bright red, snot all over my sleeve. I know she sees I've been crying. The other children, who are in line and would like to be at recess, also see that I've been crying. This is embarrassing. I am embarrassed. So I begin to cry harder, except that I'm also hiding my tears. I'm gulping sobs. "Why don't you stay inside with me?" Ms. West says. Her hand on my shoulder is not a comfort. I shrug it away. The only kids who stay inside during recess are the ones who have misbehaved, like the two boys at two separate tables, brooding here because they were roughhousing during story time.

I try to pull myself together, but I can't be done with it. My shoulders are rattling, salty tears tracing rivers down my cheeks. Ms. West dismisses the class to the aide who walks the kids to the playground. Then she kneels next to me and rubs my back. "Do you want to tell me what's wrong?" she says.

Now it's just us—and those two naughty boys who are staring at us, but no matter. I look up at her and whisper, "I can't find the end of the numbers."

Ms. West doesn't understand. "Is someone teasing you?" she asks, as though I haven't even answered—as though she hasn't even heard what I said. I start crying again. "Are you homesick?" she asks.

"I started counting and I couldn't stop," I say. My chest is heaving so I half-cough the words.

"Why don't I call your mom?" she says. And she uses her intercom to the right of our classroom door to buzz down to the office. Our new house is just a half mile away, and Mom comes to get me. By the time she arrives, the adults have decided that I'm feeling sad about the move, that starting the school year midway has been difficult for me. Mom lets me sit in the front seat of our station wagon on the drive home. I've stopped crying, but I'm sullen. Katje is singing in her car seat in the back. "Yell-ow-yell-ow-yell-ow," she coos, to the tune of "Twinkle, Twinkle, Little Star." She's so proud that she knows something. But I know there are things that cannot be known.

BY THE TIME MOM GOES into labor, we have moved into a four-bedroom ranch on a small cul-de-sac in which more than half the houses have kids around my age. Mom's parents have already arrived to help out when the baby comes.

Mom is at an ob-gyn appointment with Alice, sitting in the waiting room, when she feels something wet between her legs—a trickle and then a gush. She stands up with remarkable presence, time slowing, and walks to the receptionist's window. "My water just broke," she says. "Can I use your phone?" Around her, everyone flies into action. Mom leaves a message for Dad at his office. She calls Kermit, who is watching Katje, and asks him to pick me up after school. Alice has gathered Mom's purse and is asking about how to get to the emergency room. That's when Mom realizes she doesn't know where the hospital is yet. A nurse, sensing her rising panic, offers to drive them the seven blocks to labor and delivery.

Across town, Dad is at a business luncheon, and he has just put in his order. When his secretary gets the message, she finds him at the restaurant. Dad calls the doctor's office. He's still new in his job as an in-house lawyer for Michelin, the tire company, still meeting people for the first time. He does the calculation in his head. Mom's parents are with her. Babies take a long time to arrive. My birth had taken hours. I'd been induced because President Gerald Ford was set to pass through town, and the doctor didn't want my mom to contend with closed roads if she needed to get to the hospital. Katje had come late at night, also taking a long time to find her way into the world. Both times, he had held Mom's hand, encouraged her, waited with her so long the waiting was what he remembered about birth. So Dad finishes his steak and asparagus before he heads for the hospital. This is how he remembers it.

Their third child, however, is in a hurry. Mom labors for just two hours. After his lunch, Dad joins the other prospective fathers pacing the length of the waiting room and standing at the pay phone. A nurse's assistant passes through, and Dad flags her down: "Will you tell Ann I'm here and I want to come back?" he asks. She disappears, leaving him there for more than an hour. Then she escorts Dad back to the room just as the doctors are encouraging Mom to push. He remembers the doctor is annoyed by his presence and tells him to stay out of the way. A small fist emerges, followed quickly by a head, shoulders, and a smooth, filmy body. The doctor lifts the baby to Mom's chest to suckle. Alice hovers over Mom, who is equal parts euphoric and exhausted.

Mom hands the baby to Dad, who marvels at another new life. "Get a photo!" Mom tells Alice, who lifts the camera hanging around her neck. In the snapshot, they both look with amazement at their youngest. The only one of their children born in the South, the family's rebel.

SEVERAL HOURS LATER, A PEDIATRICIAN comes by. The baby is in the nursery, having been washed and swaddled tightly, so Mom can get some rest. It is quiet in the room, the lights turned low. Dad sits in a chair against the wall, and Alice has gone home to check on me and Katje. Mom is trying to snooze, but she wakes up when the pediatrician arrives. He perches on the side of the bed and consults his notes. "Congratulations on your new baby boy!" he says.

"Boy?" Mom and Dad both say. There must be some mistake. This baby is a girl. The doctor looks confused, embarrassed. He steps out, checks the number on the outside of the room, returns. "Oh, yes," he says. "A girl, congratulations."

Dad will remember this slip of the tongue. It won't seem like a mistake as much as a sign. The youngest member of our family is assigned female at birth. But as we grow this will change. By the time I begin The Project, I will have known him as my brother Evan longer than I believed him to be my sister. So what do I call this baby, whom the pediatrician presumed to be a boy and whom our family mistook for a girl? I tell Evan that I find this confusing, that I don't know how to tackle it in The Project. He grows impatient with me. He doesn't get what my confusion is about. "I'm just Evan," he says. "It's what I choose to be. Why is it hard to respect that?"

"Because respecting it—" I try to explain but the words aren't exactly there. "Respecting it is denying my own history." In my history, I had a little sister. This feels like truth to me for a long time. I was one of three little girls. We had round faces and long hair and wore matching dresses that my mother smocked for us. If the youngest of these three girls was not who I believed her to be, was a boy, then who was I? It chipped at the foundation of my own identity.

But something fundamental has changed for me as I've lived with Evan; I've refashioned that history. I've leaned into the emotional truth of it, and as I have, Evan has come clear. Who he was has emerged. Evan was a willful child, a kid who was always self-possessed, who arrived everywhere fist first. He was stubborn and independent, uninterested in following other people's rules. As I describe my brother to you, exactly as he was, he becomes more clearly himself when I use the pronouns he chooses.

You'll know, even as I use the word "Evan," that Evan had a name before this. It's a name I won't tell you. To utter it would be to disrespect all the work he has done to find his way to Evan. The more you get to know him, the more you'll see the pronouns, and the names, don't matter at all. Evan teaches me that there is an endless quality to truth; the external details constantly shift as we move closer to the emotional centers of our lives. And you can try to explain it, but it will be no easier than explaining infinity. Not everything can be explained. Some things must be accepted.

SIX

French Training

"Are you awake?" Dad asks. I'm groggy, the kind of jet-lagged tired when my head feels like an anvil that lobs from side to side. It's my seventh birthday, and we've just arrived in a village in central France where we will spend half a year. Mom, Katje, and Evan are all sleeping as though it's the middle of the night, but it's early afternoon. I want to go back to sleep, but I also want my dad's attention. These moments of having my dad all to myself are rare.

Dad stands at the window, surveying our new surroundings. We've been deposited at a white stucco house with a red tile roof across from a cherry orchard and a grape vineyard. The house slopes down a hill. Most of it is on one floor, but the bedroom that will belong to me and Katje is downstairs. It has twin beds, a large wardrobe, and shutters that hide a window that opens directly to the backyard. Outside, there is a small walnut tree with one significant branch forking off to the right. In one of our silent home videos from this time, I clasp this branch and try to walk my legs up the trunk while Katje circles it on her big wheel. I'm tiny with a round face and long, dirty blonde hair that falls loose and stringy. Katje is tinier, her face even rounder, her hair pulled back into pigtails that twist into curls. I stop to rest and reevaluate my position, and Katje scurries up the tree. She hangs upside down from its branch and smiles at the camera. My young-me face crinkles, blood rushing to my cheeks. I am somewhere between angry and embarrassed. I'm the oldest, and I still think this entitles me to do everything first and better.

I pull myself from bed to join my dad. He's a slim man of average height with a neatly trimmed mustache and a crescent of dark brown hair circling a slowly expanding spot that has been bald since he finished college. We walk into town together, hand in hand. He says French words and I repeat them, trying to mimic the way the vowels catch and sink down into the back of his throat. We pass a patisserie and a boulangerie. "Bou-LAHN-je-ree," Dad says.

"Bou-LAHN-je-ree," I repeat. I skip to keep up with him. Dad's stride is long, and unlike Mom, he doesn't turn to check that we are with him. We need to tell him if we're falling behind, but mostly, we know not to fall behind.

When we get down to the center of town, there's a market of some sort along the street. Dad approaches a guy and asks what's going on. I hear them murmur and marvel at the way Dad can piece together words I don't understand. It's not just the words; it's the way his body language changes when he speaks French, subtly modeling itself after the person with whom he's speaking. I resolve that I will be able to do this, too. At the market, there's a man playing a guitar and someone else playing violin. Some of the kids have taken off their shoes, and they're dancing in the road in their bare feet.

Dad squats down to my level, and he's smiling and looking directly at me. He asks if I want to dance with the other kids. And yes, I do want to, because my Dad wants me to! He bends over to untie my tennis shoes. But then I lose my nerve. As he stands up, I lean into his side, and he runs his palm down the length of my upper arm.

EVEN WHEN WE'RE CONCEALING THE most radical secrets, secrets that will grow inside us like thorns and pierce us and eventually consume us, we sometimes have seasons that are beautiful. This is what our time in France is: it's a deep breath collectively held, an adventure. I strike out into a foreign culture to experiment with new things and then retreat to the comfort of a home where I feel safe and seen and loved. I believe it will always be this way.

We have moved here because of Dad's job at Michelin, the French tire company. Even though Dad plans to spend his career as a lawyer working in Greenville, the company has a rule that no matter your role, and particularly if it involves pushing papers in another country, you must spend six months working on the line, making tires. You must *understand* Michelin's business and the culture in which it was created. Dad reports to a factory in the nearby city of Clermont-Ferrand. He wears a yellow jumpsuit over his suit and tie. He learns to make rubber and then a roadworthy tire.

Mom makes two friends, Élisabeth and Jane. They are the mothers of children in the nursery where Katje spends her mornings. They meet one day after drop-off, during which Mom often lingers just outside because Katje has terrible separation anxiety. Her teacher's only English phrase is "Do you need to pee?" Every time the teacher says this, Katje cries harder and throws herself at the door. Mom wants to cry, too, but she holds herself back, knowing this will only make it harder for her middle child. Élisabeth and Jane begin to notice Mom there, balancing Evan on her hip, and they stop to visit with her, to comfort her. Mom speaks no French, and only Élisabeth speaks English, but Mom discovers that with good hand motions, language doesn't matter that much. Before long, the three women drop the kids off and go for coffee frequently, laughing over their shared plight as moms of preschoolers.

Élisabeth is a knitter. One afternoon, she arrives at the front door with her daughter Carolle, an extra pair of knitting needles, and a large ball of yarn. Élisabeth places the needles in Mom's fingers and begins to demonstrate with outsize movements. "Comme ci," she says, executing a knit stitch. "Comme ça," she says, following it with a purl.

Mom tries to follow, and when the stitch doesn't come out right, Élisabeth leans over and grasps her hands, letting them follow Élisabeth's own until Mom has gotten the hang of the stitch. They both repeat "comme ci, comme ça, comme ci, comme ça" over and over to form a perfect row. It will be years before my mom learns that "comme ça" is not French for "purl."

MOST OF MY MEMORIES OF French school focus on what I've just missed. I often don't know what's going on. I arrive without my gym clothes on gym days. I don't have the right school supplies. I rarely line up correctly in the school yard, where we're supposed to sort ourselves by height and gender. The teacher is always calling "Jessica" but she pronounces it with a long middle syllable—Jess-SEE-ka—and it's the first time I've gone by this full version of my name, instead of Jessi, so sometimes I don't even notice she's calling me. None of this bothers me. I'm so different that I'm not ashamed of this difference. I don't try to fit in.

When I get home, Mom makes us crepes because she has noticed that Jane and Élisabeth make afternoon crepes for their kids, and then she sends us out to play. At eighteen months old, Evan is too young to be interesting to me, but Katje and I sometimes cross the street to construct elaborate games of make-believe in the cherry orchards. I'm the director of our pretend games, which follow two scripts. Either we are stranded and in danger, trying to make an escape by moving from tree to tree without touching the ground, the deep red juice of the sour cherries grinding into our palms and staining our clothes, or we are getting married. I am the husband because I'm taller and I have a button-down shirt that looks husbandly. Katje is the wife, and she wears my Easter dress from the previous spring, the red one that Mom smocked. After I commit to Katje, she balances on the back of my big wheel as I pedal us off to our honeymoon.

Other days and almost every evening, I curl into the leather chair in the living room with a book. I'm reading the Bobbsey Twins mysteries. My uncle in Boston has bought eighteen of these books secondhand and mailed them to us. I fly through them. I read before dinner and through dinner, a book tucked in my lap. I read in the car, and I read at tourist attractions when Dad points to castles and paintings and encourages me to put my book down. When I have read all the Bobbsey Twins mysteries, I start my pile over again.

FRANCE IS THE LAST TIME I remember my parents having fun with each other. They have a gentle ease. I can feel this. There is so much that is foreign and new all around us, and they are collectively figuring it out. On weekends, we travel. When school lets out for summer break, we head out for longer spells. Our old Citroën is always on the verge of a breakdown. Both Katje and Evan are still in car seats, and I sit in the middle. We pack baguettes, meat, and cheese into baskets and drive through Luxembourg, Spain, and Germany, staying at youth hostels. There are rarely any other young children at the hostels. We are an entertaining oddity for the backpackers. In Switzerland, a hostel in the foothills of the Alps has life-size chess pieces on a board mowed into the lawn. A backpacker in a bikini top and cutoff jeans challenges me to a game, which I play more like hide-and-seek than chess.

In late summer, we drive south to the French Riviera. The men and women stretch out on their towels wearing only bikini bottoms or Speedos. No baggy American swim trunks. No one-piece suits. I've never seen so many breasts, right out in the open, as if this is a normal thing. Maybe it is? All the same, it feels a little shocking. We stay at a rented apartment on the coast. I remember two things about the south coast of France. One is the light. It has an open quality to it. It's warmer than other light, lending everything a pastel shade. Also, I remember Dad's power beach walks. Mom teases him. She wants to bathe in the sun while we dig in the sand, but Dad is always looking for one of us to go for a stroll. "We know what he really wants to see!" Mom says, and I laugh along, but I wonder what it is.

Everything is funny in France. Like the time Mom and Dad are shopping with us in the Grand Marché, an everything store where you can get school supplies, flour, sugar, and cow innards for your pâté. We've been in France for a while by then. A voice comes over the loudspeaker to announce a contest. The TV show *Dallas* is very popular in France, as it has been in the US, and the speaker asks: "Qui a tiré sur JR?"

Mom smiles broadly and then starts laughing. She knows they are asking, "Who shot JR?" And she knows who shot JR! In France, the show is airing two full seasons behind what US viewers saw. Eighteen months ago, she'd watched the nail-biter episode in which it was revealed that JR's scheming sister-in-law had shot him. "I know it! I know it!" she says.

"Elle le sait!" Dad calls out, and he's laughing, too. He swings Evan onto his hip, and we hurry through the market to the manager's office, where Dad presents Mom to a man with a stern face. "C'était Kristen Shephard!" she says. The man's face breaks into a smile, and he asks Mom her name, which he announces over the loudspeaker loudly and clearly: "ANN." Then he hands Mom the prize: a red balloon.

THE FOLLOWING WEEK, DAD RECOUNTS the story of winning the contest over dinner at Élisabeth's house. She and her husband, Giles, have invited us for a meal. They live in one of the historic stone houses in the center of the village, and we make our way up a worn stairway to a living area with tiny windows and low ceilings. They've pulled the dining room table into this room and set up a card table next to it so we all fit around it. Mom and Élisabeth have grown so close, though their relationship involves so little talking. At dinner, Dad acts as the translator, telling the story of Mom's big contest win. Everyone watches *Dallas*, and they love the fact that Mom is in the know.

"Alors qui l'a fait?" Giles calls from the kitchen where he is plating our supper. Mom knows what he's asking: "Who did it?"

"Honey, don't tell them!" Mom says, gasping for air as she laughs. She doesn't want to ruin the next year and a half of TV viewing for her friends. Giles appears with a platter of meat, and I'm hungry. By now, I've picked up enough French to figure out most of what's going on, but I miss stuff. Mom places meat on our plates and carves it into pieces. "It's hamburger," she tells us so that we'll try it, and Katje starts chowing it down. But I know it's *not* hamburger. I'm listening to Giles explain that he went deer hunting. At first, I think we must be eating the deer. I take a small bite, and it's pretty okay. A little tough, not like what I'm used to, but okay. I take a larger bite and am chewing it as I listen to Giles and Dad discuss the hunt. Now they're talking about a dog—*le chien*. Their dog apparently went with them. I look around and don't see the dog. They're talking very fast, and I hear the words "shot," "fell," and "dog" in French. I look down at my food. Maybe this is why the meat is tough? Maybe this is their dog?

Just thinking about it, I'm immediately sick, but I need to be polite. I can feel the meat in the corner of my cheek, and I ask to get up. Élisabeth points out the bathroom, and I go into the tiny room and shut the door. I spit the meat into the toilet and gag and run water. I try to drink from the faucet to make the taste go away, but I can't erase the image: we are out there eating their dog. Dad is *okay* with this! Mom and Katje don't understand because their French isn't good enough. I come back to the table and sit. I don't eat anymore. I don't speak. Mom thinks maybe I've gotten sick. It starts to worry her, and she tells Dad we need to leave long before either of them feels ready to get up from the table.

As soon as we get home, my color returns. I ask for a snack. I'm hungry. Mom pulls out some crackers, and Dad sinks down at the table and looks at me: "Why didn't you eat dinner?" he asks.

"Dad!" I say. "We were eating their dog!" Then my dad is laughing and my mom is laughing. They both realize at the same time what has happened: I've only understood part of the conversation. Dad explains that their dog came with them on the hunt, that he lives at their house in the country. We were eating deer that the dog helped them catch! I want to believe them, to be in on the joke with them. Mostly I do, but not entirely. I still worry that no one but me could understand what was really going on.

IN THE FALL, WE TAKE the train to Paris. We stay in a tiny hotel room, and my parents hire a babysitter, a man who smokes all night and ignores us, so they can go out to dinner. They choose a Michelin two-star restaurant, and Mom orders the salmon. It's a thin filet of poached salmon prepared as my mother had never seen salmon made before. ("After that, anytime we went out to eat, she asked for that salmon," Dad says now. "I just remember how much she loved it.") This is one of the best dinners they ever have.

The next day, we visit Versailles. It's a quick train ride, just over an hour. We spend most of our time in the gardens, which look to me like a coloring book in which someone has stayed exactly in the lines. On the way home, Dad decides to pay a visit to his Parisian colleagues in the local office. Mom will need to take us back to the hotel on the train. Dad looks up the tracks for us, and he tells Mom we'll need to make one switch at Montparnasse.

All the way to Montparnasse, I can tell Mom is nervous because her mouth purses into a tight line and she keeps pulling Evan onto her lap. He would rather toddle up and down the aisles with the uncertain gait of a new walker. Mom's wallet with our passports is zipped into a belt around her waist, and she rests her hand on it constantly. As we ease into the station, she sees that we have landed at Track 2. According to Dad's instructions, we have only to cross the platform to board the next train. Evan wiggles to evade Mom's grasp as she clutches him on her hip and drags our suitcase with her other hand. "Go in front of me so I can see you!" she tells us. We shuffle across the platform, file into the new car, and take our seats. Sweat beads at Mom's temples. I look around and notice that there is no one on this train. A red light at the front of the train blinks "Pas en service."

"Mom," I say. "Mom." She's trying to settle Evan. "Mom," I repeat, "Mom, Mom, Mom, Mom, Mom." She looks at me and sees that I am alarmed, and I recognize something in her eyes that unsettles me: fear. Just for a moment. She blinks it away.

"What?" she says.

"This train is out of service!" I say. "It's not the right train!"

Now we are shuffling off it again, three tiny kids and an overwhelmed woman. An English-speaking traveler senses we are in distress and asks where we need to go. "Montreuil," Mom and I both say, because this is the station closest to our hotel. He glances at the board and notes that the train has switched to Track 7. Then, because he's a nice guy, he hoists our case, walks us to the train, and slips the case onto the rack above a bank of empty seats.

We make it just in time.

Dad gets back to the hotel that evening, and Mom and I recount the story of how we got turned around at Montparnasse. Mom is still upset, her eyes glazing. Dad doesn't notice this. He focuses on the twist of fate that led a stranger to help us. He tries to point us to our own ingenuity in catching our mistake. "This is what we came to France to learn! See?" he says. "We always figure things out."

Mom is angry at Dad then, and she's still angry about it when she reminds me of this story. It's been three decades, and she can still conjure her feelings as she sat there: "Your dad left me there," she says. "To get home with three little kids all by myself."

This is where the fray begins. They're looking at the same event, but they're telling different stories. They're both unwilling to acknowledge what is true and has always been true: when it comes to the matter of the train mix-up, they're both right.

SEVEN

We Will Serve the Lord

Whenever we move to a new place, we shop for a church. We're Protestant. Since Dad was raised Methodist and Mom was raised Baptist, we start with the local Methodists, but we aren't picky. We go to a few services and try to figure out which people are most like us, where our parents might be able to find their friends, and where the worship service delivers on its promise to bring us closer to God.

In South Carolina, we join St. Andrews First Presbyterian. We're charter members. My parents first join before our trip to France, when the church still meets in a borrowed space in a high school. By the time we arrive home from our European adventure, there is a newly constructed sanctuary over on Reid School Road. It's modern and light-filled with a semicircle of steps at the front that lead up to a square, wooden pulpit. Every Sunday, we gather for services and Sunday school, and then we go to lunch at Wendy's or Hardee's with other church families.

My parents sing in the choir, and Mom plays the guitar. On special occasions, we perform with her. For Palm Sunday one year, she prepares a family number with hand motions, a song called "Magic Penny" by Malvina Reynolds. We practice in the den, and all three of us belt out the lyrics, even Evan, who is just three. But then when we get to Sunday service, we all go mute—even me, and I'm the oldest. At the appointed time, Mom herds us like ducklings up to the step in front of the pulpit. I turn to see all of the faces watching us. Their attention burns. The guitar starts, and we whisper-sing while looking at our hands. I wonder if the floor will open and swallow us. I sort of hope it does. Then Mom picks up the melody. She isn't nervous. She belts out the lyrics: "Love is something if you give it away," she sings. It's a beautiful song, all about how love is like a magic penny. If you hold on too closely, it'll disappear. But if you give it to others, you'll become rich. Mom has a voice that is large and beautiful and carries. All I have to do is hold on to it. All the people out in the congregation are smiling. They like us. Katje and I are both singing now. Even Evan gets into the hand motions. We hold up invisible pennies for congregants to see and then hug them close to our bodies as we sing: "Lend it, spend it, and you'll have so many, they'll roll all over the floor." Now I'm hamming it up. We roll our arms and then thrust them forward as though our invisible pennies have fallen everywhere.

No one is supposed to clap after music at church, but everyone claps anyhow because we're all so cute, and I know it.

NOW I'M IN THIRD GRADE. This is the year that everyone, even my parents, calls me Jessica instead of Jessi. Apart from starting recorder lessons and playing with the rainbow-colored parachute in gym class, I find school boring. This causes a few issues for my teacher, Mrs. Johnson, who is probably thirty and has red hair that brushes my desk when she looks over my shoulder to check my assignments. I often finish in half the time we're given, and then I distract everyone else. Once, I make myself a challenge to complete the entire week's worksheets with my left hand (I'm right-handed). Upon looking at my nearly illegible assignments, Mrs. Johnson speaks to me sternly. Another time, I offer to help Rico. He gets work that is slightly different from mine. After I finish my own worksheets and turn in my folder at the front of the room, he slips me his worksheets, and I complete them. Other kids around us start to notice. Pretty soon, I'm doing work in my lap for a half dozen. I think I'm being discreet, but Mrs. Johnson catches on and calls my mom. We finally agree that when I finish my lessons, I can excuse myself to the library corner of the room to work on writing prompts that Mrs. Johnson gives me. These are open-ended questions that allow my mind to wander through the lead of my pencil onto the page. I invent characters and tell stories. I hear dialogue in my head that I try to capture. I love this. I speed through my work every day so I can escape to the library's shag rug.

Writing becomes my refuge. Before long, it's what other people notice about me. For the annual schoolwide writing contest, we pen essays about our professional ambitions. I write about becoming an Olympic ice-skater. I explain how it will feel when I jump into the air and spin, the wind skittering across my legs, and land on the blade of my skate without wobbling.

The winners of the contest are set to be announced at the annual spring PTA meeting. It's on a Tuesday night. There in the auditorium, as our parents gather, I wait as the principal calls out each grade's top writer. First. Second. Now I'm holding my breath. I want to win. He gets to third grade, and calls out a boy's name. It's not me. I'm glum and tune out as the principal announces the fourth- and fifth-grade winners. But then he is announcing the overall best writer in the school, and it's me. I hear my name called as if it's coming from a television in a distant room. I almost don't pick up on it. Then Mom nudges my shoulder. "Go up there!" she says. I leap up and walk up the aisle, then climb one step to the low stage where the principal hands me a silver trophy. I decide I'm not going to be an ice-skater. I'm going to be a writer.

Later this year, I get my first diary, as a souvenir, on a trip to Disney World. My parents tell us we can each pick out one thing from the gift store. I walk past the mouse ears and Pluto stuffed toys to pick up this lavender book, which has a tiny lock and key. That morning at the Disney character brunch, while Minnie and Goofy stop by to give my siblings autographs and pose for photos, I slide into the back of the booth and begin to record our trip. I write obsessively. From this point on, I keep a daily log. For the first few years, it's more an accounting of events than a reflection on them. Often, my log involves detailing which friends have slept over and whether they've come with me to church.

CHURCH IS OUR FAMILY'S SHORTCUT to an insta-community. It offers us an immediate sense of belonging. This is especially true in Greenville, where people mention their congregation just after their last name in any introduction. "I'm Ann Hempel. We go to St. Andrews!" Mom will say when she meets people. St. Andrews is open-minded compared with many of the local congregations. Our babysitter, for example, goes to Bob Jones University, a fundamentalist Christian college so conservative that its science department teaches creationism.

Despite its liberal leanings, there are still things that bother my parents about St. Andrews. At Christmas, the church holds a toy drive. Families are invited to bring in newly packaged and wrapped gifts that will be directed to a local charity. One evening, Dad comes home from a meeting to discuss church business, and he's scowling. We're watching TV while Mom puts away the toys we've strewn around the back of the den. Dad sinks down on the piano bench next to her and leans forward, crossing an ankle over his knee. "A man stood up and said that there are a *lot* of poor people," he tells Mom.

"So what's he suggesting?" she asks. Mom is scooping Lego pieces into a shoebox, and her hand begins moving faster and faster.

"He wants to find poor *white* kids to give the toys to," Dad says, almost under his breath, as though he's embarrassed.

Now I have fully turned around. I interject. "Why?"

"It doesn't matter," Mom snaps. Her tone confuses me, and my face contorts as though I might cry. I see her features soften, and she calls me over, away from the little ones. "No, it does matter," she says. She looks up at Dad: "We should explain this."

No one says anything for a minute. I can tell they're uncomfortable, but I don't know why. Then Dad picks up, with the voice he gets when he explains why we have to carry through with a chore like brushing our teeth. "We believe that white and Black people should be treated the same, and that God wants us to share what we have with anyone who has less than us," Dad says. "Do you understand?"

What does this have to do with poor white kids? Who gets the toys? I want to ask more questions, but they both seem uncomfortable. I'm supposed to get it, and I sort of do. "Yeah," I mumble.

As an adult, I'll come to understand that the price of belonging to a church community, or to any community, is accepting beliefs that you don't hold. Sometimes these beliefs are so incongruous with your own that you have to break away from that community and leave it. But when the community is how you define yourself, second only to your name, that breaking away comes with a steep price. You'll be alone. You must reconstitute yourself. You must search for new communities or build your own.

I don't know how my parents would have navigated the racism that simmers just below the surface of our church community, because a few months later, we move again. My Dad runs into some corporate politics at Michelin and no longer sees opportunity ahead in Greenville. This is disappointing, especially for Mom. They've done so much moving. But the company has transferred Dad to another office, and he now spends weekdays on the road, leaving Mom home with the three of us. One night, we're in the tub when Evan pipes up, "Mommy, is Daddy dead?" He's three. Mom scoops him into a towel, cradling him on her hip, and strides down to the bedroom where she gets Dad on the phone immediately to talk to him.

Not long afterward, they decide that staying is untenable. Dad rejoins his old law firm. We make plans to move back to Massachusetts.

I LOVE CHURCH, BUT IT'S not my path to God. I aspire to be a good Christian, and lots of people go to church who are not good Christians. I learn this from Grandpa Hempel, who remains skeptical of his son's life choices. I can tell even at nine by the way he talks to Dad. Grandpa's always pointing out good Christian things my Dad can be doing more of. He doesn't approve of my mother's clothing; she sometimes wears jeans, not dresses. He's disappointed by us kids, by how little we know about the Bible. Every time we visit, my grandparents remind me that God requires devotion and commitment. Daily prayer. A life free of sin. If you fail to honor Him, you'll go to Hell.

The summer that we move north, he and Grandma offer to keep us kids while Mom and Dad look for a house. Now that Grandpa Hempel has retired, they live in a small ranch home in the middle of a farming community in southern Pennsylvania. They grow pears, tomatoes, and other vegetables in their flat, square patch of yard, which backs up to a cornfield where the stalks stand high above our heads. Grandma cans these delicacies and stores them on the shelves at the back of Grandpa's study.

Since we will be with them two full weeks, they enroll us in vacation Bible school in the mornings. Every day at lunchtime, they pick us up in Grandpa's Cadillac, the back seat so enormous that I can stretch my arm out from my body across Evan's car seat and not touch Katje on the far side of the bench. We eat turkey sandwiches on whole wheat bread at the picnic table in the backyard, and then Grandma scoops canned pears into ice cream dishes for dessert. At first, we don't like this food. Pears aren't dessert. Also, Mom usually cuts the crusts off our sandwiches. Grandma says this is wasteful. She tells us crusts are good for us and wasting them is a sin. When we still won't eat them, she begins paying us one penny for every crust we finish. This is motivating. At the end of our stay, our grandparents take us to Kmart. I put my entire earnings—twenty-five cents—down on a copy of *The Bobbsey Twins and the Cedar Camp Mystery*.

Sometimes after dinner, Grandpa gathers us for a quiz. He names a topic, and our challenge is to recite a Bible verse that addresses it. I don't like this game. I rarely know the verses, and I'm not used to not knowing. He may say, "Truth," and then I'll stand there searching my brain, trying to remember any of the verses at all on the back of my weekly Sunday school flyers. I worry that I'm letting down my family, that Grandpa thinks less of my parents because we can't do this.

"Want me to help you?" Grandma says, and after a long time, I'll nod. "How about John, chapter 14, verse 6?"

"Good one," Grandpa will say, and then he opens the New International Version of the Bible and reads: "Jesus answered, 'I am the way and the truth and the life. No one comes to the Father except through me.'"

I try to listen, but the words take on a lyrical singsong quality. I begin to use our afternoon rest time to study for these quizzes, opening my confirmation Bible that has my name embossed in gold letters on the front. It's so big; the pages are paper-thin. I can't ever hold the phrases in my memory.

One night, during a different summer visit a few years later, my grandpa sits on the piano bench and calls us to him. "Tonight's word is 'horse,'" he says.

"I know it!" says Katje. She hops from foot to foot. This is a surprise. The only person worse than me at this game is Katje, who is nearly four years younger. We all look at her, and I grab her wrist as if to protect her from the embarrassment that is about to befall us both.

"Go ahead," says Grandpa. He's smiling, curious.

"As for me and my horse, we will serve the Lord!" she says.

And sure enough, she's almost right. Joshua 24:15: "As for me and my house, we will serve the Lord."

Grandma bursts out laughing. "Where did you hear that?" she asks.

"It's in the bathroom!" Katje says. Just next to the sink in the bathroom, there's a cross-stitch with this verse. Katje has been sounding it out each day when she sits on the toilet. She loves horses, has since birth, and maybe that's why the word "house" lodged in her mind as "horse." Now Grandpa is chuckling. And I'm laughing because I'm relieved that we have made them happy. Katje can't figure out what's funny.

IN THE BIBLE, JOSHUA IS the successor to Moses. If Jesus is the star of the New Testament, Moses is the star of the Old Testament. God calls him to lead the Israelites out of Egypt, where they were held as slaves. Moses hears this call and accepts it, even though it requires him to muster the courage to believe in himself, to believe the voice he hears. Imagine if you suddenly heard voices telling you to do something. It'd take a lot to believe them. Moses frees the Israelites. Once free, however, the Israelites are ungrateful. They don't thank God. They don't praise him. Instead, they worship false idols. For this behavior, God condemns them to wander through the desert, afflicted by plagues, for forty years before they can enter the promised land.

Grandpa explains this story one afternoon when I interrupt him in his study. The other kids are playing in the yard, and I've come in for a cup of Kool-Aid. I peer at him from the kitchen. What is he reading so intensely? He doesn't look up, so I edge in along the wall until I'm right next to him. Grandpa has enormous ears with white hairs that grow out of them. I'm standing right at his elbow when he finally glances up. He's working on a guest sermon that he'll deliver at a nearby church the following Sunday. His concentration is so fixed that he startles, and it scares me. "Come sit here, let me tell you about Joshua," he says. He pulls a chair up, and I slouch into it, prepared for another long story. Instead, he offers a short lead-up and then a question.

Moses never makes it out of the desert, Grandpa explains. He never sees the promised land. He dies, but he has appointed Joshua to lead the Israelites into Canaan, where they will finally be free—of slavery, of plagues, of all bad things. Once Joshua sets foot in Canaan, he addresses his followers. Their parents have been led out of slavery, and they have endured plagues, all for this time that God has provided in the promised land. Joshua gives them the choice: they can worship other gods, or they can serve the one true God. Then he declares: "As for me and my house, we will serve the Lord!"

Grandpa explains that through Joshua, the Lord gives all of us a choice. We can worship other gods. Grandpa believes the gods of our age are technology, consumerism, and desire. Or we can follow the Lord Jesus Christ.

Joshua has made his choice clear.

Grandpa fixes his eyes on mine: "What's your choice?"

"I will serve the Lord," I respond, because I know it's the right answer.

THIS IS THE SUMMER I get serious about prayer. God loves us and will take care of us if we have faith and pray. But if we choose not to, according to Grandpa, we'll wander through the desert, afflicted by plagues. We'll go to Hell.

I'm already an anxious child. I worry I'll get hit by a car when crossing the road to board the school bus. I'm concerned about the Cold War and whether I can hide behind the TV when the Russians break into our den to kill me. After a fireman tells our Brownie Girl Scout troop that the average American will experience a house fire at some point, I begin checking the stove every night to make sure it has been turned off. Prayer becomes my foolproof insurance plan to keep bad things from happening.

Every night, I repeat the Lord's Prayer. I resolve never to forget, and I don't. I add a postscript in which I confess my worries and reveal any lies I've told. And then a "PPS," a post-postscript: "Please look after Brandy [my dog that has died and is presumably in heaven] and Barkley [an earlier dog that has died]."

As I grow, I keep saying the prayer. When I go to sleepovers, I excuse myself to the bathroom and whisper it. In my adulthood, it takes on a Pavlovian quality. I can get on an airplane at three in the afternoon, drop into the middle seat at the back of the coach section, say the Lord's Prayer under my breath, and fall asleep.

WE FINALLY SETTLE IN THE middle of Massachusetts, landing in a town called Shrewsbury. My parents find an Arts and Crafts–style bungalow right on Main Street, a few blocks from the town center. The house number is 666, the significance of which I will only think about much later. We join a Lutheran church called Mount Olivet. The congregation is much smaller than at St. Andrews: I'm the only kid in my grade at the entire church. Mount Olivet's building is tiny and modern. Its central architectural feature is a beautiful organ with dusty blue hand-painted pipes that stretch across the right corner of the choir loft. This is the church we'll be confirmed in, the one we'll attend until, abruptly, we all stop going to church ever again.

Church works differently here. It's more casual. At Mount Olivet, people sometimes wear jeans to services. At school, most of my friends' families don't go at all. I join a baseball team, and sometimes I have to miss games because they're scheduled for Sunday mornings. Who schedules games on Sunday mornings? I wonder. Back in South Carolina, nothing was even open on Sundays.

Mount Olivet's members become our closest family friends. We celebrate the holidays together and host parties for each other. The pastor's daughter babysits us. My parents join the choir, which is led by a gentle hippie man with long wavy hair. Since they sit in the choir loft, the three of us kids often crowd into a pew with the pastor's wife and try very hard not to squirm or giggle during the service. Once when Evan is four, he gets a bad case of the wiggles. The pastor's wife grasps his hand tightly to quiet him, but he continues to move around, bringing his foot beneath him and then releasing it, so that the buckles of his patent leather Mary Janes make loud scraping noises on the bench. Then he leans over to her and whispers loudly, "Do you ever get a bubble in your butt that you just can't squeeze out?"

In South Carolina, this would have been embarrassing, but in Massachusetts, it's funny. The pastor's wife tells my parents during the coffee hour after the service, and she's chortling so hard the coffee sprays through her nose.

I like church. I like the people and the way I feel when I'm there. But I never talk about God with these folks. My relationship with God is my own business, and by the time I'm ten, it has begun to fray. There are things I can't tell God anymore. I still say the Lord's Prayer, out of both fear and obligation, but I drop the postscripts. I stop telling Him what's in my heart, and I hope that He doesn't know. I've realized my heart holds ugliness that God must not see. I don't remember the event that precipitates this, but if I had to guess, I'd say it's most likely the nighttime dreams. One dream concerns my favorite TV heroine, Punky Brewster. She's a tomboy orphan with a lot of spunk. She has black pigtails, a purple vest, and different-colored tennis shoes. I dream she comes to live with me. We share a bedroom. There's a fire in the middle of the night, and I save her. I don't even know what's wrong with this dream, but afterward, it embarrasses me to think about it.

When you endeavor to keep a secret even from God, you can be sure that you're going to Hell.

EIGHT

Our Bodies, Ourselves

In sixth grade, I love Becky Orr. She's my best friend. She has long, brown, curly hair that she parts in the middle and pins back with two barrettes, and a face like a Cabbage Patch Kid doll—round with dimples on her cheeks. We spend our time doing things that border on "little kid," like running through the sprinkler and watching *The Mickey Mouse Club*. Then we go to our respective homes and talk on the phone. When we're not talking, I'm thinking about talking to her. I can find a way to weave Becky into any conversation. For instance, if Dad mentions going to the beach next summer, I might say, "You know who loves the beach?"

"Who?" he'll say, even though he knows the answer.

"Becky Orr."

I don't really understand most of the social life starting to unfold around me. I read a lot, compose poems, and play the French horn, which I took up when all the other girls started flute and clarinet because Dad said it'd help me get into college. I'm just under five feet tall—average for a sixth grader—and 112 pounds. (I know this for sure because I write my weight in the upper corner of my journal every day.) I have a bad perm that I don't know how to take care of, so someone at school gives me the nickname "Medusa." I don't understand where the other girls get their clothes. They all wear Benetton polos, mostly in blue but a few in green.

Once a week they coordinate; someone tells someone and they all wear their polos on the same day. I'll beg Mom for one of these shirts until I finally get one, and it won't matter at all because I'll wear it on the wrong day. Once, I accidentally wear it on the same day as the popular girls, and this is way worse. They glare at me all day, but they never talk to me.

All of this is fine because I have Becky. She's my buffer, my certainty that when we go on field trips, I'll never be left to sit on the bus alone. But then it's Valentine's Day, and Becky gets a boyfriend. I'll never have a boyfriend. I know this in my knowing place. There's something wrong with me. God cannot love me because of this, and so no one else can, either. Mostly, I try to put this knowledge out of my mind. I invent crushes on people and pretend-confide in Becky about them. Becky talks about David until he finally works up the courage to ask her out at the St. John's Middle School dance, and then they are boyfriend and girlfriend.

On Valentine's Day, I make one valentine. It's for my best friend, and it says, "I love you." I remember scrawling this, not liking how it looked, starting over. I want the valentine to look amazing but also casual, as though I might have just dashed it off. I keep this valentine in my backpack and resolve to give it to Becky only if she has a valentine for me. And she does! It's handmade from brown paper with construction paper hearts, and the writing is in glitter glue. She slips it to me in homeroom. Her card also reads, "I love you." I remember the heat that rushes through my body, the way I can feel her look at me as she gives it to me. This is an easy attention. This is a discovered love. And then she wants my counsel. She pulls out a second heart, one that looks a lot like mine but is nearly twice the size. In much smaller letters, she has written, "I love you."

"Should I give this to him?" she asks me.

BEING A CLOSETED GAY GIRL in the 1980s involves hiding out in the open. It's constantly declaring your feelings to the object of your affection and getting away with it because girls are allowed to love each other. *Loving* is entirely condoned. Lusting is something of which we don't speak. I don't have a name for this way that I'm drawn to Becky. I always long to be closer to my best friends, but I don't even know what I'm longing for. To feel more? To merge into them more? To crawl inside their heads? This merging desire feels most possible when a friend is most vulnerable, such as when she is falling in love . . . with someone else.

In this way, I learn to lie to myself: when Becky calls to tell me David kissed her at the St. John's dance, I feel the universe cleave into sections, see her spinning backward from me. She'll like David better than me—differently than me. But just now, it's me for whom she reaches to share this new experience, and I want to hold on to her attention. "I'm so excited for you, Becky!" I say. "Tell me everything."

It's always this way for me with a best friend. For a brief period, I will inhabit them, and then I'll lose them.

THIS IS THE PERIOD WHEN everyone in my family begins to want things we do not have. Katje wants Nike sneakers like the ones her best friends have. She's locked in a solid trio of girls who will travel from kindergarten to high school and beyond together. They're smart and popular and kind, and they all want to wear the same shoes at school. They arrange to go back-to-school shopping with their moms, and Mom and Katje are invited.

The problem is, we're having money problems. Dad has just been made partner at his law firm, which sounds like a good thing. People congratulate him about this at church. But at home, the change stresses him out. I hear him tell Mom that he has to buy into the partnership, which depletes savings we don't have. One night, I come across Dad in his study. His eyebrow is quivering slightly, and he shows me our MasterCard bill. "Look at this," he says, and all I see is a long list of charges and a total at the bottom that is very high. "This is the sneakers we bought you in third grade," Dad continues. I can remember those Zips; they were lavender with Velcro straps, and I wanted them so badly that I'd cried in the store. Dad gives me a lesson on interest, explaining that this choice he'd made was still haunting us. The sneakers have cost us well more than their original price. Debt is the devil. "Never get a credit card," he says. But I know he's also telling me not to want things we can't afford. How much do tennis shoes really matter in the end, anyhow? The Zips haven't fit me in three years.

When Mom and Katje get back from the store, Katje is wearing the Nikes. The side door bangs, and she walks into the kitchen tentatively, her face expressionless, and she looks at me and down at her feet. The sneakers are flashy white, with a periwinkle Swoosh—Air Pegasus. The door bangs a second time. Mom trails in behind Katje, car keys jingling as she deposits them in her purse. Mom's in a mood. She knows we can't afford the sneakers, and I know it. Katje knows it, too, and I can tell she feels bad. Dad will be angry. But what are you supposed to do when you are still new to town, and you're the one mother who must look for knockoff tennis shoes at Kmart? "Next time, we're going shopping on our own," Mom snaps at Katje.

Something is changing about my mom. She used to be interested in things. She painted. She turned our laundry room into a darkroom and experimented with montaging negatives to create fusions of images. She even went back to school and got her college degree, a bachelor's in fine arts. My cousins came for her graduation, and we all wore our Easter outfits to her commencement. But now she's depressed. One day, I come across her crying in the dining room. "I'm so fat," she says. I've never thought of her as fat before. She has always looked so beautiful to me in her dresses with her hair permed and her face made up. But now she's constantly trying to lose weight. When I'm twelve, we go on the rice diet together. I don't remember the rules of this diet, but I do remember eating bowls of white rice and raisins for breakfast and dinner. "If you lose two pounds now," she tells me, "you won't have to lose twenty pounds later, like me."

ONLY EVAN IS CONTENT WITH what he has. He never tries to be like anyone else, never bends to popular opinion or endeavors to fit in. This is as true about him at forty as it is at six, when he loses his underwear at school. Mom notices this at bath time when she's stripping him down for the tub.

I've just had a shower, and I'm standing behind them in a long pajama T-shirt, drying my hair with a towel. Evan's wearing OshKosh overalls, and when Mom undoes the clasp, she sees that he is full commando. "Where're your underpants?" she asks.

"I don't know," Evan replies. He shrugs and climbs into the bath.

"Well, did you take them off at school?" she asks.

"Just partway," he says, and then he doesn't say anything more.

Evan's a stubborn, smart child who lives in his own world. He has wispy white blond hair that has taken forever to grow in, so that he has two tiny nubs where pigtails belong. From an early age, he is prone to urinary tract infections. These are uncomfortable. Mom consults the pediatrician, who puts Evan on medication. The meds help, but they make Evan have to go to the bathroom all the time. This is stressful for him and for his kindergarten teacher. She's been told that Evan will need to use the potty a lot, but Evan is still nervous to ask her. She can be stern and impatient, and Evan has already internalized guilt about requiring this patience from adults. So on the day in question, he tries to hold it. By the time he raises his hand to ask permission to use the bathroom, he has leaked a couple drops of pee.

Evan slips into the stall, a ministall intended for minipeople, and puzzles over what to do about his situation. The fabric feels wet against his body, and he's old enough to know that this could lead to another infection. He resolves to take one leg out of his underpants so that they hang more loosely in his pants. Then he hikes up his overalls, fixes the clasps, and returns to reading circle.

Somewhere between the toilet and his classroom, the underpants slip down his other leg. He doesn't feel this happen, doesn't notice where they slide out behind him. When he gets home, they're gone.

AT ELEMENTARY SCHOOL PICKUP THE next day, Mom sends me into the main office to check the lost and found. We fight about this—because how could she do this to me? Asking for my brother's pee-stained underpants? This is so embarrassing. Yes, it's the elementary school, not the middle school where I go, but Shrewsbury is small. These kids all have older siblings who go to school with me. These teachers are going to tell people. *No one must hear me ask after my brother's pee-stained underpants.* But Mom doesn't give me a choice.

I push through throngs of little kids, hang a right into the office, and there is Becky Orr with her mother. Why is she here? Becky didn't even go to this elementary school, but she's here, sitting in a chair against the wall. "Hello," I mumble, my face flushed.

"Hi," she says. I can hear that her mom is talking to the woman at the front desk. The secretary looks past her to me. "You're Ann's daughter," she says. "Can I help you with something?"

I freeze. I try to think of something to say, some other reason I might have come into the office. At first, no words come out. Then I recover. "No, I forgot something but I just remembered it," I say, and I turn on my heels.

Evan and Katje are already strapped into the back seat by the time I return. The car's engine is running. I slide into the front seat and pull the car door behind me. "Had anyone turned them in?" Mom asks.

"No," I lie.

That evening, I dream that I'm Punky Brewster, and I'm saving Becky from a burning house. The roof is falling in, and we have to climb through a window down a ladder. She grabs me around my neck as I ease onto the rungs. I wake up before I learn whether we survive.

NOW, IN CONVERSATIONS FOR THE Project, both my parents say we knew gay people. Mom mentions her guitar student, a single woman who taught school in the next town over. Dad points to Randy, the church organist, who died of AIDS in 1987. Pastor's wife gathered the ladies who sewed at church to make a square for Randy for the AIDS quilt. I remember this. I knew that Randy died of AIDS, but I never knew that he, or anyone else, was gay. No one talked about that.

I don't know where my concept of gayness might have come from, but by sixth grade, I do have a developed sense of who is gay and what it means. Maybe it's shaped by the reports I've seen on the news about a new disease called AIDS that is killing gay people. Maybe it's the articles in *TIME* magazine. I come to believe that gay people are men, that they live in group housing in dirty cities and make one another sick.

Even at twelve, I know I don't want to be gay like these men. I consider adding a clause to my nightly prayer asking God to make sure I'm straight. But I decide it's too risky, that God might learn I'm having improper thoughts. I tell no one.

A COUPLE YEARS LATER, I'm babysitting for our neighbors two houses down when I notice a book called *Our Bodies, Ourselves* on the shelf in their den. By now, I'm concerned about the way I think about girls, about how I don't ever have crushes on boys. I tell myself this is because I'm still young and some girls don't go boy crazy until high school, but I'm starting to have my doubts.

After I put the kids to bed, I pull the large volume off the shelf. It's a recently updated copy, in paperback, a reference book for everything I might want to know about my body or my sexuality. For a long time, I sit straight-backed in their maroon La-Z-Boy, staring at the closed book on my knees. Finally I open it and trace my finger down the list of contents; there, in chapter 18, is homosexuality.

I look around, as though cameras might be installed on the walls, and then flip to the page. As soon as I start to read, I'm sure. This is me. The feelings these women describe. Even the way they reject and then embrace their physical desire. I try to imagine kissing a woman. The thought grosses me out. I don't yet know about internalized homophobia. Maybe I'm a person who doesn't like kissing? Is there such a thing? I puzzle over the grainy black-and-white photos of two women with short hair, their arms slung around each other's shoulders. They're tough-looking, not girly. Will I cut my hair like that?

Then I realize I've been looking at these pages a long time. What if the family comes home and discovers me reading about homosexuality? I return to the contents page and run my finger down the list of subjects until I get to menopause. There's no way I could be going through menopause. I flip to this section of the book and then volley between the two. If the family comes home, I'll stash the book. But if they see me before I'm able to do that, maybe they'll think I'm just reading for curiosity.

From this point on, I know the thing about myself I have been trying not to know. I understand that it cannot be changed, that it is innate, like my eye color. I'm gay. One day I will need to accept this, and I believe it will end the good part of my life. It will end my ability to get along with the people I know and love. I am gay. I will spend my adult years in a dirty city, living with men I do not like. I won't have kids. But hopefully, also, I'll know women that look like the women in this book. (Would that be so bad?) Maybe, I think, I can stave this off until after high school. Maybe I can buy myself a few more years of the good life, in which I think I can be like everyone else. Maybe no one else has to know.

NINE

I Am the Problem

On Fridays, I take French horn lessons after school. Mom picks me up at the side door by the band room at three thirty. One Friday, I come out and Mom isn't there. She comes directly from elementary school pickup, so sometimes she's a minute or two late. It's a warm day, so I stand on the curb in the sun and wait. Ten minutes go by. I grab the handle of my horn case and begin pacing the length of the curb, the plastic-encased bell bumping awkwardly against my calf—tap, tap, tap. Now I am beginning to worry. My stomach turns. Has she forgotten? She never forgets. Maybe something has happened.

The teacher finishes her next lesson and comes out to get into her own car. "Is your mom coming?" she asks.

"Yes! Yes, she's on her way," I say, and I can feel the heat in my face. I stare at the sidewalk so she can't see my eyes. I decide to count to one hundred, because surely Mom will be there by the time I'm done. When I reach one hundred, I extend my counting to five hundred. Mom drives a fire-engine-red GM minivan that looks like a dustbuster. Maybe she's been in a car accident. I mumble the Lord's Prayer: "Our Father who art in heaven." *I hope she hasn't been in an accident and that she's okay.* "Hallowed be thy name." *But if she's fine, then I'm angry.* "Thy kingdom come." *Really angry. I've been standing here for more than an hour.* "Thy will be done."

Dad's traveling, so I begin to spin through the names of other adults I can call from the pay phone in the lobby. I try the school's door, and it's already locked for the day. Finally, the dustbuster swings into the lot and pulls up in front of me. There are no obvious dents in its fender. My eyes sting, mostly with the adrenaline that now begins to recede. I slide open the back door. "Mom, where were you?" I ask. I'm met with a blast of tension. Katje and Evan, belted into the back seat, remain silent.

"Sorry, I lost track of time," Mom says. She doesn't look at me. *Sorry? That's it? Who's sick? Who's in trouble?* I slide in beside Katje, who shifts in her seat and doesn't look up. Was Mom also late to pick them up?

"Mom, I was afraid you weren't coming!" I say. I'm annoyed now, and I look ahead into her rearview mirror so I can make eye contact with her reflection. But Mom is not herself. Her eyes are bloodshot, red, as though she's been crying, but her mouth is pursed.

"Of course I was coming. I pick you up every week!" she snaps. My words fall back into my throat. She's brooding now, angry-sad, emotional. I've made her mad somehow. "You have to respect my time. I can't always just come *get* you!" she says.

I didn't see this coming, and I don't know what to say, so I apologize. My stomach is turning. "I *do* respect you, I really do."

Now her voice becomes quiet. She spits out her words: "You take me for granted."

THIS HAPPENS WHEN I'M THIRTEEN, or maybe when I'm fourteen. I don't know. For several years, my memories cease to be linear. I don't remember how stories begin or end, or what events lead to one another. Everything becomes complicated.

Mom's having a hard time. Dad has recently taken on some larger clients in Germany and Switzerland, and he leaves for long trips to Europe. She's left to care for us, to keep the laundry running and shuttle us to after-school activities. She also works part-time as a receptionist at the orthodontist's office. It's a job she doesn't enjoy. And of course all of this is hard and a little lonely, but there's something else, too. Something that

people around us begin to notice in subtle ways. Late pickups. The occasional missed appointment. My parents have long been the bedrock of
any community they join. Mom leads the music at vacation Bible school.
Dad is involved in local government. They are trustworthy. They don't
flake. Something doesn't add up.

This is the beginning of a depressive episode, only none of us knows
it yet. I come to think of her depression as an occasional darkness that
rises up to smother her unexpectedly and render her unpredictable. She's
the emotional engine of our family, and that engine is sputtering, crap-
ping out, stalling . . . and then motoring along again. She's exhausted all
the time. She's angry. She's frustrated. She wonders why she's frustrated
and then she realizes: it must be me.

I'm the problem. I frustrate her.

I come across Mom on the phone with her sister in the evenings, the
cord stretched from the kitchen into the dining room so she can sit at the
table and lean her elbows forward, and she's crying. She's complaining
about me, how I talk back to her. I expect her to chauffeur me around,
and then I'm late, leaving her waiting for me. I am absentminded and
often forget to tell anyone when I've gone to a friend's house after school.
I expect my parents to pay for expensive music lessons and then don't
practice enough. I groan when she asks me to do things such as help
with dinner or put the dishes in the dishwasher. I emit long, exasperated
huffs. All of this is true, but is it unusual? I wish I could get to my Aunt
Mary, to tell her my side of the story—that I don't know what's going on,
but things don't feel right here. I think I'm a good kid. I'm in all honors
classes, and I'm acing them! I play in the band! I don't do drugs! But I also
think maybe I *am* a problem. Why else would Mom be crying?

Dad's trips extend from a few days to a week. Sometimes his flight
doesn't land until late on a Saturday night, but he's home in time for
Sunday services. The three of us kids are expected to be in the kitchen,
dressed up, by nine fifteen a.m. on Sunday mornings so we can make the
nine thirty service. Dad pulls the dustbuster out of the driveway at 9:20
for the three-minute commute over to Mount Olivet.

Church is our best chance for support, but it has become alienating. These are the adults that are expected to know us and love us, to be present for us and keep tabs on us. It's obvious something is up—only maybe it's not obvious? The adults are our parents' friends. They're checking in with our parents. If you ask anyone at church, including me, what's wrong with my family, they'll say "Jessi." This is what Mom tells Dad. This is what Dad has come to believe, too. I'm an impulsive teenager with a mind of my own, they'll explain. I'm pushing boundaries. I'm having a difficult adolescence. I'm testing my mother.

I'm going to be the death of her.

I TRY TO BE BETTER. I study her. When I make her angry, I try to memorize what has angered her, to dissect it so that I understand what contributed to it. The trouble is, it's always changing. Mom is a ride through the lush jungles of rural Cambodia: I can't tell when I'll step on a land mine and lose a leg.

After my next French horn lesson, she arrives for pickup right on time. She's smiling when I slide open the van door. She invites me to sit in the front seat, but I opt for the back. There are my siblings, eating graham crackers out of sandwich bags. I mumble "thank you" to her and don't talk the rest of the way home. I want to be invisible. We tumble out of the car, and I sit at the breakfast bar in the kitchen and begin to sort through my backpack. Mom sidles up beside me, and I can feel the heat of her body next to my body. Instinctively, I move back. "I'm sorry for last week," she says. "Of course I pick you up from your lessons. That's a normal thing to expect."

"It's okay," I say, because I don't know what else to say. But that's not why I'm nervous, and I can't explain this to her. An hour and fifteen minutes disappeared while I stood on the corner. The time was unaccounted for, and she hasn't told me where she was. This has started to happen regularly, in different ways. Will it happen again?

Mom pulls me into her in a sideways hug, smooshing my ear into her breasts. She smells like Dove Body Wash. This type of physical affection used to bring comfort, but now it makes me anxious. It's unpredictable. She's unpredictable. "I love you," she says.

MOM LOVES ALL THREE OF us fiercely, but she doesn't love us in the same way. As much as I am her challenge, Katje is her refuge. From the earliest days, when she gravitated toward horses instead of dolls just as Mom did as a little girl, Katje is Mom's favorite—her doppelgänger. It's hard to explain. Katje is just easy for Mom. They have the same humor, the same passions, the same thought patterns. They get each other. Mom has never known how to make me happy, but she knows exactly how to bring her middle child joy. When Katje is ten, Mom meets a woman who has an old quarter horse named Dolly and strikes up a deal: Mom will bring Katje to volunteer at the woman's farm every Saturday morning; Katje will ride Dolly and brush her. After this, every week, Mom helps Katje brush out Dolly's long mane. Mom shows Katje how to hold a carrot in the palm of her hand so that Dolly's lips and teeth mash right up against Katje's skin without gnawing her stubby fingers off. At the feel of the tickle, Katje squeals and laughs, and that is Mom's joy.

Why can't things be easy like this with her eldest? It's a question Mom wonders about. She asks Katje when they're in the car, on the way to and from the barn. Her children have always been so sweet to one another, and it's still true. Why do they get along so well? "Why is Jessi so nice to everyone else?" Mom says. Her middle daughter sits silent, listening, taking it all in.

WHAT IS A LIFE SUPPOSED to feel like?

Mom doesn't know. Her life doesn't feel the way she believes it should. She lives in a suburb much more upscale than the neighborhood in which she grew up. She's married to a lawyer, and by most measures, her children are impressive and successful. Isn't this how it's supposed to be? But her husband is always working, and he doesn't seem to see her. This has been building for years, now that she thinks about it. Actually, right from the start. In the earliest days of their marriage, they went in to talk to their minister about communication problems they had. It was the closest they had come to therapy. The problem they could identify was that they wanted different things—Dad wanted to get their financial life on track, and Mom wanted to start a family. On the minister's advice, they chose both. Dad went to law school, and Mom got pregnant with me. Everyone got what they wanted, but they didn't get better at communicating. For years, it felt as if they were on the verge of starting the life they wanted. They were having their babies. They were following Dad's job opportunities. They were changing cities and countries. Always, it seemed that the start of the life they would share together was just up ahead. But now the start has come and gone. They're settled. And instead of feeling that she finally has my Dad's attention, Mom feels that she has lost it.

At first, she thinks Dad has lost interest in her because she has let herself go. We can't afford fancy clothes, and she spends any extra money on her kids. She's heavier than she has ever been. She diets, and her diets take five pounds off her frame that our Dad doesn't notice, and inevitably she's so depressed about this that she then puts ten pounds on.

When Mom doesn't receive affirmation and attention from Dad, she finds it from other places instead. At some point, she begins to take in strays. Once, we come home from school to find that she has agreed to foster a one-footed duck. He swims around and around in circles in a wading pool in our backyard until she finds him a forever home. She has a soft spot for animals, and she begins to allow us to populate the house with a menagerie that grows to include two dogs, four rabbits, a hamster, and two birds. Then, Mom buys the horse while Dad is on a business trip. The woman who owns Dolly has decided to get rid of her and offers her to Mom for just five hundred dollars. That's cheap, when you don't consider the cost of stabling and feeding her. Mom is resourceful, and by asking around, she finds a neighbor who will board the horse. "What's this sixty-eight-dollar charge?" Dad asks the following month as he reviews the checkbook.

"Oh, I bought Dolly," she responds. "That's her monthly upkeep."

They fight about this, and the fighting feels good—or at least like something. At least when Dad is quizzing her about how they'll pay for this horse, he's noticing her. He's thinking about what she wants, how she spends her time. This works at first as a way for her to connect to him, but then it starts to have the opposite effect. With each impulsive decision, Dad retreats. He starts leaving the realm of Home to her.

THROUGH CHURCH, MOM STARTS TO volunteer with an organization that shelters children from the developing world while they have medical procedures done. For a while, we have a teenager from Korea with a weak heart; she is followed by a toddler from Ecuador with a cleft palate. The rush of providing the aid is enthralling, but then when they are gone, Mom gets tired. She is alone again, with only the three of us for company. We're needy and self-centered. We want her to pick us up places and drop us off, and we rarely thank her. Every morning, after school drop-off, she brings the laundry into the den and settles back in the recliner to fold it. At ten a.m., she turns on *Little House on the Prairie*. Most days, she gets the laundry put away, does the shopping, and picks us up by two p.m. But now there are occasionally days when she doesn't pull herself out of the chair. The laundry remains unfolded. Friends' parents drop us at home, and we pull Bagel Bites out of the freezer and microwave them for our dinner. I can still see her there, always with a basket of laundry that she is in the midst of folding. There is always so much laundry to fold.

As the youngest child, Evan takes all this in. He hasn't yet reached double digits, and he believes his childhood is why he remains lovable. He is cute, and he knows this. He dreads growing up. His older sisters are his models. I am so much older than him that he can't decode me. He and Katje are just two years apart, yet they're completely different. The things that come easily to her, like dressing up and liking boys and being popular, aren't things that he is good at or even cares about. They don't get along. So he already knows that, rather than the kind of tween my sister is growing into, he is more likely to be the kind of teenager I have become: Trouble. A disappointment. A disaster in the making. It's all up ahead, but for now, he keeps to himself. It's his way of protecting himself.

And Dad. Where is Dad? Traveling. Working. Traveling some more. He has started to take on more cases for clients in Germany and France, and his trips stretch to ten or twelve days. Sometimes he even misses church. When he is home, he escapes to his garden. He is a cutout silhouette, a small slice of black space retained for his eventual reappearance. Long before there are cell phones, my dad's attention feels like the attention we afford people and things when really we are furtively scrolling through Instagram.

I FEEL GUILTY WHEN I start to think there's a problem with the way Mom treats me. Mom's punishments are rarely physical. Their greatest deficit is that they are odd, inconsistent, and often delivered out of context. And, disproportionately, they're trained on me. One day, I'm in my bedroom, which is a sprawling dormered room that spans the entire third floor of the house. It has no door, just a stairway that climbs six steps to a square landing and then takes a sharp right turn, rising another ten steps. The walls are covered in lavender paper, with images of ribbons spiraling vertically down, wrapped in purple and white flowers.

I don't remember why Mom is angry initially, but I can hear her banging the pots and pans in the kitchen as she washes up. "Jessi," she calls. I opt to pretend I don't hear her. Maybe she'll call one of the others. But she storms up the stairs. It's a mess up here. I've left outfits strewn all over the floor. I'm sitting in the midst of these clothes with my headphones on, listening to the *Into the Woods* cast recording again. I pull down my headphones and look up at her, and she places one hand on her hip. Why does it feel like she's mad at me for being happy? The air hisses in and out through her teeth. "You don't take care of your things!" she tells me. We both know she's right. The Banana Republic shorts I begged her for are on the floor, and she leans over to scoop them up. Now I'm worried. I grab a pair of sweatpants and stand up to put them away. She moves her body in front of mine, and she's standing too close, towering over me. "Why do I buy you nice things if you don't take care of them?" she says. The blood has rushed to her face. Her arms are wild and unwieldy as she sweeps up these clothes—every last item—and thrusts them into our attic. "I'm sorry, Mom!" I say. I've learned that the phrase is a shortcut when she is this way, the quickest way to de-escalate any situation. But it isn't working. She twists the key in the attic's lock and pulls it out. I'm crying. "Please, Mom!"

"I'm going to teach you a lesson," she says. "They're gone for a week." She pockets the key. I know there's nothing I can say that will change her mind at this point. I can try to lobby my dad, but he's unwavering in his commitment to back her decisions. If she says this is an appropriate punishment, he will agree. Mom's domain is Home. My nice school clothes are locked up until the following Friday. I have only sweatpants and the clothes on my body.

If the point of this exercise is to humiliate me in front of my peers, it works. I'm ashamed. This shame is about having only one outfit to wear in high school, when I'm already a social pariah. Already, I don't fit in. But it's also a shame about my mom. By now, I know this behavior is erratic and unusual, that it isn't in line with how other people I know are disciplined. It feels important that my teachers don't know about it. This is something I intuit but can't explain. Beneath all of this is the deep shame that I know what I really am. Maybe God knows, too. Maybe God is punishing me, sending plagues down upon me.

I bring the cordless phone into my closet and call my best friend, who is Julie that year. "Mom is crazy-mad," I whisper into the receiver. "She's locked my clothes in the attic." I tell Julie that I'm scared of Mom, she's yelling a lot. This is true. But what exactly am I scared of? I beg Julie to keep this our secret. "Are you okay?" she asks. "Are you safe right now?" This is how I discover that in addition to bearing witness to her crushes, there's another way to feel close to your best girlfriend: invite her to be part of your emergency.

Julie brings me clothes. Normally, we don't see each other every day because we aren't in many of the same classes. She's a year older than me.

But every morning that week, we meet in the band room before class, and I slip on her Champion sweatshirt and her jeans. These clothes smell like her. All day long, I can feel them wrapped around me, and sometimes I daydream about what she might have been doing the last time she was wearing them. These fantasies are surprisingly G-rated—maybe she was baking chocolate chip cookies, something she loved to do.

Then, just before the last bell, I meet Julie again. I pass her back her clothes and assume my week's uniform so that when Mom picks me up, I'll be wearing the same clothes again. Julie hugs me. "I'm worried about you," she says. I'm letting her think things are a little worse than they are at home, but it feels worth the hug. We have a secret, from Mom and from everyone at school. It's just ours. The thought of it makes me feel warm and excited.

TEN

Help Us

I'm sitting in my closet, beneath the church dresses, when I hear the car pull into the driveway. There is lavender wallpaper inside the closet as well, and as I crouch beneath the clothes, pushing aside the water shoes my parents got me for my sixteenth birthday, I make a practice of tracing the flower ribbons, counting each bloom.

Outside my window, the abrupt cutoff of the car's engine brings my attention back—the car door slamming, the tinkle of the keys as Dad slips them in his suit pocket. I focus on my knees, how they're pulled up so close I can rest my chin on them. I can feel my head, too. It's throbbing. I let it fall forward and reach my fingers to the back of my scalp, parting my hair to feel for a lump. How long have I been here? The afternoon light has changed.

Downstairs, Mom sits in the TV room recliner. It's evening, so probably *The Mickey Mouse Club* is on. She's been crying. Maybe she's still crying, but she's also fuming, and she's so tired. She's parented the three of us—me and my siblings, who are then twelve and ten—by herself for nearly two weeks while Dad has been in Europe. We've been alone with one another, the four of us, pacing around the house avoiding one another like roommates who used to be friends and now can't get out of their lease.

OUR FAMILY'S OCCASIONAL DUSTUPS HAVE escalated into constant conflicts. It's my junior year of high school, and this dynamic with my mom has intensified. We still have stretches in which things are good, consistent. But now, the bad times have drowned out the good times. I've become distrustful of Mom even when she is reaching out to me. There are too many days like today. It's a Thursday. I'd noticed when I woke up that she was in a bad mood, so I'd gone with Julie to another friend's house after school, but I'd forgotten to tell Mom. When I don't come home, she's concerned. This concern escalates into anger. She begins calling around to friends' parents and reaches Julie's mom, who tracks us down. I'm doing algebra homework a few blocks away. It's after five p.m. by now, and I haven't realized it has gotten so late. "My mom says your mom is *mad*," Julie tells me.

Julie's got a car—a light blue Subaru—and volunteers to drop me at home. I don't want to go, but I don't really have a choice. I begin gnawing on my thumbnail, which has been bitten down to its nub. As Julie pulls up, Mom is standing on the side porch. Her face is blank. I hop out of the car and attempt to assess whether I can get past her and into the house without a conversation. We live on a busy road, and Julie has to ease the Subaru back down the driveway and then wait for traffic to part so she can edge out. She isn't gone yet when Mom grabs my right arm just beneath the shoulder, dragging me up the stairs and pushing me in front of her through the side door. Does Julie see this? I want her to, and also, I am embarrassed and hope she has not.

Mom yells at me, but I don't remember what she says. She grabs the tall wooden coat tree just inside the door, most of our jackets toppling to the floor of the mudroom, and begins whipping it down to within centimeters of my skull and then pulling it back. The dog is barking now, and Evan is there in the kitchen, too. Once, only, Mom lets it slam into the back of my head with its full force. The fact of having done so seems to scare her. She lets up as I begin whimpering. "I'm sorry,

Mom, I'm sorry," I tell her, because I really am sorry. I never set out
to upset her.

"Go to your room," she says—a constant refrain in our house and
always a relief. I flee through the kitchen and up the stairs to the safety
of my closet, where the lavender ribbons of flowers trace the same path
down the wall every day. Sometimes I zone out in this closet and entire
afternoons disappear, in a form of meditation as protection.

That's where I am when Dad arrives several hours later. I can feel my
head throbbing, a headache emerging. I'm happy. There's no *not* seeing
the bulge that has swollen up on my skull. Now I have something to
show him. I've tried to talk to him about the constant conflict, but he
doesn't believe me. Now, he can't miss it.

Dad is a distant figure, consumed by his job. And if Dad is honest
with himself, he likes work. He's good at it and rewarded for being good.
All of the problems at work are solvable. It's orderly, and no one needs
anything from him that he isn't the absolute best person to provide. Even
when he isn't off in Europe, his days are long. He wakes before six a.m.
and drives Katje a mile down the road to the barn. While she mucks the
stall and feeds Dolly, he sits in the car, skimming the *Worcester Telegram
& Gazette*. Back at home, he eats half a grapefruit and then drops me off
at the high school on his way to work, well before seven thirty a.m. He
rarely makes it home before seven thirty p.m., after we've eaten dinner.

Dad has always traveled. When we were younger, my siblings and
I gathered on my parents' king-size waterbed while he unpacked after
these trips. He brought us back hotel shampoos and shower caps and the
same box of small Swiss chocolate bars that we would apportion evenly
between us. As we aged, Dad's trips grew longer. We sometimes forget
now whether he's home or traveling, but Mom never does. She feels abandoned. Dad's return often coincides with a crisis, an emergency that seems
designed explicitly to remind him that his absence is our undoing. Today,
my failure to alert my mom to my after-school activities is the crisis.

Mom hears Dad's car as well. She lifts herself from the recliner and
meets Dad at the breakfast bar. I can't pick out her words. I pull myself

up and tiptoe down the stairs, pausing on the landing, just out of sight. I can't see her, but I can hear her tell him I'm irresponsible, that I just do whatever I want. She tells him I don't listen to her, that there's nothing she can do, that she can't control me.

"Jessi," Dad calls, and I'm there too fast. He doesn't hug me. We all know I have just overheard everything Mom has said. Time slows down as he waits for me to speak. I'm aware of where each of us stands, the way Mom has positioned herself between us. Dad hasn't taken off his suit jacket yet. "What have you got to say for yourself?" he asks.

I have so many things to say, but I'm silent. I'm looking at Mom, and I'm at once scared and sad. No matter what I say, Dad will travel again, I'll be alone in this house with her, and she'll hold my words against me. Nothing will change. Still, I've been practicing my words, speaking them quietly to myself. My headache emboldens me. I place my hand on the back of my head to be sure. "She hit me," I mumble. I'm looking at the floor because if I look at them, I will lose my nerve. "With the coat tree. She hit me."

Dad's eyes dart between us. "Is that true?" he asks Mom. I see an opening. He might believe me. I'm remembering France, that first day that Dad and I walked into town. Dad's hand was my anchor, his enthusiasm my guide. Now I want his hand, want him to reach into the murk and haze of my life and give me an anchor.

Then his knowing is gone. Mom's eyes grow confused and then fiery, her body feels large above me. "I never hit you," she says. She looks at Dad as if to ask, *Can you believe this? What am I supposed to do?* This is what confuses me. I can see she believes herself; she's not lying. And if she's not lying, then I must be.

Help me, she's asking him.

Help me, he's asking me.

Help me, I'm asking.

Only there's no one to ask. My head aches. I can feel it. I try to push words out of my mouth, but nothing comes. My dad raises an eyebrow at me, and now he's disappointed. He can't trust me. I can't trust me.

ELEVEN

It's Not You

I become too much for Julie. It's understandable. The late-night calls, the crying. The way I get upset about my parents and then make excuses for them so that she must hold the incongruity of my many truths. Julie confides in an assistant administrator at the high school, Ellen Meyers. One morning, Mrs. Meyers lays a hand on my shoulder as I enter the building and tells me to come see her after lunch.

Mrs. Meyers's office is in the basement of the high school, on an interior corner, across the hall from the speech and debate room. Between classes, when a swell of adolescents spills into that hallway, she steps out to supervise, calling people by name when they need to slow down—or just when they look as though they need to be seen by an adult. She's tall but seems taller because she's so thin. She has dark brown hair, a thin nose, and nails that are always manicured. Maybe because she's so thin, she's always cold. She's always holding a mug of hot water with lemon because she can't stomach the caffeine in tea.

Her door is closed when I arrive. I stand there, looking through the window. I'm too timid to knock. Eventually, she looks up and beckons me in. I sit back in the one chair beside her desk and pull my knees into my chest, hugging them tightly. Her eyes assess me, running from my forehead to my toes. "How are you doing?" she asks.

By this point, I'm tired—exhausted. My life has bifurcated. At school, I'm lively, engaged: winning speech tournaments, part of the pit orchestra for the play. At home, I mostly hide in my room. In between, in the final period of the day as I prepare to make the shift to home, I get sick with nerves. I grow short with people and stop concentrating. If an after-school program runs long so that there's even the possibility that I'll be late to the sidewalk for Mom's pickup, I throw up slightly in the back of my mouth.

All of this is private. It's my business. I don't share it, not even with Julie.

"I'm okay," I say. For a long time, neither of us says anything. But Mrs. Meyers has a way of using silence to elicit information. The quiet expands between us until I feel compelled to fill it.

"What's going on at home?" she says. It's a pointed question. It isn't gentle. I feel as though I'm being disciplined, as though I have done something wrong. I start talking. The words come out in a jumble, and they don't communicate what I intend them to. But the act of reaching for the words at all has its desired effect. A rush of relief washes over me. For a few minutes, I feel better.

Mrs. Meyers understands more than I'm able to comprehend about my family. She doesn't have the entire story, because it isn't known yet. But she knows enough to know where I'm wrong. Whatever is happening at my house, I'm under the impression that it's my fault: that this cloud that looms above my family is the product of my screwy adolescence; that I've become a teenager, and teenagers are difficult, moody, and disobedient. When I'm at school during the day, after I've relaxed into the consistency of a predictable schedule and before I sink into the anxiety involved in going home, I can sometimes hear the voice inside me suggesting that maybe I'm not the problem. But when I get home, I can see the pain Mom is in. I believe I'm causing it.

I begin to stop in to see Mrs. Meyers regularly. Our conversations often start the same way. "I don't really understand what's going on," I tell her. This has been my default way of putting off the process of feeling my feelings. If I could just think about it more, if I could just understand it more, then what? "I don't get it," I explain, and then I share whatever has happened. Mrs. Meyers listens. I come to depend on that quality of her attention. When all the story is out of me, she scrawls "It's Not You" on a yellow Post-it, and then she sticks it on the front of my notebook. As the weeks progress, my notebook accumulates dozens of "It's Not You" Post-its. I lacquer them down with clear packing tape and layer more on top. It becomes a code, so that sometimes I don't need to tell her what has happened anymore. I can just swing by her office, and she'll slap a Post-it on my notebook. "I'm going to keep on writing this until I know that you believe it," she tells me.

I look at that notebook, which I keep sandwiched between my French textbook and my science notes. I read those words, and I feel seen, loved. But somewhere just beneath all of this, I believe I have her fooled.

IT'S 1991, AND I'M A junior. This is the year that I become a tracker. I track two people. I track Mom because that is the way that I can best take care of myself. I learn to observe her tiniest habits so that I can determine when she is going to fly into a tirade. I can tell by her body posture in the kitchen when I first see her in the morning: whether her elbows are drawn in and close to her side instead of expansive and relaxed, whether she is looking away from us and down. Most of the time, things are normal. She's busy with the things that busy her: Katje's horse, the part-time job, church. But I can feel the air change density on the days that she is not busy, and I work to make myself scarce.

The other person I track is El. That's what I call Mrs. Meyers after we get to know each other. She's popular among the kids, and she has a few other projects—students who rely on her the way that I do. El is busy, and she rarely has free periods in which I can drop into the chair in her office and hang out. She worries about me. She has set me up to talk once a week with the school guidance counselor, Mrs. Garvey. But if something happens, something that is Significant, she finds time in her own day.

I begin to test this. I invent things that happen. I embellish real events, adding details that I assume are necessary in order for something to qualify as Significant. I show up at her door, peering in until my eye contact signals to her that it's Really Important, and then get a pass to miss French class so that I can sit in her office and try to explain the emergency. Often in these moments, there isn't an explanation, at least not one that justifies an emergency. Because how do I explain that the emergency is just that I need an adult to anchor me, to see me and love me as I am and assure me that everything is going to be fine?

One day, I'm walking to French, passing El's office, when I see that her door is shut at a time when it is not normally shut. I slow down, peering just a bit too long, and inside are my own mother and father. Why are they there? I think I'm going to puke. Why don't I know that they're there? I trust El, and I trust that she believes me. But she hasn't told me my parents are coming in. I sit in my French class and don't hear a thing the teacher says. I'm obsessing, running over in my mind the ways that events might transpire, worrying that right then, El and my mom are piecing together that I have lied about everything, that shortly everything will be *over*. That El will take back her Post-its and cease to love me.

Later, my stomach in knots, I poke my head into El's office. I tell her that I saw my parents in there: "What's going on?"

"I couldn't tell you," she says, shrugging. She looks stressed. "I had to take the meeting, and I couldn't tell you." I never find out what happens during this meeting, but afterward, our family starts counseling—me, Mom, and Dad.

AS I EMBARK ON THE Project, Mom and I revisit this period in our lives. We've never spoken about it. There are too many things on which I'm certain we still won't agree. There are too many things I just don't want to dredge up. Even now, Mom holds on to the idea that I was a difficult teenager, and I suspect I really was.

"Did you ever have this kind of trouble with the others?" I ask her. Katje and Evan were in middle school then, watching from the sidelines.

"They didn't push as many buttons," she tells me. I ask her whether she remembers going to the counselor, and it's all kind of hazy to both of us.

"I remember this guy . . ." I begin.

"It was a guy?" Mom asks.

"I don't remember," I say, and then Mom jumps in.

"There was one therapist—she was *miserable*. Really poor at what she did. I wonder if that's the one we had for the three of us . . ." she says.

Here's what I remember about therapy: We go on Wednesday afternoons at four p.m. Mom and I drive from home, and Dad comes from the office. We sit silently on the way there. We sit silently in the waiting room while we wait to be called. I don't remember the gender or the age or the demeanor of the human who treats us. I do remember that the first time we go, this person asks to see me alone before my parents join. They tell me that if I'm being hurt in my house, I can speak up. I remember this for its absurdity. For one, no one is physically hurting me—not often or much, anyway. But more absurd than that is the theater of those meetings. I'll be with this therapist for an hour, and then I will go home with my parents, and I can only assume that I will pay a price for whatever I reveal to this stranger in front of them. By this point, I have lost my bearings. I don't know what's normal and not normal, what is a secret and what is worthy of sharing. I resolve to share nothing.

My parents join me, sitting on either side of me on a very long couch. I don't remember what we talk about, only that I have a sense that my parents don't talk to each other about important things or even little things. This hour we spend together in a room is as much time as they devote to their shared parenting conversation, at least in front of me. So how is anything supposed to get better?

IN TRUTH, MY PARENTS ARE no more clear about why our family life is unraveling than I am. I've stopped trying to talk to Dad. I'm taciturn and surly with Mom, and then I go to school and tell another woman the things Mom wishes I'd talk to her about. One day, we're on the way to pick up my friend to go to play practice, with a theater group I've joined. Mom pulls the car to the side of the road. "What have you been telling Mrs. Meyers?" she asks me. I mumble a response, or maybe I say nothing. I don't recognize her countenance. She isn't angry or depressed or out of control. It's something else, a desperation, holding back tears. This next part is engraved in my mind: "What happens in our house is our business," she says. "Maybe it's not perfect, but you've got it pretty good. If you keep telling people all these things out of context, you just wait. They'll come and take you away from us. Do you want that?"

Then she pulls back into the lane. We drive around the corner and pick up my friend. In an effort to keep my friend from noticing the heaviness that engulfs the car, I become overly boisterous on the way to the theater. I laugh too loud at a joke she makes. I ask her a lot of questions. But inside, I'm reeling. Mom is threatening me, trying to scare me, scaring me.

And Mom, she's scared. She's losing me, even if she doesn't lose me to foster care. She has lost me emotionally to a stand-in mother she didn't select or invite. She is losing her grip on her family and on her role within it. She doesn't know why.

WHEN MOM AND I REACH the end of our conversation about my teenage years, she arrives at the conclusion I've long held: maybe it wasn't me she was mad at. "It was probably a muddled mass of anger at your dad. You know, I was mad at him for so long. Not knowing why. And not channeling it enough to know why I was angry," she says.

The truth of this sits between us. She apologizes. But I don't need her to apologize. She tells me how proud of me she is, how she was the one who lost her cool. "I mean, you were a normal teenager, honey," she says. I've been waiting for this final affirmation, this "It's Not You" to arrive for so many decades, since the first time El slapped that Post-it on my notebook. "I remember being so jealous of her," Mom says.

I'm on the sofa in my Brooklyn living room. I've been hiding the depth of my relationship with El so long that I'm nervous when Mom brings her up, but what she has to offer is resolve: "I'll be forever grateful that she was so supportive of you."

I think this revelation will feel different, that it will come as relief. But it doesn't. El is dead, gone two years now. She had an awful cancer but hung on long enough to witness my marriage and the birth of my son—two things she wanted for me. I'm grown, launched. I've been absolved of the conflict of my adolescence, assured by both my mom and my stand-in mom that things were hard, and it wasn't my fault. And I still don't totally believe it. I can't tell you what parts I made up and what parts happened. Some small and still shrinking part of me, a part that will never completely disappear, believes I might be lying.

TWELVE

All of the Ways We Pretend

Hugh is the first gay guy that I *know* that I know, but we never talk about this. He's tall with dusty brown hair and a wiry frame, and it always seems that he's slouching, as if maybe he could just will himself to take up a bit less space.

We meet at practice for the regional theater, where I have a very small role in *The Miracle Worker*. This is just before my senior year. Hugh and I have a lot in common. We were born exactly one day apart. And both of us have trouble with our families. Hugh lives in a town on the other side of Worcester from my town, Shrewsbury. I only ever go to his house once, to pick him up for rehearsal. He's from a Catholic family, born somewhere in the middle of a pack of five kids. He has grown up on Saturday Mass and catechism class, and he found his way to theater earlier than I did. We make jokes and play pranks throughout our rehearsals in the run-up to the show. We all give one another shoulder rubs, and I love the feeling of Hugh's strong fingers digging into the spot at the bottom of my shoulder blade.

The week before our performance is tech week. We're expected at the theater every night. We eat pizza and play cards in the green room. There are inside jokes and, as the night wears on, shared confidences. I don't remember anything about the performance, but the cast party is a blast. We hug one another as though we've all just been to another planet together and now we must return to earth. The letdown will be inevitable. I hug Hugh last, on purpose, and we hold on longer than anyone else. As we pull away, he looks me in the eye. "You have my number," he says. "Call me."

Hugh and I become phone friends. Our first conversation is awkward, but then gives way to something as close to comfortable as I ever get with anyone. Pretty soon, I'm rushing home from school to call him. I never quite figure out Hugh's living situation. He lives at home, but he also stays in Worcester, in the fancy apartment of this older man, Donnie. Donnie has this Daddy Warbucks vibe. He lives alone, and he has a busy job and a packed social calendar. I can't figure out what his interest in Hugh is. Donnie's apartment is huge and fancy, the closest I've ever seen to anything that might qualify as rich. Hugh has liberal use of it and use of a credit card while he stays there, as well as a car. At the end of an early phone chat, he asks me what I'm doing on Friday night. "Want to get together?" he says.

"Like, a . . . ?" I almost say "like a date," but I don't. I'm sprawled on my back on the carpet in the middle of my bedroom, the cordless phone tucked behind my ear. We talk about how everyone is dating someone and how neither of us knows anyone at our high schools that we want to date. We're too busy for that, busy with our school work and the French horn (me) and the theater (him). The things that are important to our peers are not the things that are important to us. We get drunk on each other. We say things like "I like you so much!" that exist in the ambiguous place where the "like" could be platonic or another kind of "like." The truth is that I *love* Hugh because I feel seen by him, close to him. I know it's not romantic love. There's no rise in my body temperature when I think of him, no heart skip, but there's great relief when I credibly tell my friends: "I talked to Hugh for two hours last night." They've never known me to have a boyfriend, and now they're left to assume that Hugh is one. I live in the quiet shadows of these assumptions other people make, letting their stories about me become my temporary truths. So to the Friday night invitation, I say, "Yeah, totally, what do you want to do?"

"Donnie has a hot tub," he says. He lets these words drop. A hot tub. This has a sexual vibe. I don't know what's supposed to happen in a hot tub. It scares me. What's he asking?

That Friday, I drive Dad's old Honda Prelude over to Donnie's apartment, and Hugh meets me in the parking garage to show me where to put it. We're nervous around each other, shy. He lets me in, and I follow him through the master bedroom and into the largest bathroom I've ever seen. The hot tub is just as he described it, big enough for four people and with a television on the left edge. Donnie is in Los Angeles on business, and we're alone.

We stand there a few minutes, not talking. I can feel myself blushing. *Be normal!* He leans forward and turns on the bubbles. He isn't looking at me. I let down my backpack and open it. Inside, I've stashed a bathing suit—a one-piece navy suit with green horizontal stripes on top. It was my just-in-case suit, and now it feels like a relief. I yank it out and he smiles, his eyes finally meeting mine. He disappears into Donnie's bedroom and comes back in trunks.

We use Donnie's credit card to order Chinese food—so many takeout containers of dumplings and salty lo mein. And we sit there in the hot tub in our bathing suits, slurping noodles and watching *Say Anything.* Diane's father asks Lloyd Dobbler what his future plans are, and both of us recite his line in tandem: "I don't want to sell anything, buy anything, or process anything as a career . . ." I know this film so well. I've watched it a million times with my friends. He stumbles here, but I keep going: "I don't want to sell anything bought or processed, or buy anything sold or processed, or process anything sold, bought, or processed, or repair anything sold, bought, or processed." And then he sings out the final phrase: "Kickboxing! Sport of the future!" Is anything in life this good, ever? I have rarely felt so comfortable with another person. I intuit that we share the same secret. And I know that we have the same need—for a story to share with our friends, to have for ourselves.

I'll tell my friends about this evening, and I won't make anything up, but I will leave things out, and I'll let them believe what they want. This is the best date I've ever had.

THE ONLY WAY OUT OF pain is to address the wound. This is as true of spiritual and psychic pain as it is of the physical variety. But sometimes the price of tending to what hurts is too great. We shut down our intuition. We push away our feelings. We suffer, and we don't even see the way that we cause others to hurt as well. That pain can be acute, as it was in the combustible years of my early adolescence. But for long stretches, the pain can also be tolerable. A dull ache. A longing. A sense that there is an unrealized greater version of our lives ahead of us if we address what hurts, wrestle with it, accept it. But maybe there's also a good enough version of our lives in which we honor our commitments, follow the rules, and make peace with what we don't have. This is what it means to live in the closet. Isn't it enough to enjoy good takeout and a movie in a hot tub on a Friday night?

This is the chapter of our family's life when we're all trying to make everything okay, and for a while, it works. Things feel easier at home. For one, I've begun to see an exit plan. I start to receive thick marketing envelopes from colleges and universities. Dad brings home the bricklike compendium that is the *US News & World Report*'s college rankings, which lists every school along with its size, its SAT requirements, and a short description. I sit at the dining room table, working my way through the book and highlighting my top choices with a yellow pen. Do I want a small school or a big one? Urban or rural? Should it have a conservatory? A writing program? I have only two hopes for college, both unarticulated. I want to go far away. And I want to cement my straightness. For this reason, I am drawn to the Deep South. William & Mary. The University of Virginia. Davidson. Washington & Lee. I only add Brown because El says she can see me there.

Mom's depression has let up. Is it because I've grown out of my difficult phase? Or because counseling has sounded the alarms for our family, and Dad is traveling less? I suspect she can also see just how close we kids are to grown. Her baby is in the sixth grade now, a middle schooler, old enough to stay home alone while Mom takes Katje to muck out stalls in the afternoon. Mom is already wistful, wishing for things to be different and better in these last months before I go to college.

Meanwhile, Dad is trying to show up more. He plans a southern college tour, which he combines with a family vacation. I can imagine him sitting with the paper in the morning in the car as Katje shovels out stalls, trying to figure out where to take everyone. That's where he gets the idea. He and Kat have always had a tough relationship, strained. He's looking for ways to connect to her. I suspect he calls a travel agent from his office to investigate whether it's even possible. It is! And if he uses his corporate discount for the hotel, maybe we can do it. He waits until he's holding the folio with the hotel reservations to introduce the idea. Mom's getting school lunches together. He and Katje have just gotten back from another morning trip to the barn, and Dad stops her before she dashes into the bathroom for a shower. "Who wants to go to Chincoteague Island for pony penning day?" he asks.

Mom drops the brown paper bag she's holding and looks up. She's smiling, and it's a real smile, big and inviting. They had talked about trying to do this several times before. Katje looks at Mom's smile and looks at Dad. "Me!" she says. "Me, me, me, me, me!"

Everyone in our family knows about pony penning day, even Evan and I, who aren't really into horses. Mom read the children's classic *Misty of Chincoteague Island* with her own dad, and then she read it to us when we were kids, sitting on the back porch of our house in France. Misty is part of a breed of feral ponies that live on a small island off the coast of Virginia. Once a year, volunteers round them up and force them to swim across the channel. The babies are auctioned off, and the ponies are returned. Mom has always wanted to go to Chincoteague Island, and now Dad has suggested it!

THE ANNUAL RUNNING OF THE horses starts the third week in July. On Saturday afternoon, a group of volunteers called the Saltwater Cowboys begins rounding up the wild ponies. A couple hundred of them gather in a corral on Assateague Island, where they wait until Wednesday morning. If you drive up on the island and park in the lot by the beach, you can catch a look at them. You'll notice how small yet sturdy they are, with salty, shaggy, windblown hair that has never been brushed by little-girl hands. Over the next few days, these ponies are checked by a vet. The point of the auction is to control the size of the herd so it doesn't become too big and overrun the island. It's also a fundraiser for the Chincoteague Volunteer Fire Company, which will use part of the proceeds to fund veterinary care throughout the year.

In the end, I can't go watch this spectacle because I have to take the SATs. I'll fly down at the end of the week to join the family in time for a visit to the University of Virginia. So most of what I know about this part of the trip is pieced together from Mom, Dad, Katje, and Evan.

That Monday, they drive eight hours to Virginia. They stay at the Comfort Suites, a hotel just off the bridge that connects Chincoteague to the mainland. The atmosphere in town is frenetic. Tens of thousands of tourists have come in for the festivities. Everywhere there are ponies, and postcards with ponies, and T-shirts and stuffed animals. A nightly Volunteer Fireman's Carnival has games and raffles. The local theater offers free showings of *Misty*, the film based on the classic book. It's hard not to get swept away in the excitement of the moment. "Honey, I think we need a pony!" Mom says as they walk around town that first afternoon. The first time she says it, it doesn't sound serious.

The pony swim is Wednesday morning. Mom wakes Kat and Evan up before the sun rises. They're groggy but powered by adrenaline. Even Evan is excited now, because the whole town is on edge, as if collectively holding its breath. For the entire week, without the pressures of friends and school and my presence, Katje and Evan have been getting along. They pull on their sandals. Dad drives two miles to the Assateague parking lot, where they leave the car so they can wade right down into the water to watch. The Saltwater Cowboys have gathered the ponies at the edge of the corral. They're waiting for the slack tide. This is a short window of time—about thirty minutes—between tides when there is no current. The water is as still as it ever gets. The gates .open, and then all Katje and Evan can see are pony heads and necks, moving in a pack through the water like synchronized swimmers. They all make it across—even the little ones that seem too tiny to be so strong. These horses are so tiny you want to wrap your arms around their necks and hug them. But they are feral. They'll rip out your guts with their hooves in a flash.

After the swim, the ponies are given a rest. Then the Saltwater Cowboys round them up and parade them down Main Street to the carnival ground, where the auction will happen on Thursday morning. I imagine Mom with her camera at the side of the parade, snapping photos. Dad holds Evan's hand to keep him close. Mom's favorites are the dappled baby ponies, so miniature they'll look like big dogs when they're grown. "Look at that one!" she says, pointing to a tiny marcher. "Maybe we should bid on him!"

THAT NIGHT, DAD CAN'T SLEEP. He remembers tossing and turning, wondering what to do. His wife and kids have spent all day "choosing their pony," as Mom keeps saying. She talks as if they're going home with one. But that was never the deal. How can they afford that? They can barely afford Dolly's care, and next year he'll have to pay part of my college tuition. They're *not* going to get a pony. They can't.

The next morning they squeeze into the bleachers to watch. It's crowded and East Coast humid, with droplets of sweat beading up on their foreheads and at their necklines. As each pony is led to the block, the auctioneer speaks quickly, his voice like a runaway train. Then Mom sees the one from yesterday's parade. "That one!" Mom says, pointing to a dappled gray colt.

"How would we even get it home?" Dad asks, and he thinks he has the upper hand here because they haven't made any plans. But he doesn't realize that Mom has already figured it out. The previous afternoon, she spoke with vendors all over the fairgrounds. She'd called Dolly's barn to see whether there was an extra stall for a second horse. She'd even found a man who makes a business out of hauling horses home for buyers. When they leave Chincoteague to pick me up at the airport in nearby Newport, Virginia, this man will drive the new charge north.

Dad understands that she's serious. She wants a pony. And, really, a pony might be great for them. It'll make her happy. He wants to do that. And it'll help his relationship with Katje. She's jumping up and down beside Mom. She didn't really think this was going to happen.

But now Dad takes control. It doesn't occur to him that part of what is going on here is that Mom wants to pick this pony. He doesn't like her choice. He doesn't think the pony is a good value; he doesn't believe that this tiny runt of a horse will grow large enough to ride. Mom and Dad have left the bleachers and are walking from stall to stall, Katje and Evan struggling to keep up with them. "How about that one instead?" he says. He points to a dark brown colt. Mom is so surprised by his sudden willingness that she doesn't question his choice in the moment. Then Dad sidles right up next to the auctioneer. The man is calling out the numbers. "Oh, do it, honey!" Mom says, and Dad lifts his hand to bid. Neither of them believes it's happening. And then they are there, in Virginia, with a pony. He has knobby knees with a black mane and a white streak down his nose. They agree to call him Bandit because he has deep shadows around his eyes. It looks as though he's wearing a mask. These shadows, it turns out, are just baby fur that sheds as Bandit grows. Every living thing evolves.

THAT FALL, EVERYTHING FEELS AS if it has momentum. Each of us is pleased with the present, and planning for the future. I hang out with Hugh whenever we're not in school or at theater practice. I bring him to meet Bandit. We're all busy with Bandit, who needs more consistent care than Dolly has needed—training and daily socializing. He gives our family a collective purpose. As Bandit grows, Katje gets right up on him. I marvel at this. I would be terrified, but she isn't.

In the winter, college letters begin to arrive. I get into Brown. Through the school's admissions office, I arrange to stay overnight with a student. She's smart and funny, and she takes me to eat at the dining hall with a big group of friends, including one woman with an Ani DiFranco T-shirt and a shaved head. "Is she a lesbian?" I ask when we're back in my host's room.

"Does it matter?" she responds. I blush. I don't answer. We talk about something else, but when I get home, I get Hugh to go with me to the record store. I buy my first Ani DiFranco CD, a 1993 album called *Puddle Dive*. Now letters begin to arrive from campuses in North Carolina and Virginia. What will be important to me about the next four years? I have no idea. At Davidson, there's a laundry service, and everyone joins so-rorities. But the more I listen to Ani DiFranco, the more I want to spend time with people who know all the words to Ani's spoken-word poetry and songs. I decide to enroll at Brown.

WHEN I LEAVE FOR COLLEGE, I'll stop going by the name Jessica, introducing myself as Jessi for the first time since kindergarten. I won't keep up well with anyone, even Hugh. It's a way that I'll try to forget who I was before I discover who I am. Four years later, when I'm home for my final college break before graduation, Mom will hand me Hugh's obituary, which she has snipped out of the *Worcester Telegram & Gazette*. The column of news-print will say he died of an apparent drug overdose. I won't know whom to call because I never really knew his parents, and I never met Donnie in person, despite all the Chinese food I ended up having at his place. I'll sit at the dining room table, stare at the small piece of newsprint, and cry. Mom won't know what to say or understand what's behind my tears, but she'll sit there next to me, and it will be a comfort. I will wonder then as I wonder now: Did Hugh ever come out?

THIRTEEN

Both Hands

"The Q is for queer," says the guy at the front of the room. "But some people think it means 'questioning.'" He reminds me of Hugh, times one hundred. I'd thought "queer" was a bad word, sort of like "fag"—a pejorative word for gays, one that had been turned into a put-down, as when someone says something idiotic: *That's so queer.* But this guy says we can reclaim words, that we can decide on their meaning.

This is the LGBT session for Brown, and it's mandatory for all first-year students. Along with my dormmates, I'm crowded into the dusty student lounge in the basement of Andrews Hall, sitting cross-legged, shoulder to shoulder. I'm between a blonde-haired prepster from New Jersey and my roommate, a Filipina American premed. I'm wearing a striped polo shirt, jeans rolled at the ankle, and Bass penny loafers. And as I look at our moderator and his two assistants, I'm disappointed. This first month of college is about deciding who I'll be here. I'm in the process of picking people to spend time with based on my own self-perception: Do they dress like me? Think like me? Talk like me? These LGBT moderators do not. There are two men, both with long hair and sways to their walk, lilts to their speech. And then there is a woman, a lesbian. She has dyed black hair and bangs trimmed high and straight across her forehead. She wears a black T-shirt, a short black leather skirt, and thick eyeliner. Her backpack is a metal lunchbox. This is the person assigned to educate us on lesbianism? All three of them speak, but I watch only her. She sits on the table, her legs swinging back and forth, as the three of them go through the resources available on campus. She pushes her body back on the desk, her legs spread. And then I notice. She's not wearing underwear. I'm embarrassed that I'm looking, but it's impossible not to see this. I glance to my left and my right, and others are noticing, too. Now I'm uncomfortable. I don't want to be like her. I'm not like her. I must not be a lesbian.

MY FIRST YEAR OF COLLEGE begins like summer camp and turns into a reeducation program in which I discover that I cannot stop looking away from the things that make me uncomfortable. Eventually, I'll need to tend to them. In my first journal entry at Brown, I write, "I heard college referred to once as a federal witness protection program for adolescents. I can be exactly who I want to be and am." But those things—who I want to be and who I am—turn out to be different. I find classes difficult. I've never struggled in school, but now I'm surrounded by private school kids who have a much more coherent approach to their education. They seem to know what classes to take. I sign up for philosophy on the premise that it will address my philosophies of life, and I am perplexed to discover the dense and confusing work of old dead male authors like Kant. I nearly fail the class my first semester before an adviser suggests I drop it.

There's another thing that begins to emerge. College doesn't feel right. The days don't feel right. There's a cycle I'm used to at home that is missing, the catch and release of tension, the fear that I'm always on the brink of an emergency. Every day is the same here. I'm in charge of how I wake up, when I sleep, and what happens in between.

And there's no one for me to track. I've spent years watching from the side of every room, evaluating how my mother or El is behaving. When things were bad, and also when they were good, I was trying to figure out, Who did I need to be in order for one or the other of them to love me?

At school, I have a great roommate and a group of friends on my hallway. I have a predictable schedule. I babysit for extra money. There's no one to track. Nothing is wrong, and it panics me. I don't know how to live this way. Absent the drama of uncertainty that has accompanied living with my mom's depression, I'm lost. I grow depressed.

In October, everyone comes to visit for parents' weekend. On the Friday, Evan sleeps over, and we stay up until two a.m., hanging out in Leisha's room. Leisha is the resident counselor for our dorm. A sophomore, she's been trained in basic peer counseling and gets a single large enough for a couch. She leans back on it, strumming her guitar while Evan, who is in eighth grade, tells us about a crush he has. "Are you going to tell him you like him?" Leisha asks my brother. She takes him so seriously, and I watch him work through an elaborate series of thoughts that total up to "probably not."

"Well, you should. Maybe he feels the same way," she says. He considers this, and his raised eyebrows suggest he doesn't believe her.

The next night, Katje sleeps over, and we crash early and wake up at six a.m. to go for a run together. As a ninth grader, she can feel that things around her at home are off. Even when Dad is there, he isn't there. She tests him constantly. She tells me about this one time: He's sitting at the breakfast bar, eating his grapefruit and reading a paper. She pulls out his Grape Nuts, the cereal he doesn't like to share, and pours herself a bowl. He says nothing. Just beneath the cereal in the cabinet next to the breakfast bar, our parents keep their liquor. Neither he nor Mom drink much, but they have a collection of fancy liquors on hand. Katje opens a bottle of cognac and sits it down next to her bowl. He doesn't look up. She uncaps it and pours it over her cereal. He doesn't notice. She doesn't even put it back, just leaves it there next to the bowl as she starts to eat. Dad says nothing. Her belly turns and her head aches, and she regrets all of it immediately. Mostly, she regrets testing Dad and having to learn that really, truly, he isn't paying attention. It would be better not to know.

I worry a lot for my siblings. And eventually, I start to talk to Leisha about my worry. She's supportive. One evening, very late, I knock. I've

had a call with my sister, and I'm upset. It's twelve fifteen a.m., but I can
see the light beneath Leisha's door. She's already in bed, trying not to fall
asleep over a textbook. She invites me in. I plop onto her couch and tell
her about my family—how I'm still not 100 percent sure whether my
conflict with Mom is my fault, how my dad is checked out, how I worry
about my siblings. Leisha listens until no more words come. It's late now,
maybe two a.m. She's almost falling asleep, and so am I. "Here, just come
sleep in my bed," she says. I cross the room and snuggle in next to her,
and it is the rightest feeling.

I HAVE A CRUSH ON Leisha. I'm certain of this. But I don't tell her. Instead, as
my malaise deepens, I seek her out. Often, I don't have anything to say.
I just want to be around her, to feel her energy. She's an athlete, and she
plays guitar and sings in a band. She's got this amorphous-gender quality to her movement, purpose and strength that comes from the tennis
court blended with the emo lyrics she puts to her guitar chords. I like
to study in her room while she writes music. And does Leisha like me?
She worries about me. It's her job. She calls the dean of student life, who
schedules an appointment to talk. I'm reluctant. I want to stay in my
federal witness protection program as long as I can, to deny and ignore
what has happened before I arrived on campus. But then Leisha issues an
ultimatum. I need to go if I want to continue to talk to her. And she even
volunteers to go with me.

   A few days later, Leisha and I sit in the waiting room of Dean Carla
Hansen's office in a small brick building a block off the Main Green.
Dean Hansen is running a few minutes behind. I can hear her muffled
voice on the phone on the other side of the door. I tap my leg and look at
Leisha and turn back. I wish I hadn't agreed to this. Then the door opens,
and Dean Hansen appears. She's tall, with shoulder-length platinum-
blonde hair, a square jaw, and sparkling eyes. She invites me in, and I
take a seat. On her desk is a picture of her and another woman, with two
redheaded little girls. She tells me they belong to her and her partner,
and I key in on the word. This woman is gay. This accomplished woman

with a cool job and normal clothes and children—who doesn't carry a metal lunchbox and is probably wearing underwear—is gay.

Dean Hansen refers me to psych services, where I start therapy, the first time I have visited a therapist on my own. I don't remember much about the appointments, only that in that office I first acknowledge to another person that "I think that maybe it's possible I might like girls."

WHEN I FINALLY COME OUT, at the start of sophomore year, I will wonder why it took so long. I've been accepted into the resident counseling program. It's a guarantee that I'll have a plum housing assignment, and I land a single in a newly renovated dorm right on the Main Green, Littlefield Hall. The week before fall classes begin, I participate in leadership and peer-counseling trainings to learn what to do if first-year students have any number of problems, from eating disorders to family crises. When I arrive for these trainings, I try on the identity. "I'm questioning," I tell people. Questioning is its own category at Brown, a liminal period during which one is free to not know. It's being gay with take-backsies— the ability to say, nope, I was wrong about that. There's even a group that meets on Sunday evenings for people who are questioning. I gather a couple of the first-years in my dorm to come with me. We all sit in a circle, our legs crossed, and look around at one another, wondering, Do I have a crush on you?

That fall, the air comes whistling out of my secrets. One Sunday, a woman walks me home. We wander from Keeney Quad, through Wayland Arch, and then swing down past the main dining hall to my dorm. "Do you want to come up?" I ask, and she follows me up to the lounge on the second floor. I microwave two cups of hot water for tea, and we bring them back to my room. Nearly half of the floor space is taken up by my single bed. I'm confident I know why she is there, but I don't really know what's supposed to happen next. The mechanics of a kiss are mysterious to me. It's not just that I've never kissed a woman before, but that I've never kissed anyone. I pop a mixtape into the stereo and up comes a song from Ani's first album, *Both Hands*. The music is so angry, all about the end of love, and I've been shout-singing it ever since I confessed my crush to Leisha and she didn't return my feelings. This woman on the edge of my bed is not the end of love or the beginning; she's just a similarly curious person, trying to figure things out. I sit down next to her. She leans forward and presses her lips against mine. Her mouth is soft and delicate, and it tastes like the Trident gum that I can tell she has just swallowed. Now I know one thing for sure: I like this kind of kissing.

A YEAR LATER, I FINALLY fall in love with someone who loves me back. It starts as a crush. Jen is a short, dark-haired midwesterner whom I meet in Education 100, one of Brown's more popular courses. We're in the same five-person study group that meets four or five times a week throughout fall semester, but that's not enough for me. I want to see more of Jen. I endeavor to be everywhere she is. I join the Ultimate Frisbee team because she plays. I sign up for Intro to Economics because I notice it on her course list for the following semester. (Really, this is the only reason. No one at Brown is making me take economics.) I keep track of where she moves throughout the day on campus and begin to show up in these places.

Jen is an introvert, someone who is deeply okay with silence. If I land next to her on a sidewalk for the seven-block walk back to the part of campus in which we both live, she may not say anything for the entire walk. Her silence inspires silence in me. This is not my natural state. When we finally get together, it's all I can do to keep from telling her—and everyone else I know—how I feel about her all the time. I try to restrain myself, to record these thoughts in my journal instead. I still have every note, card, and email she sent me during that first spring, printed and pasted in this journal, along with descriptions of how I felt upon receiving them. I try to describe every night we spend together, every adventure we take. All of this cliché first-love stuff becomes unpleasantly banal to revisit, but here's a taste. On May 3, 1996, my entry begins, "I derive satisfaction from the simple act of writing her name," followed by twenty-one lines of her name, written out: Jennifer Jennifer Jennifer Jennifer Jennifer. I will love her in this way for a long time.

I'M OUT NOW. SHORTLY BEFORE my twenty-first birthday, I shave my head. I grow to love the way the wind feels skittering across my scalp when I run down the Frisbee field. I've embroidered a pink triangle on my backpack, and I keep my hair short or shaved. I dress differently, too. The polo shirt and loafers never made it past freshman year. Now I wear button-down shirts and men's corduroy pants from Goodwill. I've made a tight group of friends, most of whom are queer. I become the treasurer of the LGBT Alliance. A friend starts calling me the BDOC, the big dyke on campus, and the name sticks. By senior year, I'm living off campus in a run-down three-bedroom flat where I throw a party in April 1997, when Ellen DeGeneres comes out on national television. So many people show up that I have to borrow TVs from neighbors for the kitchen and bedroom. I still run into people who remember watching culture change in my living room. However, somehow I miss the exact moment. I've enrolled my closest friend, Heather Rowley, in monitoring the door. She stands on the front porch, making sure we at least know who is coming into the flat. Just as the opening credits start to roll, she shouts back at me. "Jessi, is that your car?"

I look out the window, and there's a tow truck backing up to my car, which is very obviously parked in front of a hydrant. I grab the keys and run down to the street, where the guy has already started the process of filing the ticket and can't rescind it. "Please!" I beg, as he tries not to make eye contact. Suddenly, a cheer goes up so loud that we both stop what we're doing to look up. "You at a party?" he says.

"Hosting it," I reply, and I want to cry. I walk upstairs with a $180 ticket in my hand, wondering how I'll pay for it, glad that he at least didn't tow my car away. There are so many people I can't even get into the living room, so I lean against the doorframe. Heather throws an arm around my shoulders. "I can tell you what happened," she says. "Ellen said she was gay."

———

MY PARENTS ARE THE FINAL frontier. I work up the courage to come out to them in a car when they're driving me home on a break during sophomore year. They're getting along okay. If I had thought about them much, I would have seen that they were unhappy. But I don't think about them much at all because I am too obsessed with figuring out myself—eating at the co-ops, studying Russian and calculus and the sociology of gender, taking poetry workshops, dipping my toe into all kinds of identities that don't quite fit in search of something more solid.

When they show up, Dad is driving the black Jeep Grand Cherokee that they've recently gotten to replace the dustbuster. I notice it has leather seats. Fancy. Things are changing for them financially as Dad becomes more senior at his firm. I have scripted what will happen next. I've even tried it out on a friend. The ride from Brown's Providence campus to our Massachusetts home takes just under an hour. We are all wearing seat belts; no one has to look at one another. I make my announcement with a force that doesn't at all reflect my internal doubt: "I'm pretty sure I'm gay," I say, focusing my eyes on the headrest in front of me.

In the front passenger seat, my mother begins to cry. She tells me it makes her sad because I won't be able to have children of my own. Then she says she thinks maybe my cousin Charlie is gay because he is very emotional. Charlie is eleven at the time. Then she tells me that she still loves me and always will love me.

Dad stares straight ahead, hands on the wheel at 10 and 2. He says nothing.

The next morning, I'm eating cereal at the breakfast bar in our kitchen when Dad walks in. He pours a bowl of Grape Nuts and adds skim milk. "I thought I was gay once, too," he says, so casually he might be telling me that he also wore oversize sweatshirts in college.

"Really, Dad?" I respond. "What did you do about it?"

Dad drains the milk out of his bowl with a quick slurp and stands to grab his briefcase. "Well, I married your mom," he says. Then he heads out to the office.

If there's a moment when the fragile lining that holds the five of us together and maps our relation to one another begins to fracture, it's now. I remember the sound of the screen door hitting its frame as Dad leaves, the hum of the fan in the living room window, sucking in the springtime air, the barking dog. I have heard each of these noises before, but that morning they sound different, distinct. My father is more than my mother's husband, more than my dad. He is a man who once had thoughts about the direction of his life that had nothing to do with me. I want to ask him about this, how he met my mother and whether he fell in love with her. But he is gone. And even if he weren't, that small window of opportunity has evaporated. It will be three more years before my father's sexuality comes up again. When it does, in a flash, all five of us will be thrust into a new world with no rules and no familiar signposts.

PART THREE

Hurt

FOURTEEN

Outing Dad

All change is abrupt, even the change that happens slowly over time. There's always a singular moment that defines it. It's the flip of a switch, the wrong turn, the letter opened, the instant of knowing. Afterward, you search back to see who you were in the seconds before the change. You try to experience the feeling of the life you have just left. But it's as impossible as trying to conjure the feeling of snow in summer.

In the run-up to my family's implosion, I'm traveling. I've been out of college for a year, and I've spent that year exploring with Heather. We pass a few months living in a hospital community in Haiti. After visiting us there, Heather's parents help subsidize our next adventure, a hiking trip for both of us in Nepal and India. It's 1998, and for almost a year, I don't have good phone or internet access. This is deliberate. I need the distance to figure out who I am absent my connection to my family. I write letters. I reach out by fax every few weeks; my parents can't really get in touch with me. Katje is gone, too, off to her first year at Ithaca College. Only Evan is home with our folks, and even he is almost never there. He's a junior in high school, working part-time at Westborough Savings Bank and learning pointe at dance class as he prepares to apply for college.

Do any of us see what's coming?

Things are not great between my parents. Mom and Dad appear to coexist in the same house but have little to do with each other. Mom has become a music teacher, like her own mother. It started with a few guitar students, but now Mom has a roster of nearly forty piano and guitar students. She's really good at it, patient with children and genial with the adults. But she's tired at the end of the day. She eats dinner early, then retires to the tan recliner in the family room, where she watches television until she falls asleep. When he's not traveling, Dad gets home from work at seven or eight, and then disappears into the computer room. They've stopped going to church as regularly. They're both depressed, but they don't have a language for that, so they're nothing.

That summer starts off with momentum. Dad is set to turn fifty, and this presents a reason to celebrate. Mom plans a surprise party for him, and the act of party planning is a pick-me-up. It's nice to have something to rally around, a reason to feel excited. His birthday is in August, so Evan will be home from Camp Calumet, the Christian summer camp that he attends for ten weeks every summer. I'll even be back for the party, treading water between my travels and the start of a teaching job in New York City. Mom will throw this party in the church basement at Mount Olivet. All of the church friends will be invited, but many others as well. Kat has an internship in Dad's law office, so she figures out whom to invite from his work. Mom calls his sister Martha to invite her. His best friend from Middlebury will probably even travel up from Pennsylvania.

As summer gets underway, only Katje is living at home, back from college and around to help with invitations and plan the menu. She has a new boyfriend, Jake, who lives in Vermont. They've been together since January, and she really likes him. Every minute that Katje is not at work, they talk. Calls are expensive, so mostly they instant message each other on their laptops. The software they use is a 1990s classic, ICQ. Its logo is a little spinning daisy. Their transcripts are recorded, and sometimes if Katje is missing Jake after they've spoken, she'll dip back into those transcripts and read them again. One Saturday afternoon in late July, she's chatting with Jake when her laptop abruptly shuts off to download some new software. She counts as the time goes by for the laptop to reboot, but it's impossibly slow. Maybe it's broken. So she goes into the guest room, where Dad has set up the family desktop. It's one of those large computers that rests vertically on the floor. A cord runs to a monitor on the desk. Katje clicks on the ICQ window, and up pops that chat box. She logs into her account and looks for Jake online. But then someone else says "Hello" to her, and that's weird. He asks what time he should come over. She notices that Dad's alias is still logged on, so this person must think she's Dad. Who would be chatting with Dad?

"Who is this?" she types back. And just like that, the voice stops. The disembodied chat-head seems to have realized that someone else is in front of the computer, someone who is not my dad.

Kat is savvy enough with software to pull up Dad's profile. She finds that he has two accounts, one of which he uses to talk to her and people she knows. The other is a mystery. On his profile, she clicks on "history." She discovers transcripts between this man and my dad, and then she knows. There are many men. There are many conversations, sexually provocative conversations, banter that makes it clear that Dad has been talking to men on the internet and maybe meeting men out in the world.

There's so much gay porn.

Katje's breath gets caught in her chest. She wonders if she's drowning. She kicks the computer, and when it doesn't budge, she wallops it again with her foot, hard, so that it falls over, the screen going dark. She sits back in the chair and pulls her knees up. What do you do if you stumble across your father's digital life and discover he's not who you thought he was?

MY PARENTS ARE IN THE car, having just finished furniture shopping, when Dad's brick-size Nokia cell phone begins buzzing. They're booking it home because Mom's sister Mary and her husband, Karl, are arriving from Illinois for a weeklong visit. Dad is driving, so Mom answers. On the line,

Katje sounds wild, upset, like she might cry-scream, her voice swallowing a warble as she spits out her words. "Where's Dad?"

"He's right here," Mom says. "We're on our way home. We're almost
pulling into the driveway."

Then Katje speaks. Everyone remembers this story a little differently.
No one remembers the name of the man who was messaging on the
computer. Was it Johnny? Or was it Ed? Let's go with Ed. All three of
them recount with complete certainty the next statement: "Tell Dad Ed
says hi."

TELL DAD ED SAYS HI. Dad puts it together immediately. His hand on the wheel
begins to tremble as he tries to maintain the fragile vessel of his known
self. He knows Katje has been on his computer. Katje has stumbled into
his shadow life. He has not fully acknowledged his shadow life to himself, but now his daughter has seen it. He's thirteen again, stepping up to
account for his actions in boarding school. He's twenty-four, trying to
tell a therapist one truth about who he might be. *No, they are saying, no,
you just need to grow up.* He's forty-nine, a partner at a prestigious firm, a
member of the town's finance committee, in the choir at church, a father
to three children, a husband. He also believes he is a pervert, and he was
always a pervert, and now his middle child knows.

At first it seems reasonable that he can lean on Katje to keep this a
secret. This is absurd, but he isn't thinking straight. "Hold on," he tells
Mom to tell her, "I'm almost there."

He's pulling the car into the driveway, and he can see Katje standing
on the side porch. She has car keys in her hand, and she's on the phone,
probably talking to Jake. Just as this is happening, a pickup truck pulls in
and edges up behind him. Mary and Karl have arrived. Mary is waving,
her hand moving double time from side to side, her smile no match for
their scowls. This is a lot to manage, but Dad is a master of managing.

As he hops out of the Jeep, Katje clicks the phone off, sets it down
on the porch, and slips behind the wheel of her own car. She's been cat-
sitting for church friends. She's going to feed their cat, she announces.

Her voice is expressionless. Aunt Mary stops smiling. Dad looks from his daughter to his sister-in-law to his wife, who is so surprised and confused that she is silent.

"I'll come with you," Dad says to Kat, and before she can refuse, he slides into the passenger side of the car. His goal is to try to figure out what she has learned, how much he can still hide. Immediately, he can see that this is futile. She has seen too much. Even one exchange would have been too much. And what has been seen cannot be unseen. The jig is up: secret Paul is not a secret. They drive in silence while she waits for him to start talking. But he can't think of what to say. When they reach the house, he follows her inside. "Do you hate me?" he asks.

"No, but you have some fucking nerve," she replies. He has never heard her swear.

MOM KNOWS THE WORST HAS happened, but at first, she doesn't know what the worst is. She watches her daughter and husband pull away and then turns to help Mary and Karl with their luggage. Everyone can tell Mom and Dad are in the middle of a crisis. Mary is a decade older than Mom, and Karl—my mom's beloved older brother-in-law—has been married to her sister since Mom was ten. Mary is a short, round version of my mom who has spent her nursing career taking care of the tiniest babies in the newborn intensive care unit. She cries when she's happy and hugs as though everyone will be gone tomorrow. Karl is a witty Swedish American engineer and farmer who named his dachshund after his favorite beer, Miller. They are the rock on which Mom has always leaned when things become unsteady. And now they're standing in the driveway with her, witnessing her watch her husband and daughter leave.

She knows they can see that she is not herself. She is sadder and heavier than she was the last time they'd seen her, a year earlier. She knows they have watched her become less of herself now for years. Something is happening—only what's happening? Who is at the heart of it? Like so many people, they have stood by as this family has come disassembled, without understanding where the problem is, what needs to be fixed.

Mom lets them take over. Mary goes inside to put things in order. The phone is ringing, so Mary picks it up. A man is asking for Dad. Why? Karl beckons to Mom to get into his car, and they drive down to our local pizzeria. Karl orders two coffees. They sit there like that, not drinking their beverages, as Mom puzzles over what might be going on. Has Dad cheated on her? He must have cheated on her. Maybe Katje discovered this. But who is Ed, then? Something awful has happened. It has been happening for a long time, but this is the first day she *knows* it.

ONCE OUR FRIENDS' CAT HAS been fed, Katje drops Dad back at the house, stuffs her backpack with essentials, and leaves. She needs to go away, to go somewhere where she can process this for herself, to go somewhere where she doesn't have to see them—see him. Jake lives with his father in Vermont, and he invites her to stay the rest of the summer with him. She doesn't ask our parents, and she doesn't even tell them. Her keys jingling in her hand, she hugs Mary and Karl without making eye contact. Then she slips Alanis Morrisette into the car's CD player, turns up the music so loud she can't hear herself think, and hits the gas. That evening, once she has arrived, she calls our parents to let them know where she is and that she's safe. Mom gets on the phone, and her voice is quiet, monotone. Dad has told her. "It's going to be okay," she says.

"I'm staying here," Kat says.

"How about your job?" Mom replies.

"I'll figure it out." Kat doesn't plan to quit her internship at Dad's office. She'll commute more than two hours to Boston and sit in a cubicle three doors down from Dad, just so that he can be reminded every day that although he may have blown up their family, he hasn't destroyed her. She won't acknowledge him when he passes by her and won't respond to his emails. It'll be impossible for colleagues to miss the way she ices him out, but no one will ask. This thick daily tension will last for another three weeks.

But that first night on the phone, Mom is still trying to convince

Katje that all is not lost. "It's going to be okay, it's going to be okay, it's going to be okay," Mom says.

This turns out to be true, but it will take a decade.

IN OUR CONVERSATIONS FOR THE Project, I ask Mom what she remembers about this day. By this point, we've been having regular conversations for months. My questions are starting to feel repetitive. How many times can I ask her—or ask Dad and Katje and Evan—to describe the most challenging days of our lives together? And this morning, we are having technical difficulties. She can barely hear me. "I think it's my phone," I say. I check the Bluetooth settings and remove the headphones.

"Nope, it's mine," she says. "I listen to the *Ten Percent Happier* podcast in the mornings and his voice is so loud," she says. "I always turn the volume way down." I imagine my mom now, a month before her seventieth birthday, listening to the ABC anchor Dan Harris explore meditation, creativity, and joy. She walks her dogs a mile each morning for exercise. She watches what she eats. She plays cards with her best friend on Tuesdays. It's a good life, one for which she is grateful. I wish this version of Mom could assure her younger self that things might turn out this well. She turns up the volume on her phone so we can hear each other better, and then we return to our conversation. She repeats, "So you're asking what I remember about Dad coming out and that whole process?"

"Yes," I respond. "But what was *your* perspective?"

She takes a long time to answer, the details arriving in layers in her mind. Now she can conjure the floor plan of the kitchen. Now she can see where she is sitting on the stool at the breakfast bar when she and Dad have the conversation. Mary and Karl have left. It's just the two of them. She's panic-stricken, already terrified they will get a divorce. What does she have, if not this life? She waits for Dad to tell her what's going on. Then he does. His voice is distant and clinical. He tells her he has been chatting with men, that he has broken the covenant of their marriage.

He confesses to everything. He tells her he's sick, he's sorry, he'll fix it. The news arrives so fully out of nowhere that Mom doesn't know what questions to ask. Silence falls between them. Neither of my parents knows what is supposed to happen next, and then Mom knows. "One of the first things I did," she tells me now, "I looked him in the eye and said, 'You're going to help me call everybody, because I am not throwing you a surprise party.'"

A few days later, Mom asks Dad whether he has made the calls. Dad shrugs. He hasn't. Mom takes half the list. They both hope that mostly they'll get answering machines, which is what happens. "What do I say?" Dad asks Mom.

"You'll say what I say," she responds. "Due to unforeseen circumstances, the party for Paul Hempel has been canceled."

SPEAKING TO MY PARENTS ABOUT this time is difficult. For one thing, it's been two and a half decades, and none of our memories is sound, so time lines don't always align. But more than that, by this point in their decaying marriage, Mom and Dad have lost all compassion for each other. They no longer perceive each other as thinking, feeling humans. They're unable to give each other the benefit of the doubt, to see each other as the fresh-faced young adults who made this bargain with which they now live.

I've heard it said that in any marriage, there are three characters. There is each individual spouse, and then there is the marriage itself. Each needs tending, and none is to be elevated over the others. But here they are, and their marriage is a villain. It has sucked the soul out of each of them in an effort to maintain itself. In this situation, if the marriage should die, they can see no other alternative: They will die with it. There will be nothing left. But as it is, they're barely surviving. They've been living this way for so long that even if they endeavor to preserve the marriage, they have lost each other. They know each other too well and not at all. Mom believes Dad is a wily, two-faced cheater; Dad believes Mom is erratically emotional. Their stories about this time still highlight the

weaknesses each sees in the other and showcase the ways in which each
felt the other was trying to exploit them.

What really happens?

ON AUGUST 14, 1998, my dad turns fifty. That day Mom goes to speak with
Pastor. He's a jovial, middle-aged man, just slightly older than my parents, with a graying mustache and cheek creases that are frozen into a
permanent easy smile. He knows the birthday party has been canceled,
and Mom asks for his discretion. He invites her into his office, just outside the church sanctuary, where she falls into a chair and tells him the
entire story. I imagine that in the twenty-two years Pastor has then been
at Mount Olivet, he's heard many people relieve themselves of their secrets and shames. Does this make Mom's revelation any less astounding?
Mom still remembers, word for word, his response: "I'm shocked," he
tells her. "I mean, you could knock me over with a feather."

Dad is driving to New Jersey. He shares the same birthday as his
oldest sister, Martha, who is turning fifty-six. Just as he did when his life
first fell apart thirty years earlier, he heads in her direction. Now she and
her husband live in the woods outside Princeton. She is a family practice
doctor and a trained psychoanalyst, and her kids are grown and gone.
Dad and Martha sit on the screened back porch in the evening, looking
through the late summer twilight at the deer that have crept into the
edge of the yard. Dad tells Martha everything that has happened. He
explains that he loves my mom, that he doesn't want to break up his marriage, he wants to make it work. He confesses to his explorations with
men. While limited almost entirely to the computer, these transgressions
of his marriage cripple him with so much guilt that he doesn't know how
to begin to ask the question: Am I gay? Do I like this? Desire can lead us
to bad ends. How can anyone experience pleasure in this setting?

Martha has always been a listener. It's her psychoanalytic training.
Or maybe it's the product of her own complicated life: when her kids
were young, she quit her job as an organist and fought her way into a
medical school that, in 1982, was uninterested in accepting a mother of

nearly forty. She knows the pain that comes with being out of alignment in one's life. She says little and judges little.

When Dad is done talking, Martha takes a breath. "Well," she says. She and Dad have the same detached, pragmatic quality to their words when they chew on big thoughts. She asks him a question he will not be able to answer for a long time: "You need to think about, when you are retired, and you are sitting on this porch with someone in the future, would you rather be sitting here with a woman, or a man?"

FIFTEEN

Can I Have the Keys?

Looking back, Evan can trace the first clue to visiting day at camp. Evan is a camp kid, one of those teenagers who puts in time at school and home so they can escape to the structure of an orderly world run mostly by other teenagers whose parents have topped up their offspring's snack bar cards and left them with enough bug spray and underwear for more than two months. Every summer, our parents drop Evan off at Camp Calumet on Lake Ossipee in New Hampshire. Calumet is a Lutheran camp where children learn archery and sailing and attend vespers every evening. There are clusters of freshly painted red cabins and tents on platforms, shaded by grandfatherly pine trees. The camp's main clearing, set beside a serene lake, is bookended by a great hall, where kids gather for talent shows and worship, and a dining hall, where a bell signals activity changes every hour or so. Katje and I also attended this camp, but we never fell in love with it the way that Evan has. Still, I remember the swell of Luther Hall, the way it reverberates during assembly when every child and adult sings together, "Freedom is coming, oh, yes, I know." The teenagers sit in the rafters, stomping their feet so that the whole building shakes. You feel part of something larger than yourself. This feeling is what Evan loves. It keeps him going.

The summer that Katje outs Dad, Evan is a counselor. He has just finished his junior year of high school and plans to spend ten weeks at

Calumet. Already, in small ways, he's more independent than his peers. Once a week, counselors get a day off, and usually they hike down to the camp office to call their parents. Evan doesn't call, and he doesn't write. He doesn't hear from Mom and Dad at all. He doesn't think much about it.

At the start of August, Mom and Dad drive up to visit Evan on his day off. It's a three-and-a-half-hour drive, and they arrive just before lunch. They bring my brother's favorite dog, a dalmatian mix named Tory, which is nice but also a little unnecessary. Tory isn't used to being leashed, and she jumps all around until Evan tackles her to the ground and scratches her belly. It's a sunny Tuesday, and some of the younger kids' parents, who are staying across the street at a family campground, stop through for lunch. There's a barbecue on the sandy stretch of beach at the edge of the lake. Evan, Mom, and Dad work their way through a buffet line and sit at a picnic table, the dog leaning up against my brother's ankles. Evan sneaks pieces of his hot dog down to feed Tory. Mom and Dad are being weird. They're sitting too close together, being affectionate with each other. Dad slings an arm around Mom's shoulder. Then out of nowhere, they disagree about something that neither of them will disclose. This annoys Evan, who is also gently aware that some of his friends may be watching.

"I think we should tell him," Evan remembers Mom saying.

"Let's wait," Dad says.

This back-and-forth continues through lunch. It's conversation but also body language, whispers, and asides. They're having their own drama right out in public, except that Evan is barely paying attention to them. He's thinking about where he'll go hiking next week; whether he'll be invited to go with the older kids to a nearby waterfall he loves; if it's true that two other counselors are dating; whether he can scoot out later in the afternoon to read a few more chapters of his summer reading assignment, *A Prayer for Owen Meany*. After just an hour, our parents get back in the car. The visit seems quick, and Evan wonders why they didn't stay longer, given the long drive. As they pull back down the long dirt driveway to the main road, he considers what they decided not to tell him. Are they getting a divorce? Then a friend walks by and asks him to pick up an extra lifeguard shift that afternoon. Evan doesn't think about this interaction again until the last day of camp.

THE WEEKEND BEFORE LABOR DAY, camp wraps up with a huge bonfire. Evan doesn't want to leave. He has been on campus since June. He was supposed to come home for a weekend for Dad's fiftieth birthday, but the party was canceled. Evan doesn't know why, and he doesn't care. It's a bonus weekend at the place he loves best, with the people by whom he feels known.

The campers leave on a Saturday, and the counselors have one night to themselves before they head out, too. They stay up too late on that last evening, after they've put the mattresses up and helped close the dining hall for the season. They're singing and telling inside jokes. It's already starting to get chilly at night, and Evan pulls his arms inside his oversize Calumet sweatshirt, the one he won't take off all fall. Someone builds a fire, and someone else plays a guitar. There are lots of marshmallows left in the dining hall kitchen, and a few Hershey bars, but the camp is out of graham crackers. Kids improvise. No one wants to be the last person to go to bed.

The next morning after church, parents arrive to collect everyone. Alyssa goes. Zach goes. Each Taurus and Volvo that pulls away engenders tears and promises to stay in touch, and then it is two p.m. Evan is standing there by himself. Our parents have failed to come for him. He asks to use the phone in the office and dials our number, but it has been disconnected.

EVAN DOESN'T REMEMBER HOW HE gets home that summer. He calls our pastor. Pastor calls friends of our family. Someone comes and gets him, or else someone at camp gives him a ride. What he remembers is walking into our house, dropping his duffel bag and sleeping bag, and there are our parents, apologizing for the confusion. They messed up the days. They need to talk. He follows them into the TV room, the room where most people spend most of their time in our house. Only this feels like a very awkward, formal meeting; the familiar is suddenly unfamiliar. Mom sits in the large easy chair, and Dad sits on the piano bench, leaning forward, his elbows on his knees. Evan drops onto the couch and thinks about how long this will take before he can ask for the keys to the car to go visit his school friends. He hasn't seen them all summer.

Nothing can surprise my brother by this point. He is beyond surprises. For many years, no one has lived up to his expectations for them, so he has stopped having expectations of them. For a long time now, our parents have been quiet tenants of the house, each sinking back into worlds that don't include Evan. He's figured things out for himself. He is resourceful. He, too, is very close to Mrs. Meyers, whom we both now call El. She's a consistent source of adult affection and guidance. She has moved offices since I first sought her out and now has a sprawling room just inside the main entrance to the high school, where Evan looks for her, even when it's summer and kids aren't in school. The point is that he's getting by. Our parents cannot surprise him because he's beyond surprises.

But then our parents level up. They surprise him. Evan remembers that Dad looks at the floor and begins speaking in a rote, pragmatic sort of way. The essence of his speech is something like this, according to my brother: "When I was a little kid, I was molested, and that made me gay." Before Evan can make sense of this, Dad continues, "I thought I had taken care of it, but I hadn't." Evan glances at Mom. She sits there in the chair, her face a cloud of emotion, her tears absent, which is weird. She is a crier, but this is so big that there are no tears. No one looks at Evan. Dad keeps going. "I'm trying to figure that out. We're going to try to figure that out together."

Then Dad stops talking, and he and Mom both sit there, looking at Evan, who is mostly very confused. Evan is familiar with homosexuality. He knows I'm gay, and it's a cool thing. He's proud of me for it. He's maybe just starting to think that he could be gay, or something. But this isn't what Dad is saying. He seems to be saying that he is broken in a way that has manifested as gay, that it is a problem to be fixed. Our parents want to know if Evan has questions. He shows no obvious emotions. "Okay, so, are you getting divorced?" he asks.

"No," Dad says. Mom stares at the wall.

"Dad, are you going to live somewhere else?" Evan asks.

"No, I'm staying right here," he answers, too quickly.

Evan shrugs. "Can I have the keys?"

AS FAR BACK AS EVAN can remember, things have been out of alignment—his body, his home, his family members' relationships with one another. He has learned to deal with this misalignment by carving out his own path, navigating his life independently. Once Kat and I left the house, he moved into the third-floor bedroom that had been his and Katje's as toddlers, then mine as a teenager. Sometimes, now, it seems as though this room is an apartment, and he is a tenant, ignoring the chaos of the landlord's family. He gets good grades, particularly in math and science. He has a few friends, though he's not one to gravitate to groups. He's on Student Council, but only because he ran unopposed and it'll look good on his college applications. His friends are often fellow oddballs.

As the school year gets started, Evan attempts to hold things together. Three afternoons a week, he continues his job as a bank teller. The other two afternoons, he dances ballet. Dance becomes his refuge. He's not close with the other dancers in his class, who have forged a tight friendship based on their collective dreams of playing Clara in *The Nutcracker*. He holds no professional ambitions, as they do. He doesn't aspire to look like a ballerina. He just knows how perfecting his pointe positions makes him feel. "I could spend hours in the basement studio, focusing just on being able to absolutely control every last twitch of my body in a world that I otherwise couldn't control at all," he says now. "I couldn't control that I was growing breasts. And I couldn't control that I was expected to be a girl. And I couldn't control what was happening with our family, but I could control my grades, and I could control my body when I danced." It's the same for him with food. He has started eating less and less, not because he wants to be skinny, but because it's an input he can master.

This is an important thing to understand about my brother at seventeen. He doesn't like who he is becoming, but he doesn't understand that he has an option to be anyone else. He feels entirely out of control and quite sure he isn't meant to be alive, because where are the other people like him? So he finds any way he can to keep himself in check. This is what he loves most about dance.

The fall is a blur. It becomes clear that our parents don't sleep in the same room anymore. Things happen that lead Evan to draw conclusions, but no one ever tells him what's going on. Sometimes this is because our parents don't share information with him. They want to protect him from something they can't define. Sometimes it's because no one else understands what's going on either. For example, someone will allude to something that reminds Mom of the seizure she'd had over the summer. "Mom, you had a seizure?" Evan will ask, and only then, Mom will tell him that her epilepsy has kicked up, probably as a result of stress, and she collapsed while visiting Aunt Mary in Illinois. Now Mom's not allowed to drive for ninety days. That leads him to another question: "Mom, you stayed with Aunt Mary this summer?"

A FEW WEEKS INTO THE school year, Evan comes home to discover Dad in the kitchen in the middle of a Thursday afternoon. "Come on, we're going to visit your Mom," he says.

"Where's Mom?" Evan replies.

Mom has been hospitalized. Katje is driving back from college. Evan asks whether Mom is sick, and Dad equivocates. Yes, and also no. "The important thing," he says, "is that she's going to be all right." It's about twenty minutes from our house to St. Vincent Hospital on Vernon Hill in Worcester. What Evan remembers most about the drive is the silence— not an uncomfortable silence so much as a natural pause, a content energy between them. This is part of a connection that Dad and Evan share; they can both sit in silence comfortably together.

The hospital is an imposing white structure with six floors of windows that have air-conditioning boxes hanging out of them. In the lobby, a receptionist directs them to Mom's room. They take the elevator up three floors and emerge into an area that is nothing like hospitals my brother has visited before. Evan realizes what he's looking at. "This is a locked ward," he says, having no context for this. Dad nods. A woman with a key unlocks the door and the two of them follow her down a hallway lined with tiny rooms that culminates in a large common area. "There are people doing repetitive motions and sounds. There are people screaming," Evan remembers. "It's frightening."

They are shown into Mom's room, which is a tiny box with two beds. Evan remembers nothing about her roommate, only that the zombie look in Mom's eyes, which had been present since he came home from camp, has been replaced by a flicker of . . . something. What is it? She has bandages from her elbows all the way to her thumbs. Of all of the things that have happened so far, the weird and intense moments and unexpected situations, this is the least normal. And yet, there is Mom, acting normal. She asks Evan if he is all right, and he shrugs. "Yes," he replies. She tells him about the art project she's been working on, with popsicle sticks that she has by her bedside. Evan takes the popsicle sticks in his own hands and begins to turn them over. Inside, a piece of him flies backward, retreating out of his body and out of the room and looking down at the scene: There's Dad, standing in the corner, looking down at the ground. There's Evan's own body, long blond hair in a bun for dance, oversize Brown University sweatshirt. Evan asks himself, *What is happening?*

BACK AT HOME, DAD ASKS Evan to cancel Mom's music lessons. Ev works his way down her roster, explaining to the students that she's under the weather. She won't be able to teach for a couple weeks. These conversations are awkward. Dad never asks Evan to lie about what's going on, but he can see plainly that neither Mom nor Dad is sharing the details of their dissemblance with most of their friends. So Evan is cryptic in his language: *She's under the weather.* At first Mom's students and their parents are alarmed that she's ill. A few know she's in the hospital, and they wonder whether she has cancer. But as the weeks go by, it becomes clear that

Mom's absence isn't brief. She starts teaching again and then must cancel lessons again when her depression takes hold. The students stop asking as many questions, and many of them drop lessons. Everyone suspects some sort of unexplained breakdown.

There are people who continue to show up. A few women from church refuse to be shut out, even when my parents stop attending—even when news finally gets out that something has happened, and neither Mom nor Dad will return phone calls. During the week that Mom is in the hospital, a bright, even-keeled woman with short black hair named Peg Harbert finds out Mom is there. Peg is a stalwart, always ready to help out. She sings in the choir with our parents; our families have celebrated Christmas Eve together for more than a decade. Peg researches visiting hours and comes by, but she's not allowed in because she's not family. She convinces the staff to ask Mom to go to the window. Six floors down, Peg stands in the bushes, holding a white poster board sign that says "Get well soon!" to cheer Mom on.

Peg also drops food by the house. When no one picks up the phone, she just stops by, and Evan answers the door. Peg puts the plate in his hands. She looks worried when she sees him, and she asks how he's doing. He says, "Okay." Evan's not sure how he's doing, and he doesn't believe that telling Peg will change anything. The only person with a full accounting of Evan's days, his inner thoughts, his aspirations, is El. She is the person who pieces together the broken fragments of events that Evan brings to her and explains what's going on to him.

Around this time, El sends me a letter. "You really should reach out to your brother," she writes. It's rare that El tells me to do anything. Her language is usually replete with words of love and acceptance. I read the stern tone in her prose and recoil. I don't write her back. Doesn't she know that I do reach out to him? I call Evan a lot that year, and I rarely get him. When I do, he's always unforthcoming. He never tells me anything.

SIXTEEN

You've Reached a Number That Is No Longer in Service

During the summer of the great reveal, I'm at a teacher training program in Houston. Teach for America has created this program to help prepare me for a two-year commitment at an elementary school in Central Harlem. I have chosen this course because I'm interested in education, but also because TfA lays down some rails for young people finishing school. TfA will help me with my school loans and give me an on-ramp to a credit card, and even more important, the program provides a prepackaged answer to the question "What are you doing after college?"

I arrive at this program directly after traveling in India, and I've been away from home for a long time. I don't know much about what's going on there. I've needed to be away, to escape from the chaos. I can't yet see how I've carried the chaos with me, and I'm acting it out in the jobs I pick, the relationships I embark upon, the friendships I nurture. That understanding will come later. It is the lesson I will spend the next decade learning. For now, I spend six weeks practicing classroom management techniques and studying teaching strategies for beginning readers. Every so often, I call home. No one ever picks up, so I leave messages. I'm so busy that when anyone in my family calls back, I'm never there to catch the call. We continue on like this, missing each other, until the day that I call and the phone has been disconnected.

This disconnection is strange. There are two weeks left in the program, and I wait for someone to call, to leave a message explaining what has happened, to share a new phone number. I think about how I've had to sign an emergency form listing a backup way for TfA to contact my parents, and I could always go find it. I think about calling Pastor. I panic. There's a place inside me that has been waiting for the bottom to fall out of my life since I was a child. It's a familiar panic, the same feeling that I remember experiencing when my mom didn't come to get me that time after my music lesson in middle school. In a short period, I've become very close to my roommate, Sarah, with whom I'm sharing a tiny dorm room for the summer. I try to explain the situation to her, but it doesn't make sense, even to me. I feel young when I'm telling her about my family, as though I may be revealing that I'm still a child, still subject to my parents' will. But this moment, as I prepare for my first job, my first apartment, and my first credit card, is my entrance into adulthood. I'm grown. I decide not to think about the disconnected phone. I'll figure it out when I fly back to Massachusetts in two weeks. Instead, Sarah and I head down to the cafeteria for dinner.

AT THE END OF MY training, I fly home. Both of my parents come to pick me up from the airport in Boston, and they're holding hands. I see the resolve in their clasp and think, *They're getting divorced.* But they're not getting divorced. Instead, as we settle into the car for the hour-long ride, they fill me in on the past two weeks. I'm not Evan, their youngest child. I'm an adult already, and I've come out of the closet. They talk to me differently. They don't spare the details. They tell me about Katje's foray into Dad's virtual life, about Mom's mental health crisis, about how they're each deliberately attempting to stay in the *not* knowing, whatever this means. Also, Mom says Dad's upcoming birthday party has been canceled.

Dad talks quickly all the way home. Everything is going to be okay, he assures me. People can be gay and be married, he says. He's not even sure he's gay. It might just be an unhealthy streak of something he can fix with the proper therapy. He's trying to figure out what it all means.

He's not going to use the computer anymore. Some of these men from the computer have Dad's phone number and have tried to call him. So that's why they changed the number.

"That was two weeks ago," I say.

"Was it?" says Dad.

"Why didn't you tell me?" I ask. It feels like a mean-spirited question. There's a lot going on. No matter how miserable they've been privately, I've never known my parents to let the story of their marriage spin out of control, but now it's clear things are out of control. Katje has decamped to her boyfriend's house; she knows everything. Evan is still at camp; he knows nothing. When we get home, Mom is sullen, taciturn. I have this impulse to try to comfort her, but I don't know how. Having had such a hard time with each other for years, we have no common ground. Dad is overly familiar. He has joined my team! He's out! It's all he wants to talk about. And although his sense of self is crumbling, he's discovering a few things as well. Around this time, he goes out to eat with a male friend at a restaurant in the next town over. The two men sit over dinner and talk. Dad marvels at this, the idea that he can share a meal and the intimacy of a chat with a man in public. Of course, men and women go out to dinner together. Two women may go out to eat. But men? According to my dad's original framework for making sense of things, men don't share this kind of intimate public space.

I'm scheduled to be home for two weeks before my teaching assignment in New York starts. But after the first weekend, I've had enough. I stuff my hiking pack with everything I can carry and get my parents to drop me at the bus depot in Worcester. There, I catch a Peter Pan bus to Manhattan. My college girlfriend, Jen, lives with a childhood friend in a tiny one-bedroom apartment on the Upper East Side in the '90s. The bedroom is just large enough for the red aluminum bunk bed they share. Thankfully, Jen has the bottom bunk. Somehow, my family's crisis allows both of them to declare a special circumstance, and I'm invited to stay for a few days and share Jen's bunk with her.

For the past three years, Jen and I have had a dramatic relationship, and that drama has mostly been instigated by me. I love her very much, but I pick fights with her. It's the only way I know to feel that she loves me. We break up a lot. This intensity sustains me and destroys me. We get back together but don't call it that. She travels in China, and I travel in Haiti and India. Now, after several years of loving each other, of first romance, of long-distance letters with poems and mixtapes, I'm finally moving to New York City, where she lives, and we are fully breaking up. Or rather, she is breaking up with me.

This has to happen.

Later in the fall, I'll send her a letter in which I tell her that my life is too heavy and I'm sorry for that, but also, we both want a break from me. I wish I could take one, too. But on the August evening that I arrive, she slings an arm around my shoulder. I lean into her, and the objects around me take form again. Reality solidifies. I relax. The next morning she gets up to go to work, and I don't want her to leave. Her roommate has already gone. I'm crouched at the foot of the bed, watching her brush her teeth and fish out socks from the closet, and I can see that with every move that involves taking care of herself and wading back into the routines of her daily life, she's moving away from me. I panic. That's the only word that describes what happens next. I pull my knees up under my chin, and tears leak out of my eyes. I have no plan for the day, no one who expects me to be anywhere until the following Tuesday, when Teach for America's New York orientation begins.

"Are you okay?" Jen asks, even though she sees I'm not. I can tell she's hoping my answer will be yes, that she can go on to school. But every step she takes toward the structured consistency of her own daily life is a step away from me. Now I'm rocking slowly back and forth. I am silent-screaming, the way you do when you open your mouth and the sound travels in instead of out. When I think about this now, I can feel the rush of blood into my shoulders, the fight-or-flight response taking over my body. I am behaving like the child I was, but I have become an adult. I can't breathe. I can't make any sounds. This is a panic attack.

It's also a test.

Will Jen love me more than her job? Or will she abandon me?

Jen calls to say she'll be late. Once again, I have succeeded in making my emergency into our emergency. I am not alone in it. The adrenaline begins to leave my body. Even then I understand that with every shared emergency, I'm driving her away from me.

AFTER ORIENTATION, I GO HOME for a weekend to gather my stuff, which Dad has agreed to drive to New York. Being there is weird. Katje's back at Ithaca. It's just Dad, Mom, and Evan, who is home from camp. I notice Dad looks different. Has he shaved his mustache? Yes, but that's not it entirely. The wide ring of brown hair with its minuscule comb-over is gone: he's shaved his head! That night, the four of us sit down to dinner together at the formal dining room table. Dad has made corned beef and cabbage in the slow cooker. We're talking about what has happened, and it's a relief that we've broken the silence around it. Dad says he's thinking he'll stay married to Mom but also come out. Mom doesn't have a lot of agency here. Like the rest of us, she's waiting to see what will happen. But I have questions. I'm confused about how this is going to work. He's slurping his cabbage, and I notice he's the only one who's eating. He explains he doesn't want to leave Mom. He's *married* to her, and he never stopped to consider that marriage was anything other than a permanent arrangement, for better and for worse. It's the covenant he made with God, the promise. He thinks he can keep some structural parts of their life together, that we can keep being a family in the way that we've been a family.

"Dad, you need to join a group for married gay men," I tell him.

"That's not a thing," Dad says. He really does believe there aren't many people like him. At least, he hasn't met them.

"No, it is," I reply. "Here, hold on."

I happen to *know* it is because I pick up *Gay City News* from the street-corner boxes in the Village, and these groups are listed in the classified section in the back. You can find them through the local LGBT Center. I get up from the table, Evan at my heels, and I go back to the computer room. Evan is looking over my shoulder as I pull up a web browser and open a search screen. I plug in "gay married men." Five minutes later, we are back at the table with a printed page that has the contact information for a group that meets in Boston on the second and fourth Wednesdays of every month.

"You should go!" Mom says. She and Dad are both surprised to see that a resource like this exists, that there are evidently more people like them, women and men who are trying to stay married and navigate this challenge. Maybe it would help.

Mom's permission here is crucial. Dad accepts it, and he begins to attend. He drives to Boston twice a month, for more than a year. Through the group, he learns just how many original approaches to marriage people can take. At the time, I don't think to look for a support group for Mom, a shared community of women whose husbands are coming out. That's the thing about coming out as queer. It's hard, but you're also entering into a community. There are people there to catch you, if you look for them. When you are the spouse of someone who is coming out, it's hard, and you are being left. The thing you have in common with others, if you can even find these others, isn't an identity you want to nurture. If we'd plugged "wives of gay men" into a search bar, would a group even have come up?

The next morning, we rent a U-Haul and pack it with my clothes, my bed, and the desk I got in middle school. Dad drives me back to New York. I've agreed to live with my friend Kim, whom I met in India. She's a dancer and yoga teacher who waits tables at a restaurant across from the American Museum of Natural History. With her limited income and my teacher's salary, we need a two-bedroom for under $1,500. Even in 1998, this isn't a lot of money, but with Dad along to cosign our lease, we find a railroad apartment on West 109th Street. Everything in the apartment is miniature—the toilet and shower setup, the stretch of counter that contains an oven and fridge, the corner where we put Kim's orange velour love seat.

We flip a coin to see who will get the bedroom with a window, and

I lose. My bedroom is an internal room with a pocket door, just larger than the double bed within it. At first, I don't think this matters. I only sleep in there. But as the days drag on and I shuffle between this room and the tiny living area that looks into an air shaft, I will lose sight of the difference between day and night, until the year becomes one long night.

WE RE-CREATE THE INVISIBLE PATTERNS in our lives until they are revealed to us. We live the same cycles of love and loss, over and over again. So it's not surprising that my professional life with Teach for America becomes a mirror of my family life. I'm assigned to a fourth-grade classroom in Central Harlem at a school that is failing, only everyone is pretending it's not. The days are long and hard, and the children are cute. My classroom is on the fourth floor, room 403, and on the day before classes start, I find a mouse. Due to a lack of resources, I understand that I will need to take care of this mouse myself.

This year is a crisis, because things are always a crisis at PS 92. I start the year with twenty-six students. Two have special needs and are accompanied every day by paraprofessionals, but the school isn't prepared to help them properly. Regularly, the elevators are broken, and these students can't get to the classroom and must spend the day in the cafeteria. In the winter, a guy is shot and killed in front of the school. This happens shortly after dismissal, so most of the kids are gone, but no one cleans up the blood that has soaked into the snow to the right of the main entrance. This blood turns a crusty brown and freezes on the ground. For the next week, we all walk by it. In the spring, another fourth-grade teacher quits. Her class is divided in two and distributed between me and a colleague. After that, I have thirty-eight students.

DURING MY YEAR IN NEW YORK, my parents rarely call. To be fair, I'm very hard to reach. I don't have a cell phone. I'm at school during the day, usually until late. My apartment is depressing, and so I often spend the evenings with a friend and then, because New York is time-consuming to navigate, stay over and go back to school from there. I try to call every day, but I usually get the answering machine, and after a while, it's full. I have to call several times because no one is there to pick up the phone. Then when someone does, I often learn something bad has happened, and no one has thought to tell me.

On the day that Mom is admitted to the hospital and Dad brings Evan to visit, no one calls. A couple of days go by, and I can't reach anyone. So I call early in the morning before I leave for school. Dad picks up. "Your mom's in the hospital," he says. "She tried to hurt herself."

"What?" I ask. "When?"

"Last Tuesday," he says. I'm trying to process this.

"Why didn't you call me?" I ask.

"Your sister drove down," Dad says, as if this is a logical reason.

"Do you need me to come?" I say. This is a half-question. I mean it, and also, I don't.

No is always the answer.

Thank God it is. I've designed my life so that I can't come, so that the emergencies I face every day are so demanding that I cannot get away to help with the emergency at home.

There is one phone on the ward, so I need to schedule ahead to talk to Mom. Dad tells me that Mom will call me that afternoon at five p.m. I am nervous about her call. I sit on the living-room sofa and wait, and then the phone rings. It's Mom, and I'm so relieved to hear her voice. I pledge to myself that I will try never to be difficult, that I will be more of the daughter she wants, if she will just get better, just stay with us. Mom sounds good. She tells me about the art therapy program they have at the hospital, that she has painted an apple for me. I don't remember much more about the call, who said what, but I remember the unsettled feeling in my stomach. Now I know that Mom, who has been depressed for so long, is capable of hurting herself.

OVER CHRISTMAS BREAK, I FLY to the Bay Area to visit my friend Heather. Her parents help me pay for the ticket. Karen and Tom Rowley are doctors who raised Heather and her sister in Oakland and then Berkeley. I first get to know Karen and Tom when they visit Heather and me in Haiti right after college. We break away from the hospital community where we're staying and have a magical weekend stay at the Hotel Oloffson, a Gothic gingerbread mansion in Port-au-Prince that had been popular with writers and artists in previous decades. We drink wine over dinner and tell stories late into the night; Heather talks to her parents as if they are friends, and by the end of the night, so do I. After that, Karen and Tom send me cards and check up on me. Their younger daughter is at NYU, and when they visit New York to see her, they make a point of taking me to dinner. Now as my own parents struggle and my work consumes me, I ache for some adult guidance. I'm nearly as excited to see them as I am to see Heather.

The December weather is dreary and frigid back in New York, but here in California the sky is bright and I don't need a jacket. We spend the week taking walks on the fire trails, so far up in the Berkeley hills that when the fog has cleared, we can see the Bay Bridge stretching its way to San Francisco, the Transamerica Pyramid rising from its skyline. Heather's life is unfolding so differently from my own. She takes me to Point Reyes to hike by the ocean, and we trace a thin path across a field that ends in a spill of rocks. When traffic isn't bad, it takes less time for her to get here than it does for me to get to Brooklyn.

On New Year's Day, I wake up in a sleeping bag on Heather's friend's floor in San Francisco. We have brunch outside on her back patio and then wander three blocks up to Dolores Park. Here, I pull out my journal, which I always carry in my backpack, and pen my intentions for 1999: "Find a way to live every day like this."

Two days later, I take a red-eye back to New York. I sleep badly and land before six a.m. on the first Monday morning of the year. In a bathroom stall at JFK, I struggle into the one suit I own. I don't usually dress up for school, but it's helpful when I'm tired. The kids behave better. I pay $29 for a taxi and make it into my classroom in time to scrawl the day's schedule on the blackboard before the seven forty-five a.m. bell.

YOU KNOW THAT FEELING WHEN you prop your legs up on a desk while you're doing something, and it's comfortable enough until they suddenly go numb? They've fallen asleep, and they can stay that way for quite a while, but when you make an effort to return blood flow to them, it's uncomfortable. They tingle. They cannot hold your weight. This is what happens to my life in the spring of 1999. I don't even notice when I stop being able to feel it. I am lonely. I know my ex-girlfriend will not take me back. I am worried my mother might die, and there's nothing I can do about it. I know things will get worse at home. And I go numb. I sleep anytime I'm not with friends. When I'm awake, I sit on the ugly orange velour love seat in our living room and stare at the wall. I am without instructions. Until this point, the decisions have been made for me: go to school, go to college, finish it off with Teach for America. But now I must make my own decisions. I must figure out what I want from my life and find the energy to propel myself toward it. And all that I want is a nap.

School is a distraction. It requires me to step out of my depression and show up. But one afternoon in May, my student Jason throws his chair through a window and shatters the glass. The chair drops four stories to the courtyard below, narrowly missing a person. I call the principal, who takes Jason to the office, and I don't see him again. A social worker has gotten involved, and Jason is placed in temporary foster care. I don't learn the details about why. The next day, his mother comes to the building, and she's carrying a gun. Her eyes are rolled back in her head.

The woman starts up the stairs toward my classroom, but the school administrator has called the police, and by the time she gets to my door, they are there, too. The kids watch her bob and weave. As the police take the woman away, she yells threats at me, names the people who will come for me. She tells me that everyone in her building knows I am the rat who took her son away. I stand in front of the kids until the noise is gone, and then a little longer, and then I ask them to line up. It's time for dismissal. No one at school checks in with me.

Later, I take the subway home and try not to think about my day. The next day is pretty normal. No one mentions the incident. Jason doesn't return. The day after that is Friday, and I decide to help the kids process any feelings they might have. I gather them in a circle on the rug, and I remind them that two days earlier, Jason's mom came to our classroom with a gun. They might have some feelings or questions, and so we're going to talk about it. The kids seem to take this in stride. Gun violence is part of their lives in a way that I'm not able to understand then. "Does this make you think of anything?" I say.

Someone makes a fart noise, and everyone giggles. That's when the tears come. My tears. I can feel them stinging at my eyes, and I realize I'm in trouble. The emotions are coming for me. I hold it together long enough to open the door between my classroom and the next so that the neighboring teacher can listen to my kids. Across the hall, the science teacher has a phone in his room. I use it to call the New York office of Teach for America to explain what has happened. I'm still not sure if I'm overreacting, if these unruly feelings are out of proportion. The community around me seems to have normalized these events. I tell the woman on the phone this when she picks up, and she tells me she can be at my school in about thirty minutes. When she arrives, we meet with the school administrator.

Until this point, I haven't been afraid. I've taken the subway to work early in the morning when it's dark and cold, and I've stayed late, leaving at weird hours. But now, I'm afraid. I feel that people look at me differently, that they know I'm the teacher whose actions led to a child being removed from his home. Did I even mean to do that? I am a white teacher in a school that is almost entirely Black, a young teacher among seasoned professionals. What are my credentials? My ambition and work ethic are not enough. I don't feel that I belong here. There are just a few weeks left of school, and Teach for America offers me the option of taking leave. But one day, I come in to find a note in my mailbox, written in pencil with lots of twirls and decorations, that reads simply, "Ms. Hempel. If you leave, teach me first." I resolve to finish out the year.

IN THE END, HEATHER'S PARENTS throw me a lifeline. Shortly after the gun incident, Tom comes to New York to visit Heather and watch Cal's Golden Bears face off against Clemson in the final game of the National Invitation Tournament at Madison Square Garden. He invites me to join them. I don't know anything about basketball, but I go. Tom is silent, concentrating, as we watch the players race up and down the court. It's a close game. Then at halftime, he leans back and turns to me. He's a barrel-chested man with thick white hair and a bushy mustache. "Well, Jess, Karen and I have been talking," he begins. He and Karen call me Jess, even though most people go with "Jessi." I love this. It makes me feel special. "We think you should move to California." He says they'll put me up while I figure things out.

A flood of relief washes over me. All I want is for someone to tell me what to do with my life, and here's a directive. The game picks back up, and we turn our attention to the court. But I'm already beginning to plan, thinking forward. What could I do for work? Where would I get a car? Could I defer my student loans? By the end of the game, I've decided. I'll go. The Golden Bears win the championship by this point. Cal fans are ecstatic. We tumble out of the Garden, surrounded by people throwing their fists in the air and yelling, "Go Cal!" Tom buys me a Cal hat. For the first time since I arrived in New York, I have a sense that maybe things will be okay.

The next day I email my Teach for America supervisor to submit my resignation, effective at the end of the school year. She doesn't hold me to the program's two-year commitment. I'm free to go.

SEVENTEEN

Three-Headed Monster

Immediately after Dad comes out, even before I move to New York, Mom and Dad start couples counseling. Once a week, they visit a doctor in Worcester. He has an airy office on the fourth floor of a large brick building. There are two wingback chairs and a couch opposite the guy's leather chair, and my parents always sit side by side on the couch, their bodies not touching. Mom thinks Dad talks too much and doesn't listen. Dad has no memory of the content of these sessions, except for one: they both remember the conversation about the murders.

The topic comes up by accident. They're discussing trust. It's the word that comes up in every session. Is it possible to rebuild trust that has been so fundamentally dismantled? Mom looks down at her lap, or up at the guy, anywhere but at her husband. She says she can't trust Dad. She says it's a familiar feeling, one that she has had before.

"When?" asks the therapist. Dad is fidgeting. He's trying very hard not to cross his arms in front of his chest, and despite his best efforts, they keep inching back up his body from his lap.

"Well, I guess Ypsilanti," she says. "Around the time of the murders." The word hangs. Now both men are sitting up a little straighter. The therapist is precise in his language and his timing. She notices his in-breath, feels his stare.

"What do you remember about that time?" he asks. He's pushing. Her heart begins to race. She can't think straight. Now Mom is upset, and she can't talk about it. The sounds of the room begin to amplify—the ticking of the wall clock in the corner, the motor on the fish tank. There's too much talking, too much talking! "Ann?" the man asks. Mom is crying. It's messy, blathery crying. She rushes out the door and hits the button for the elevator. No one comes out after her. She pushes it again, digging her thumb into it over and over. When the elevator doesn't come, she looks around, and there's an emergency exit to the stairwell that she pushes through. But now she is stuck in the stairwell. There's no reentry. She sits on the top step and waits for her breathing to return to normal.

Maybe she can push the many-headed monster down. Maybe she can make the black hole that is expanding in front of her recede. Breathe. Breathe. Breathe. When no one comes to look for her, and she can feel her physical body again, she walks down four flights of stairs and gets into the front seat of the car. She waits for Dad there. They drive home in silence.

Later that afternoon, the therapist calls Mom. He tells her he believes she has post-traumatic stress disorder. He tells her she needs to see her own therapist, to work on this, and he recommends someone. At first, this annoys Mom. Dad is the one with the problem. But what choice does she have? Mom begins to see a therapist, a woman whom she will see for seven years. Maya will save her life. Maya will give Mom the tools to save her own life. But it will take a very long time.

BEFORE MOM FEELS BETTER, she'll feel a lot worse. A couple months into her work with Maya, things get tough. This is the time that Mom's hospitalized, when Dad brings Evan to see her. Evan remembers visiting her there. I hold on to a fragment of our phone conversation, how her voice was thin and crackly. Katje can still feel the rush of adrenaline that came from speeding home from Ithaca to sit with her. But only Mom can recount the specifics of how she got there. The way she remembers it, she doesn't understand the consequences of her actions. She cuts herself. She slices into the fleshy part of her skin between her left elbow and her wrist. She draws the razor down so that the blood drips down her arm. There's an addictive quality to seeing this blood emerge. It's an outward sign of the roil of emotions that's tearing her up. Inside of a life and a body that feels numb to the point of nonexistence, it's proof that she exists.

Until the point when she doesn't want to be alive. Then she draws the blade lightly across her wrist. Not with enough force to squeeze out blood, just enough to form a small red scratch. She can feel how easy it would be to press down, to hit the gusher that would lead her veins to empty themselves. She can slide into the bathtub in the back master bedroom, run some warm water, let it all go. She knows this thought is poisonous, dangerous. She shakes her head, hard, walks out of the bathroom into the bedroom. *Stop it! Stop it!*

Mom picks up the phone beside her bed and punches in the first three digits to a number she's memorized, a number she's used already a few times. Then she drops the phone in its cradle and walks over to the mirror where she looks at herself. She doesn't recognize the person looking back at her, the way her dark hair falls nearly to her shoulders, refusing to hold the curl it once held effortlessly. Her skin sags in places she doesn't remember it sagging. Her carved-up arms are scary to her. She can't push the many-headed monster away. She returns to the phone and dials Maya again, this time completing the number.

Maya asks whether Mom feels she can keep herself safe, and when she says she's not sure, Maya urges her to go to the hospital. From here, nothing goes as Mom expects. When she gets to the emergency room, Maya isn't there. She's alone, and these people are telling her that she has to stay. The place is sterile, nerve-racking. People watch you all the time, even when you take a shower. But as otherworldly as it all is, there's a piece of Mom that relaxes. She has pulled the rip cord on her life. She is safe. She can rest.

Mom is in the hospital a week, maybe a bit longer. This is the place where she is diagnosed with major depressive disorder, where she is first given meds. Katje drives down from Ithaca to be there, so thankfully Mom's not alone. Dad and Katje come to pick her up and drive her home. When Dad arrives, and Mom sees him, she doesn't feel anything. Just numb. She has withdrawn inside herself, and she's aware that she's a soul, looking out of a person's eyes, watching Ann Hempel's life as if it is a movie—a movie with a long sad stretch in the middle and an uncertain ending. From here, she'll enter a therapeutic day program. She's glad to have a plan for the very next day, a place she knows she needs to be. As she leaves, she hears one staffer tell another, "Oh, she'll be back."

FOR MOM, THIS UNEXPECTED FRACTURE in her marriage is an ending of a sort, even if it isn't an end to the marriage. It's an end to a life that she thought she wanted, one in which she had—at least from an outsider's perspective— what everyone else had. She had a partner for Trivial Pursuit parties with the other families from church, someone who covered life's expenses, whom other people admired. And yes, she felt like an alien in her life at times, but for Mom, the problem wasn't the marriage. It wasn't the people. It was me, or Dad, or her.

But for her husband, this marital fracture is a beginning. Before too long, he appears lighter, snappier. He moves his belongings into the guest bedroom. He's not moving out, he assures her. If she wants to stay married, he does, too. It just needs to change, to be a marriage in which they each can be more complete versions of themselves. Dad starts to populate a life in that guest room that doesn't include her, right in the middle of their shared home. Everything becomes rainbows. There are rainbow towels and a set of six aluminum rainbow rings on a chain that Dad sometimes wears around his neck. He is starting to look different. There's his shaved head. A while ago, he fixed up his bike, and now he puts on tight spandex outfits and goes riding with friends on the weekends. He goes out places in the evenings, and if she asks, he'll always tell her where: A support group. A volunteer organization to help gay teens. A service at a church called United Church of Christ that—get this!—is for queer people who've been disinvited from their other churches. A party. A date. Mom stops asking.

Dad gets a boyfriend, a guy named Steve who lives with his wife and kids in Southern California but travels to Worcester often for work. Mom learns that Steve has an arrangement with his wife, so this relationship is totally sanctioned. She wonders about this other woman, who she might be that she's decided that this arrangement works for her. Mom wonders if she can ever become a woman like this. She misses Dad, not the man in the guest room, but the guy who took her to a Michelin two-star restaurant in Paris where she had the most delicious filet of poached salmon she'd ever tasted. Sometimes when Dad's not home, she'll go into his room and pick up the framed photograph on his dresser, the one in which he has his arm slung around Steve. They're hiking outside somewhere, and she wonders, *When did he ever go hiking?* One day, she's looking through photographs, and she cuts her own head from the family photo in our album. She goes into his room and picks up the frame. She flips it, moves the little hands aside, slips out the photo, and glues her head on top of Steve's body, so that Dad's arm is draped around her.

"Ann! What is this?" Dad says, when he gets home later that evening.

"What?" she says, waiting for him to articulate what he is seeing.

"This photo! What'd you do that for?"

"It's a joke," she says. "Can't you take a joke?"

WE ALL WANT MOM TO be okay. More than anything, and certainly more than any anger we feel toward her, we want her to survive. We want her to want to live. This takes different forms for each of us. I'm paralyzed by Mom's depression, aware that it is a sign that El was right in my adolescence: it wasn't me. But discovering that I was right does not feel like the vindication I'd hoped it might.

Evan is witness to the moments of this depression, wondering where she is when he doesn't see her at home after school. When asked, he helps out with life's banal tasks that would otherwise go undone.

And Katje. She is the person to whom Mom turns, the one who gets her, who steps up to the responsibility of helping out. Katje is Mom's cheerleading squad, the person who remains in her corner when it seems to Mom that no one is in her corner. Katje is the first call.

This year is when the game of Pretend begins. In the game of Pretend, Mom narrates how our family life looks and feels, and the three of us try very hard to live our own lives while allowing her to nurture her own vision. We do this because we don't want her to kill herself. We love her. There is tension here. There are entire topics that we don't discuss with her and that, for years into the future, we will not discuss with her. Long after she has recovered and is thriving, we throttle certain conversations. When I let Mom read the early chapters of The Project, she finally says to me, "It's such a relief."

"What?" I ask. I'm confused.

"For years, we didn't talk about this. Now I know what your story is."

Why do we pretend for so long? We are afraid that honesty will break her. In the end, we underestimate her.

MOM IS STRONGER THAN HER breakdown. As the year progresses, she struggles. But the struggle is significant. It's the process of not giving up, not giving in. She joins a suicide support group, where she gets a boyfriend for a little while. He's not a great guy, so she cuts him loose. She has no vision for her future life, but she's stopped having a desire to end things.

In the background, she obsesses about whatever happened to that guy from high school, the one she had a crush on, the one who scared her. She's just becoming computer literate herself, and the first thing she does is google his name, repetitively. Nothing comes up. Then she googles "Ypsilanti Slayer." She discovers that the man who went to jail is still in jail. But Arnie isn't mentioned. He was involved, she's sure of it, and now he's on the loose—out and about. This is a fast path to feeling awful, terrible. Sometimes she perseverates on this thought. She wallows in the awful, but something stops her from talking about it. She doesn't even bring it to Maya.

But Maya does make her feel better—worthy. Maya encourages Mom to draw, and she begins to keep a journal. Mom is a gifted artist. Sometimes she draws things in this journal that she can't speak, that she doesn't fully know that her mind is processing: images that scare her or make her feel sad. But when she gets them down in the journal, she can let go of them.

One afternoon, Mom and Maya have just finished a particularly helpful session. Mom is feeling a bit lighter than usual, less like she wants to weep. The brick that so often sits on her chest is not there. She smiles at Maya, thanks her. She considers Maya such a marvel of a human, a woman close to her own age. Maya has a lovely life, at least as far as Mom knows. "How did you get to be such a with-it person?" she asks.

"Do you think therapists go into this field just because they want to?" Maya asks her, or at least that's how Mom remembers it. It is the first time Mom has considered that Maya is something other than the healthy one in their binary pairing of the healthy and the unhealthy. It's the first time Maya reveals, without disclosing, that she has struggled, too—that the struggle was the gift, that it gave her the skills to help others. "We're all here because we are wounded healers," Maya says.

When Mom finally starts to think about her own life as a path independent of the lives of her children and her husband, she decides to go back to school, to get a master's. She's feeling better than she has felt in years. As hard as this time has been for her, the result of the work she has done—with Maya and on her own—is freedom. She'll pursue a clinical social work degree. She wants to be an art therapist. In time, she'll become the reason that other people find hope and purpose.

EIGHTEEN

I Don't Even Remember the Fight

When summer comes around again, Katje and I drive across the country. She's twenty and I'm twenty-four. We look alike that summer; we wear cargo shorts and cutoffs, tank tops and hoodies. My hair has grown out so that it falls just beneath my ears; hers spills down her back. We both fold bandannas into headbands to keep the hair out of our faces. I've just gotten a tattoo of an elongated "om," the Sanskrit symbol, on the inside of my right wrist. She has a tattooed sun rising from the base of her spine.

I'm moving to Berkeley, California; Katje is going to stay with Jake, who is on the West Coast for a summer internship. We meet up at our parents' place and spend a couple of days visiting with them. Since Dad now lives in the guest room, I sleep on the springy pullout sofa in the basement. I'm darting through the house, still discovering things. While no one has said as much, I suspect my parents won't be living in this house when I next return, and I'm trying to collect a few odds and ends that I don't want to lose—journals, favorite childhood books. Kat's a light packer by nature, and she's trying to make her belongings even smaller so that they can be wedged into the back of my ten-year-old tan Honda Civic alongside camping gear, food, my French horn, and two duffel bags. Just as we get the car loaded, we get into a fight about something I don't remember.

There's a feeling that's familiar to this time. We're going along and things are good, and just when they're good, we ruin them. The fight itself is the catalyst for our closeness. We can't simply let the prospect of a solid stretch of good time together carry us through the summer—we need to punctuate it with rage. I am still trying to understand this.

This fight consumes us, delaying our trip and confounding our parents. I cry. Then Katje starts to cry and I stop, my lips tightening. "I don't even know if this is a good idea," I tell her.

"I don't know why I agreed to this," she says. Or at least it goes something like that. Up until the moment we leave, I'm fairly certain we're not going. Dad steps in as peacekeeper, trying to reason with each of us, and this makes everything worse. We fall asleep angry, and we wake up hungover from our anger. We don't make eye contact. Mom fills my Coffee Exchange travel mug with coffee. Finally, because it really does seem to be the only option either of us have, we get into the car and pull out of the driveway. We simmer like this for a long time. The car's tape player is broken, and we drive along in silence for the full span of the Massachusetts Turnpike, passing into New York State. Somewhere around Albany, we begin to hear a sound. It's a low hissing, as if a gasket has blown or someone has left the television on in another room, and it's steady. I am already a comically slow driver, and I slow down. "Do you hear that?" I ask.

"What is it?" Kat responds. She is listening closely, her head cocked. *Pssssssssss.*

"Is it coming from the engine?" I ask. I've so far driven only very old cars in my life, cars that have died on me while driving. I'm nervous this one will, too, on day one of our trip.

Katje gets very still. "I think it's coming from inside the car," she answers, and her eyebrows fold down in concentration. We keep going like this for a while, but the hissing doesn't stop, and now we're both concerned.

"I think you should pull over," Katje tells me. Her voice is strong, quiet and steady, the way that it gets in a crisis. There's no one as reliable as my sister in a crisis. I pull over on the side of the highway, just far enough to be safely out of traffic. I turn off the engine, and that incessant hissing persists. It sounds as though someone has planted a bomb in our car, and it is counting down. I panic. "Get out!" I say, and we both fly out of the car and back ten feet away, watching it, waiting for it to burst into flames along with all of our belongings.

When the car doesn't blow up, we inch back toward it. I let Katje go first. On the floor on the passenger side is a small pink Sony boom box, a childhood relic that I'd tucked in at the last minute so we'd have some music. Katje's foot must have brushed against it, hitting the button on the AM radio; it's playing static at a very low volume. It's not a bomb. Relief floods over us. We drop Ani DiFranco into the tape recorder, crank up the volume, and pull back onto the highway.

IT IS ON THIS TRIP that Katje tries to tell me about who she has become, but I refuse to listen. I already know who she is. I have very little tolerance for her confessions and perceived vulnerabilities. Katje has embodied with grace everything to which I have aspired, and succeeded at everything at which I've failed. She never walked into an eighth-grade bathroom to discover her name was last on a popularity ranking scrawled on a piece of notebook paper and taped to a mirror. In high school, she was invited to formals constantly—she was invited to the sophomore semi, the junior prom, and the senior prom every single year. She played varsity field hockey and had a tight circle of best friends with whom she has been close since kindergarten. She had a high school boyfriend who adored her, and once she got to Ithaca College, she had a college boyfriend who adored her. And perhaps most significant, she got along with my mother.

In the story of our family's struggles, there are two distinct early chapters—rough periods before Dad came out. There's the chapter that seems to be about me. I am the problem. I am the difficult teenager, the challenging and terrible adolescent, the defiant and disobedient child. This is mostly the narrative that exists for people outside our family when I am in middle and high school. This is what my parents' friends at church and in our community believe. Katje is witness to this period, often caught in the middle as both Mom and I seek comfort from her. I own hardship in the first chapter of this narrative. I believe it's mine alone, that I'm targeted in a way she and Evan are not. I have so much trouble believing this myself—believing that I have a right to my feelings—that I condemn and put down anyone else who attempts to claim hardship, such as Katje. I have no empathy for her role in our family.

In the second early chapter of this story, I peace out. For many years, my relationship with my parents and siblings is restricted to occasional letters and calls as I finish college and then travel. I have very little energy for trying to help my family. As my mom's depression deepens, my sister is saddled with the challenge of being her ally. After my dad comes out, when I begin teaching in New York, my sister is the one who takes Mom's calls when she is depressed and thinking about hurting herself again. Katje is the person Mom tells the things she says to no one else.

There's another thing, too—something that Katje and I haven't ever discussed, although she knows Dad told me. It's something that Kat struggled with secretly in high school but could no longer keep hidden in college. Her first semester, she fell into a depression so disruptive that the school called our parents. After that, she got counseling. This all happened before Dad came out, while I was out of the country, living in places that didn't have reliable mail systems or internet. I found out about it from Dad in short updates when I'd call from a pay phone in Delhi or Kathmandu. This was 1998, before we had cell phones, and I didn't have a reliable way to reach my sister then. It was all so unsettling that I put it out of my mind.

Even after I return, Katje and I don't talk about our past. Partly, it's just all too close. These are the events that have programmed us, and yet we don't have the distance or the maturity to understand them or to begin to heal from them. We are each other's witnesses, and yet, we are both denying aspects of our own experiences. But when we do attempt to talk about any of this, it devolves into a series of one-ups.

I got Mom's wrath.

Well, I got Mom's sadness.

Well, I got hit.

Well, I missed my math final to check Mom into the hospital.

She loved me, but she didn't like me.

She loved me, and she liked me too much.

Well, I came out of the closet.

This is where the conversation stops because—see?—I win.

KATJE AND I MAKE QUICK time across the East and the Midwest so we can stop to explore the West. We speed down the long empty stretch of highway that runs across the bottom of South Dakota, stopping to camp near Mount Rushmore. We trace our way across the northeast tip of Wyoming into Montana, where we stop at a Walmart to buy long-sleeve shirts. There's a photo of us camping next to the side of the road in Missoula, Montana. Montana is the most beautiful, different place that either of us has ever seen. We head north all the way to Glacier National Park. By this time, five days of driving long distances, sharing meals, and setting up tents have softened us with each other. We are living in the moment. If we're angry about the larger things we cannot name, for the ten days we travel together, we'll just have fun. We'll indulge the new together.

When we get to Glacier, there is snow, and the worn tires on my old 1990 Honda Civic will not take us up the mountain. We're devastated. We stand there talking to the park guide at the visitor's center, and we're not sure what to do. Then two older women ask if we'd like a ride. They're driving a pickup truck with four-wheel drive. The driver has short spiky gray hair, and her companion is not her wife. "We're Thelma and Louise!" they tell us, and we both feel completely fine about hopping into their truck cab, squeezing in between them on the bench. Katje perches on my lap as we crawl our way up to the top. I remember the feel of the dry cold air on my face, what cold smells like, and running around in the snow in my T-shirt, the bright sun keeping me warm.

ON OUR FINAL DAY IN Montana, I have booked for us a half-day rafting trip on the Gallatin River. Neither of us has ever been rafting. We rise early, pack our tent, and motor off to the spot just outside Bozeman where we are set to meet our guide. I've chosen a course labeled "less challenging," something called the half-day classic. We'll join a group of eight others in a large orange raft that mostly floats down the river. The guide, who is a young guy working the river during a summer off from college, gives us a quick primer on what happens if we fall in. He encourages us to double-check that our life preservers are fastened. This is obviously just a matter of course for him, but I start to get nervous. I have chosen this course because the rapids are manageable and the boats are big.

We hit a few spots of whitecaps, rapids with names like Hilarity Hole and Screaming Left. I sit in the middle of the boat, every muscle of my body tensed, braced for impact. Every time I look at Katje, she is smiling as though the water itself has lifted her up. She has an impressive sense of balance, and I can tell she'd enjoy being right at the front of the boat, drinking in the spray of the rapids. Instead, she sits next to me, placing one hand on my knee when we go through a rough spot, as if she could hold me in the boat.

At the end of our float, we reach a swimming hole. This is the photo moment that the tour has advertised. It's secluded and calm, and there is a rock ledge that juts out over the hole, about six feet up. The guide encourages each of us to get a running start and hurtle our bodies over the edge so that we explode into the water; then, because we are wearing large, orange life jackets, we will bounce up like buoys and bob in the sun. The other family goes first, and then there are only Katje and I, standing on the ledge, looking down at the water. Katje is hopping from one foot to the other. She's excited. She won't overthink this jump. But I'm in my head. I'm afraid of heights and physical challenges. I don't trust my body. I don't trust that I won't jump too close to the edge and hit my head. I hesitate as everybody stands there watching me, cheering me on. I want to tell them they're making it worse. "Go ahead," I tell Katje, but she won't go. She doesn't want to leave me there, on that cliff, high above the water.

"I'll go after you," she says.

"No, I don't really . . . I don't want to do this after all, I'll wait in the van," I say. I am now mumbling, incoherent, embarrassed. I have rationalized the return to the van. I know this is just a swimming hole, that people do this every day, that it is marked as "easy" on the flyer. Then Katje gets right up next to me and tells me that I am going to jump. She is going to count down from three and then I will jump, and after that, she'll follow.

"Three, two," she says, and I hold on to her voice. "One."

Then my body is aloft, flying in the air and free-falling down so that I am briefly aware of my powerlessness against the force of gravity. It's a rush of excitement and freedom. I pop up in time to see Katje sail after me, jackknifing down to see whether she can make the force of her body weight drag her below for more than a quick second.

"We did it! I did it!" I say, as she pops up. We're bobbing along in the clear water, and we're both smiling.

THE NEXT DAY, AS WE cross the state line into Washington, Katje brings up high school. We've settled into day six of car travel, and we've listened to our mixes of the Indigo Girls (me) and Alanis Morissette (Kat) so many times that we have to take a day off from music. Our belongings have spread out through the car so that we've had to make our bodies smaller to slide in between the Dopp kits and pajama bottoms and Kit Kat wrappers that are everywhere.

I can tell Kat wants to talk about something that is hard for her. Her face has softened, and her eyes have turned in. This softening alienates me, pushing me to clam up. I don't want to hear it. I've made a fragile peace with the adolescence we have both just endured, and to revisit it in any way may cause that peace to falter. Her emotions are scary to me, as though they might suck us both into a void out of which neither of us will emerge.

To protect myself, I deny their validity. I believe she's weak. I don't know how I can believe she's strong enough to rescue me if I drown in a swimming hole after jumping off a ledge in Montana but also weak enough to drown herself in her emotions and take me down, too. But I have just spent the previous two years running as far away from feelings as I could get. I threw myself into the daily challenges of international travel. I spent a year immersing myself in fourth graders' crises so that I didn't have to experience the feelings of the crisis of my own adolescence. New York left me depressed, wallowing in the kind of sticky stuckness in which I zoned out, missed periods of time, and sometimes considered not getting out of bed. Life is finally moving in the right direction. A new direction. Any direction at all! And right this second, in this car flying by Spokane, I am alive! And I am great!

And here is Katje, trying to tell me that her first year of high school, just after I left for college, she experienced sexual violence at a party. She's trying to tell me the degree to which this event diminished her, the way she hollowed out inside and hid from herself. She's trying to tell me about the alienation involved in having to go to the doctor by yourself when you are just fourteen because you have gotten an infection that you didn't invite and don't want to explain, even to the doctor. She wants me to know how it feels to keep this secret, why she subsequently collapsed into her high school boyfriend as though he was the life jacket that would allow her to bounce back up, like a buoy.

I freeze up as she says these things. The emotion drains from my face. I don't say the right things or really much of anything at all. The easy connectedness that has existed between us dissipates. Until this conversation, we'd fallen into the belief that we were traveling to the same place, and we were: Berkeley, California. But now, it starts to feel as though we are going different ways. I will stay with Karen and Tom, who have invited me to live with them while I start a new job, finish out the summer, and then move into a room that is opening up in their daughter's house. Kat will join her boyfriend, who has a job as a radio DJ in Los Angeles. They'll drive south and then back across the country to the Ithaca College campus, where she'll continue to play rugby and study psychology and art.

THIS TRIP IS ONE OF the first things I ask Katje about when we start talking about The Project. She's not feeling certain about my endeavor, but she's agreed to let me attempt to write it. It's September, a dry warm month in Portland where she and her family live, and she's on the couch, the phone tucked under her chin. Her infant son, who refuses to nap, is nursing while we chat. He gurgles just frequently enough to remind me that we aren't fully alone. Now that Kat and I are both parents, this is always what life feels like. Conversations are piecemeal, broken up by someone who needs milk or a toy. Attention is fleeting, so I think she's not fully paying attention when I tell her, "We were fighting when we first got into the car, and I don't even remember the fight."

I expect she'll say the same, but she does remember. "It was stupid," she says. "It was about our itinerary." I'm still at a loss. I remember the itinerary. It was a great trip. I'd bought a computer program and book from Barnes & Noble, and planned a northern route across the country. We'd visit one of my friends in Oregon and stop to see our cousins in Illinois. I remember slipping the disk into the computer and charting the time it would take us to drive from city to city. I am searching back through the archives of my memory to think through this plan, and then it crystallizes. I can see exactly what Katje is trying to tell me, just one minute before she says it: "You had built the entire itinerary without getting my input. And I felt 100 percent controlled by it."

As in that famous moment during *The Wizard of Oz* when black-and-white Kansas shifts into technicolor Oz, I can see the entire trip differently. There is Katje, starting to emerge from the time in her life when she catered to me and catered to Mom and had no voice for herself. And there I am, deciding what we can talk about, what is allowed in our relationship, even exactly where we will go. She is gentle with me now, her baby falling asleep after feeding so she has time to focus. She almost doesn't want to tell me, but then she says it:

"It was a conversation in which I was asking myself, looking back now, would I be able to be in relationship with you—and still be me?"

NINETEEN

Family Conference Call

In California, I live with Heather and a third friend, Becky, in a tiny Craftsman house in North Berkeley, just at the intersection where Cedar Street meets San Pablo Avenue. The scent of fresh bread from the bakery across the street fills the house every morning. It has a miniature front yard and a back patio with a wooden barrel hot tub. In the evenings, we strip naked and sink into the steaming water together. As an East Coaster, I never don't find this remarkable—that there's a place where the weather is reliably pleasant 365 days a year, where people live as though the outside were an extra room in their house.

After spinning through a few jobs that don't last, I land a role at a school reform nonprofit, where I'm an inadequate but well-intended administrative assistant. Every day, I pick up a ride into San Francisco through the casual carpool, and I take the BART train home. This is a place where I feel welcome to experiment with presentation. I shave my head again and dress in vintage pink corduroy bell-bottoms and thick-soled Vans tennis shoes. On the weekends, I go hiking on the fire trails with Heather and her parents. Berkeley is the first place my life takes on a routine without family outbursts, crises, and the chaos of teaching. I don't need to be afraid that everything will come apart all at once while I'm not paying attention. I can relax. I think this is what I want, why I've come to California. But it makes me uncomfortable.

I remember this one night. It's a Tuesday night. I've finished work, and I shut down my computer. I head out and start up Third Street toward Market Street. It's still light out, so it must be late spring. I think ahead to the evening in front of me. Will Heather be home? What am I going to have for dinner? Maybe we'll watch TV. Then I'll go to bed. I remember noticing this moment, really paying attention to how it felt. This is how it must feel *not* to be stressed out about going home. How predictable it all seems! But also—how very boring and unsatisfying.

Whenever my parents call, I don't pick up. I screen their messages and call back when I feel I have the bandwidth to listen. Mom's often sad. Dad's calls focus on details, usually about Mom. During this time and for many more years, my relationship with my parents will feel one-sided. I listen. I very rarely share anything significant about my own life—nothing that makes me feel vulnerable. Instead, I attempt to be a sounding board as my parents work through who each of them is becoming. Even much later, when I become aware of this dynamic, when it's a crutch that no longer serves me, I can't figure out how to discard it.

CONTRARY TO WHAT I HAD expected, Mom and Dad continue to live in the large house where we were raised. They tell me about their boyfriends, and this starts to be less weird. Dad dates a married man who lives between Massachusetts and California. Once while visiting, the guy organizes Dad's socks by color in his sock drawer. After they break up, Dad tells me this was proof the man was too tightly wound. Mom dates a much younger guy she meets in her day program. It doesn't take her long to figure out that she wants more for herself and to drop him. Despite these experimental attempts at new romance, both Dad and Mom spend most of their time with each other out of loyalty and familiarity and general uncertainty about what is supposed to happen next.

This liminal space has persisted for too long, and it has become exhausting for the three of us kids. It has been sixteen months since Kat uncovered Dad's secret, nearly a year since Mom was hospitalized. The two of them have weathered holidays together, propping up the uncomfortable myth that their union is unbreakable. Each of them has tried to make the family into a vessel that allows them all of the things they want. Dad wants to come out and stay married. He's stuck in a perpetual rainbow phase of being gay, in which everything in his orbit—bumper stickers, candles, re-frigerator magnets—is intended to scream "PROUD." But he's not proud yet, at least not most of the time. He's embarrassed and ashamed. He feels so guilty. In contrast, Mom still holds out for the possibility that there exists a path through this mess where her life looks something like she expected.

The holidays come around again, and I stay in California. Kat's a ju-nior at Ithaca. Evan's in his first year at Oberlin. Both spend Thanksgiving with friends. Neither knows what to expect when classes let out and they get home for winter break. But they walk into Hempel Family Christmas Extraordinaire. Every tradition is upheld. Andy Williams is singing "Silver Bells" on the record player. Mom has pulled out all of the decorations, the ornaments marked with our names and years. She's placed our collection of German nutcrackers on the windowsills in the dining room. She's hung embroidered stockings. "My kids have come home for a family Christ-mas!" she says, and she appears so happy! She and Dad are civil to each other—even lovely to each other—but also, no one talks about anything.

Evan and Katje have never gotten along well. They're so different. But this nails-on-a-chalkboard holiday bonds them. The first night they're home, Mom and Dad retire to their separate rooms after dinner. The record player is still spinning Christmas tunes. Evan shuffles into the dining room where Kat is sitting at the table, cracking walnuts with the nutcrackers. She picks the broken nut pieces out of the shell and chews on them a long time before swallowing. Evan sits and reaches across the table to the bowl. He's allergic to walnuts, but he starts cracking the shells, picking out the pieces, and handing them to Kat. The record ends, and there's just silence. "This is nuts," Evan says.

"Nuts," Katje replies.

Evan looks at the bowl on the table and then at my sister. "Nuts, nuts, nuts," he says. They both begin chuckling.

This phrase becomes shorthand for the rest of their visit, and it comes up the rest of their lives. Whenever anything is not as it appears, is trying too hard to maintain a facade, they exchange a quick text, a knowing glance: "Nuts, nuts, nuts."

I TALK TO KAT AND Evan a lot, if separately. They each tell me about the holidays, about the strange way that our family home has begun to fossilize; the children are gone and the parents are changed, but everything has stayed exactly the same. There's no new furniture. There are no framed photos added to the collection, towels to replace those that have worn out. There's nothing that carries momentum into the future in this house, only a brittle sense that the mirage will dissolve. Surely, it can't stay this way. Each of us, in our way, is carrying some of the emotional weight for our folks. Each of us is exhausted. Mom and Dad are treading water, and therefore so are we. Not long after Christmas, we kids announce a family meeting.

All three of us remember this call. Katje is out visiting me for the final week of her winter break. Evan is on break, too, only he is knocking around an empty campus in Ohio. His dormmates won't come back for a week. He remembers taking the phone into the lounge, the way the cracked leather chairs feel against his sweatpants, the eerie quiet of a dorm without students—as if ghosts are whispering all around him.

In Berkeley, I bring the portable phone into the dining room by the landline so Katje and I can sit next to each other. First, we call Evan and go over our plan. Mom and Dad aren't expecting to hear from us, but we know they're both home at this time on a Sunday morning. Neither of them goes to church regularly anymore. We put Evan on hold and three-way in our parents. Mom answers, and she's surprised to hear from all three of us. Katje asks her to fetch Dad, and then we're all there, together.

This hasn't happened in nearly two years.

I do the talking. I don't really remember what I say, but the gist of it is that we think they should divorce. We are, as a trio, officially declaring the family's union over. We don't want to know all the details, I explain.

All of us are struggling under the weight of their challenges. This is the best thing for our family, we tell them. We're asking them, for their own good and for ours, to begin to attend to the process of moving on.

NEITHER OF MY PARENTS HAS any memory of this call. I suspect it's because their marriage—their relationship and its intricacies—was never about us. So of course, our announcement that we are ready for their divorce is not its punctuation. It will be more than a year before they file for divorce.

These first couple of years after my Dad's coming out are a mess for my parents. They live together in a house with no kids and no love, only the well-worn paths of habits that no longer serve them. Each of them is trying to stay alive. This is not an exaggeration. They try to cultivate private lives, to tend independent spaces in their hearts and minds without physically leaving the other, a person to whom all access has been expected and given for nearly three decades. It's a weird time. Now that they are being more honest with themselves, each is also more honest with the other; they know each other better than they ever have, because who can really know us when we don't know ourselves? Yet every breath they take is carrying each away from the other. There's no grace in this scenario. There's only hurt.

At first, Mom and Dad think they can work out a plan. After the pain of that first year, as they begin to reenvision their sense of selves, they believe they can be new people while living a version of their old life. They're both community leaders. Mom has served on the school board. Dad sits on the town finance committee. Before the crisis, they used to be involved in church; they were the kind of stable individuals other people called on when in trouble. Dad has just left his law firm to become the general counsel at a small pharmaceutical company. Mom still teaches music when she can.

That first year, their friends are still present—some of them, anyhow. But by the winter of the second year, people have fallen away. No one knows how to help. No one can stomach the charade, and neither my mother nor my father can articulate what might really be going on. By then, it's just Mom and Dad in the big house on Main Street, alienated from each other but unable to leave.

EVERY CHRISTMAS, DAD WRITES A letter with updates on our family. He prints it on our home computer, and Mom slips it inside the cards that she addresses and sends. Starting when I'm in middle school, Dad writes the letter in the voice of the family dog. This is a funny gimmick for a long time; the dog gives updates on the status of the pets, and the number of walks he gets. But as things grow strained, it's remarkable how little Lucky, our elderly spotted dalmatian, is able to comprehend and communicate about what's actually happening for anyone. The year that my father gets found out, my mother is hospitalized, my brother gets left at camp, and my sister runs away to Vermont, Lucky gives this chirpy update: "Mom and Dad seem to be making some major changes in the way they live and work, and I get the impression it's been an eventful year for them, too." *Oh, really, Lucky? Is this all you've noticed?* He finishes the letter with great cheer: "Dad is spending more time at home doing things with Mom and just enjoying our company."

This is Lucky's last letter.

By the time we hold our conference call, something is finally sinking in for my parents. This year, their Christmas letter doesn't go out until March, and it's more of a news briefing. Dad writes on behalf of the family. The letter opens with several paragraphs about the adventures of the children and the many, many places that he and Mom have traveled the previous year. They somehow made it to Mexico, Vancouver, Alaska, the Florida Keys, and Paris. Reading between the lines from twenty years in the future, I can see them desperately attempting to stoke a fire that has been out so long there are no embers left. Dad doesn't mention his sexuality. Instead he writes: "On the more figurative side, we've been struggling with what some might call midlife crisis for several years since the girls [sic] began to leave home." He explains that tensions have escalated beyond what is comprehensible, so they plan to separate. Then, of course, a final sentence: "At this time, we do not plan to divorce."

They're not going to get divorced.

That spring, they begin to decouple their physical lives. One afternoon, they walk through the house together, laying claim to various pieces of furniture. The dining room table (Mom). The slow cooker (Dad). At first, they're concerned about how they'll decide who gets what. But once they begin to talk about it, it becomes obvious they want different things. Dad moves in April of that year. Mom's house needs a bit of work, but she moves in June. Dad is obsessed with fairness and always has been. It's a core value for him. He still has the ledger sheet mapping out the exact number of dollars invested into projects to get their homes ready. In the end, there's an eight-dollar difference—Dad's house down payment and move costs $18,272, and Mom's costs $18,280.

These new places to live reveal a lot about how different their ideas of home are. Dad finds a two-bedroom condo in Worcester, which will be a stopover until he gathers the courage to move to Boston's gay mecca, the South End. He's drawn to cities, to nightlife, to new friends and new experiences. Mom falls in love with an old farm about a half hour west, in a tiny town where she can make a fresh start. It has wide floorboards, a claw-foot tub, and a barn for the horses. This is the first time since Dad's secret was revealed—and since even before that—that she remembers being happy.

She's by herself there on the farm, and I worry about her. I ask whether she's lonely, but in truth, she is less lonely than she has been in years. "I don't feel lonely, because I have my animals," she tells me. In addition to the horses, she's got two dogs. Over time, the menagerie grows to include a cat, two goats, a pony, another horse, peacocks, chickens, ducks, and a pig with sore feet named Daisy.

EVEN AFTER THEY MOVE, for another year, Mom and Dad remain each other's chief companion. They live in separate houses, in separate towns. They have left their mutual friends and abandoned their church communities. Dad leaves God when he leaves church, because what kind of God would allow this to happen? Mom doubles down on God, because she believes that as doors close everywhere around her, God will be the one to open the windows. But she doesn't look for a new church. She prefers to find her faith from self-study, to read her Bible. Even with a half-hour drive between them, they remain the people they speak to the most, not out of love or even habit, but because to let go of this lifeline would be to spin forward into a world without rules about how life is to be lived.

Then, sometime around the holidays in 2000, they decide to divorce. There's a moment that crystallizes the decision for Dad. Mom is driving him to the airport for a business trip. They routinely do these types of things for each other, even though it means Mom must drive a half hour to his house to pick him up. Dad remembers looking over at her hand on the steering wheel and noticing that she doesn't have her rings on anymore.

"Where are your wedding rings?" he asks.

"Oh, I took them off and gave them to the girls," she replies. "I didn't want them anymore." And he wonders, *How am I still married to someone who doesn't want to wear her ring?*

The final family Christmas letter goes out at the end of 2000. It's shorter than usual. Dad authors it and doesn't directly imply that it is from Mom, too. He provides her new address, adds updates on each of us. Like any good corporate press release harboring news that will shake the stock market, the letter breaks that news in the penultimate line: "Although we have decided to divorce early next year, we remain friends." This is not so much a declaration as a fervent wish for the future.

IN THE END, IT TAKES my parents only three years to work their way to a new, better version of themselves. Is this a long time or a little time? From a distance, this doesn't seem long for the amount of work involved in reexamining every belief you have ever held. My parents come out of their divorce with new friends, new spiritual beliefs, and new career aspirations. They've accrued three years' worth of marriage counseling, individual counseling, and support groups. If they don't come out of their divorce better, they at least come out with an understanding of how they can make themselves better.

Yet our family still feels fragile.

Here I think about the conference call—how Katje, Evan, and I all remember it. While I'm working on The Project, I stumble across a book I'd forgotten about. It's called *Families like Mine: Children of Gay Parents Tell It Like it Is*. It is published in 2004, just a few years after our conference call. The author, Abigail Garner, interviews both me and Katje for this book. I tell Abigail about the call. I'm twenty-seven at the time, recalling something from just a few years earlier. And here's my quote, just as it's published: "We called them on a conference call. We told them, 'We are your children and we need to make a few things clear. We can't take on your burdens. We need to know you are okay. We think you should divorce, and we know it will be on your time. We don't want to know the axis of your crisis; we just need to know you're okay. We want to know you have good therapists. But we really can't deal.'"

This small piece of my personal history preserved is a gift.

When people we love go through hard times, we often want to make things better for them. We usually can't. This is even more true when those people are our parents, our children, our siblings. Often the only thing we can do is love them enough to maintain our own boundaries so that when they emerge, we aren't so angry at them and broken by them that we cannot be in relationship with them.

In this passage, I can see what I didn't remember, that our call was not in fact to tell our parents to divorce. It was to tell them how to treat us, where we belong in their lives, what roles we are willing to play. It doesn't matter now that they cannot remember it. It doesn't even matter that we cannot. At that vulnerable moment in our family's history, Katje, Evan, and I took care of ourselves instinctively. This is a way that we took care of our parents as well.

PART FOUR

Heal

TWENTY

Transformation

It's silent inside the lobby of the Marriott conference center in Durham, North Carolina. In front of me, two volunteers give out name tags from behind a makeshift table. It's a Wednesday evening, and I've come from San Francisco on an early morning flight so that I can take this course. I've borrowed a car from my friend Eryn, who has also footed half my plane ticket. Now, I'm five minutes late, and these volunteers will not let me in.

I've signed up for this course because Eryn—my most sarcastic, antisocial friend—has recently become content. Happy, even. What's more, she's become involved in things, a leader. She's organizing her med school class so they'll agree to collaborate rather than compete. This isn't Eryn. It doesn't add up. I want to figure out whatever she's figured out. I'm not content. I'm depressed. I'm anxious. Sometimes, for no reason at all, I cry. I've started therapy, but I don't know why I'm going or what I'm supposed to be getting out of it. I want to be in love with someone. I think that'll make me feel the way I imagine that I want to feel. But if I'm honest with myself, I don't believe I'm lovable. Coming out hasn't changed that. And I don't fall in love with the women I date.

Eryn tells me about World Works. It's a series of workshops designed around the idea that we limit ourselves by our understanding of what we're capable of. It's an offshoot of Lifespring, a program that trickled down from the human potential movement that blossomed starting in Southern California in the early 1970s. Its premise is that our limits are in our minds. Our minds are our greatest enemies. I've signed up for this three-day training called the introduction. The lesson plan for the weekend is "transformation." And now as I pace back and forth in front of the name tag table, it's getting off to a bad start.

It's not my fault that I'm late. The problem is that my flight was late. I got to Eryn's house, and it was another forty-five minutes' drive to this hotel. I'm at the sign-up desk at 5:08 p.m. And the trainers say I'm not allowed in?!? I'm not the only one. There are other late people gathering behind me. It's almost quarter after the hour, and there are five of us. As a block, we're mad. "I paid for this," a man says. And this unlocks all of our ire. "You owe me this training," I say. I remember what the indignation feels like in my body, the warm pulse through my chest, the hot head. The angrier we get, the less bothered the people at the desk are. They don't seem to care.

Thirty minutes into the training, the trainer comes out to get us. She's a tall woman with long, dark hair and shiny white teeth that flash when she smiles. She's not the least bit bothered by our anger. What kind of customer service is this? She brings the five of us into the large conference room and lines us up on a small elevated stage in front of about one hundred people. Now I'm embarrassed. What's going on?

The trainer stands in the back, behind the audience, who stare at us. "Why were you late?" she asks. Silence hangs across the room. Then she prompts us: "Anyone can start."

For a few moments, no one says anything. Then I speak up. My words are vituperative, resentful. My arms are crossed over my chest. "I flew here from California, and my flight was late. I didn't even land until two thirty," I say, and with that, I make myself the example for the lesson she is trying to impart.

"So you still had two and a half hours to get here," she responds. "Why were you late?"

"I had to drop my stuff with the friend who is hosting me and shower," I say.

"So it was more important to you to take a shower than to be here on time?" she answers. I really don't know where this is going. What the hell kind of question is this? Of *course* I'm going to take a shower. I'm about to sit among one hundred strangers for several days.

"Yes," I say in an almost mocking, I'm-smarter-than-you tone. "It was more important to be clean than to be absolutely on time."

Now she pulls out the contract I signed when I registered for the course. It has only four agreements to which I have committed. The first reads: "I will not be late."

"It's your word," the trainer tells me. "Your word is what you have." She's making the point that we make choices about how we act, subconscious choices that we aren't always aware of, that these choices constitute our lives. At any time, we can make them differently. You are the only one who needs to be okay with the choice you've made, she implies. If you break the agreement, understand what is more important than keeping your word. She's exposing the underlying beliefs that control us. For the rest of the weekend, every single person is on time for every single session. Do you know what it feels like to be part of a group like this? Everyone holds fast to all four rules, which also include "don't interrupt," "don't take notes," and "keep your word." After a while, it feels as though you're part of one, living organism. You aren't lonely anymore, because you aren't alone. You aren't anxious anymore, because nothing is your responsibility. You trust the people around you.

It's freedom.

THE WEEKEND IS PACKED WITH experiential learning processes like this. Most are positive. Most have to do with showing us something we'd always assumed to be true in a new way so that we question that truth. In one exercise, the trainer asks us to mingle around and come to a stop in front of the ugliest person in the room. The idea of this makes me want to crawl into my skin. That's me. I know it. I'm the lesbian here. I've got funky green glasses and short hair that has grown in spiky and unshaped after a recent shave. I wear a black faux-leather belt with holes in it. I'm going for a bike-messenger-punk-rock vibe, which plays well in the Bay Area—but not here. Also, by my own standard, I'd like to be five to seven pounds thinner, and my face is too round. I want to beg out of this exercise, to hide. But there's no hiding; everyone walks around the room until they've found the ugliest person. Two dozen people are standing in front of me, more than for anyone else in the room. I pause here, take this in. I'm right. They think I'm ugly. Something unfamiliar is coursing through my body. It's relief. Because who cares? It's kind of fine.

Then the trainer asks each of us to make eye contact with the person we've chosen and say why they're ugly. Here it comes. I'm waiting for it. A few people list physical things they dislike: my glasses, my haircut. Most people, however, pick up on my body language. I don't make eye contact, they say. I'm not friendly. I was rude to the trainer, right at the start of the program. I don't seem as though I want to be there. I scowl a lot and seem angry. All of this is true. My fear has created the circumstances I fear. But now, there is nothing to fear. I feel connected, relieved, seen.

The retreat goes on this way, and every night there's homework. Our trainer tells us that you can't take responsibility for the present until you've felt your feelings about the past. Events are neutral, she says. Our interpretations of events give them power in our lives. Resentment is a burden, and forgiveness is the path to freedom. We're asked to go home and write a very long letter that starts, "Dear Mom, Dad, I got my power back. I forgive you for . . ."

By day three, I sit in front of a stranger, making eye contact, talking to her as if she is my mother. Only this version of my mother is someone who can hear everything I have ever felt without judgment. I read my letter, and I start to cry. Big heaving waves of sorrow pulse through my body. I don't know where they're coming from. The room is full of dyads in which one person is sobbing. The trainer walks around with a box of tissues until there are no tissues left. I get to the end of this crying, and I'm exhausted. I want to sleep. But now there's another feeling that's new. I'm lighter. I discover that I don't need to say anything to my mom, that the forgiveness has happened.

On the final afternoon, we're given the most uncomfortable homework. We have just one hour to make amends with the person we struggle most with. By now, I've bought in. I know that the trainer is asking the impossible. I know it's impossible only because I *believe* it's impossible. I take my cell to the parking lot and sit inside Eryn's car, which she has lent me again today. I know whom I need to call. She should be home, done with her classes, not yet cleaning out the horse stalls. I dial the numbers, and the phone rings three times before she picks up. "Mom?" I say.

"Jessi?" she replies, and she probably thinks something is wrong. I don't really call her. She calls me.

"Mom," I say, and I'm not even nervous about getting the words out. I've been filled with the spirit of the moment. I've become convinced that I can rewrite our history. "I know we had a really hard time, and I forgive you for anything you did that hurt me."

These words access something different in Mom. She doesn't know I'm in North Carolina, doesn't know I'm at a conference. I listen to the trainer's words in my mind. *Enroll her in the relationship you envision.* I can still hear her say this. "I envision a friendship for us," I tell Mom.

Mom has been apologizing to me since we learned to talk to each other. She doesn't even know what she's apologizing for, only that everything was so wrong for so long. "I'm sorry," she says, only I don't need her sorry. And I don't even want to explore her sorry, because what if we don't have a shared understanding of the past? Let's forget the past. Let's focus on the present. Let's dream up a better future.

By the time we hang up the phone, I feel freer than I have ever felt. The weekend is drawing to a close. The trainer tells us we're off to a good start. We've begun the work of transformation. But if we really want to change, we'll need to sign up for the intermediate course.

I BEGIN TO CALL MOM more regularly. Until this point, I've never thought much about her history. Now that I'm less angry, I begin to be curious about her. I begin to think about her not just as my mother, but as a woman with a life that has outstretched my own. She's undergoing her own transformation. She's still in regular therapy, but she is also training to be a therapist. She has a live-in boyfriend, an older guy who makes her feel special. She has started to take in pets that have come to a crossroads in their own lives. She has forged a quirky life for herself. She has started to want this life again. One evening while we're on the phone, she tells me that one of the things she's working on with her therapist has to do with the Ypsilanti Slayer, the murderer who was on the prowl when she was in high school. She tells me that when she was in the hospital, this was the thing that haunted her. She knew things about this case that other people didn't, she explains.

The conversation is short on details. She claims not to remember that much, and besides, it all feels so fantastical. "Our marriage therapist thought I have PTSD," she tells me. I change the subject. I don't want to talk to Mom about her marriage. It's not productive. It drags me into the past. World Works has helped me be proactive about this.

But I wonder about this frightening figure in Mom's past.

A week later, I'm at a poetry reading at Barnes & Noble, and I'm still thinking about the Ypsilanti Slayer. The store has a true crime section—three shelves packed thick with books detailing horrible events committed by infamous criminals. There, halfway along the first shelf, is a book entitled *The Killers Among Us, Book 1*. A British criminology writer has created a comprehensive guide to every known serial killer up until 1995. It's a small paperback, sized appropriately for macabre beach reading, with a grainy, generic crime scene photo on the cover. I lift the book from the shelf and slide down the wall at the end of the aisle, drawing my knees up into my chest. Right there in the store, I pull out a pen and began marking up the text.

In the decades that have followed, that book has traveled to seven different homes with me, tucked into a small box of my most important things, the box I'll grab in the event of fire. Its pages have yellowed, its back cover crumbling off entirely. I can still trace my early curiosities in the notes I've written in the margins: On page 79, next to a detail about the killer's mother weeping, there are three exclamation marks. Farther down the page, in a section about women accepting motorcycle rides from the killer, black, loopy pen marks record that "Mom did that."

I'VE JUST REGISTERED FOR THE advanced weekend of World Works, writing a check that wipes out my savings, when I learn that Evan has torn his ACL playing frisbee. He'll need to have surgery on his knee. It's an outpatient procedure—he should be in and out the same day—but still, it's significant.

I find out about this a week beforehand when I call him to catch up. "Who's going to be with you?" I ask him. It's a reasonable question, but one without an answer. Mom isn't coming. Dad isn't coming. Yes, he's let them know. He has a friend who has agreed to be there.

Evan is a conundrum to me. He's a lockbox. It's impossible to tell exactly what's going on with him, because he doesn't call. He rarely returns phone calls. He doesn't appear to feel that anyone in our family is available to him. He doesn't seek out any of us to open up to. Having had my recent transformation, I'm a fountain of self-knowledge, a bad self-help cable show playing on a loop. He won't listen to me, and I can't fix him.

But here he is, at nineteen years old, having surgery on his own in Oberlin, Ohio. When you are nineteen, you aren't grown yet. Sure, you aren't a child. But you don't know the contours of your adulthood, either. Where are my parents? I wonder this without saying it out loud, because isn't there a point when they finally show up? Like, when things get bad enough, don't they come through in the end?

"Do you want me to come?" I ask him. I've just started a new job. I've already had to miss a few days for all of my World Works trainings, and

I'm pretty sure I have no vacation yet. Maybe he can hear the hesitancy in my voice.

"Uh, no, that's okay," he tells me.

"I should come," I say.

"There's going to be nothing for you to do here."

"I'm going to come."

"Okay," he says, and he doesn't thank me.

THE OBERLIN CAMPUS IS A grand group of brick buildings arranged around a central quad slapped down on land intended for cornfields. It's as flat as anything I've ever seen, perfect for Ultimate Frisbee. He and his friend Jamie have picked me up at the airport. Jamie looks me up and down, then moves a step closer to Evan, who doesn't smile or hug me when he sees me. She's cagey, protective, and I wonder, *Is she Evan's girlfriend? Why are they so mad at me?*

Evan and Jamie drop me at his dorm, where I'll be staying, and then Evan goes to Frisbee practice. His room is a small square box with a bed on each wall, but his roommate is already gone for the summer. The room has a barren quality, his half-packed bags sitting out on the empty mattress. From his window, I can see him below, hobbling around the field on his crutches. Surely he doesn't need to be at practice today. Why doesn't he want to spend time with me? Alone in his room, I look for clues. I turn on his computer, and a document on his desktop is marked "Journal." Even as I'm opening it, I know this is the worst thing I can think of doing. As I read it, the blood rushes hot to my face. I need to stop reading, but I can't. It's all about his youth, things that have happened to him. I'm caught in the loop of his story, uncertain what to do with it. It's not mine. At once, I can see my brother's hard time. I think back to where I might have been while he was struggling through his own adolescence. College. Haiti. India. Trying to shake free of my own shadows, unwilling to reengage. How do we apologize for not showing up for each other?

I resolve never to talk about any of the things I've read. But maybe I can create an opening for him to tell me.

EVAN'S SURGERY IS THE NEXT DAY. Jamie drives us to the outpatient surgical center and drops us off. I sit in the waiting room for the four hours that it takes a doctor to reconstruct the ligament in his knee and make sure he's on the path to recovery. He's arranged to spend a week in an off-campus house that belongs to some of his friends on the guys' Frisbee team. There are no stairs, and the bathroom is easy to negotiate. No one is around because school has just gotten out. For the next few days, I keep Evan company. He hasn't fully warmed to me, but we have both relaxed. We compare mix tapes. (He likes Ani DiFranco as much as I do.) We watch game shows on cable in the middle of the day. We find ourselves laughing together. As time passes, I look for ways to get Evan to open up. "You can talk to me," I tell him. It's awkward, because there's no space for this statement.

"Huh?" he responds.

"About anything that's bothering you," I say. "If you want."

"Okay," he says, and then he flips to the next channel. *The Price is Right.*

When Evan is hobbling around again, I'm ready to get home. He remains as distant as the day I arrive, and I still don't know how to create the environment to talk about our childhood with him. What would my World Works coach say? I draw a blank. I don't know. I resolve that I'm going to call all the time, that I'm going to find a way to create a space for Evan to confide in me, that I'm going to fix him.

IN THE ADVANCED PROGRAM, World Works promises that my transformation will go deeper. I sign up to continue the training, which is three weekends, in a new location, the Orange County headquarters. At first, I don't think I can swing it. I don't have the money to be buying plane tickets or footing bills for hotel rooms. But then the people in my group volunteer to help me—to host me and cover a plane ticket. The group of us who have chosen to build on the introduction and transform our lives more fully is smaller now, maybe a dozen. They include an engaged couple, a married couple with two young children, a single mother. At twenty-five, I'm the youngest and the only one who doesn't live in Orange County. I keep returning because I'm getting so much out of it.

But there's one part of World Works that turns out to be exceptionally hard for me: enrollment. A critical component to transformation is convincing other people to pay five hundred dollars to take the introduction course so that their lives will also be transformed. The trainer has a method for explaining why this is part of our curriculum. She references Martin Luther King Jr. If he hadn't been able to convince other people to believe in his ideas, he'd have been just a man with good ideas. It was by *enrolling* people in his vision to the extent that they'd take action through peaceful protest that he succeeded. "Do you think Martin Luther King Jr. would be Martin Luther King Jr. without the 'I have a dream' speech?" she asks.

I consider this. I purchase the complete audio DVD set of King's speeches, and I listen to them all. I try to enroll my friends in traveling to Orange County to be transformed. They aren't interested. No one knows what to make of my sudden, directed transformation, my insistence that I get along with my family now, my certainty that I'm happy. I'm *happy*. I'm really truly happy. "I think I'm just too skeptical of a person," my friend Craig tells me when I explain that he, too, could find value in the program.

One day, I call another friend, Erin, to suggest she enroll. Because truthfully, by now, I've committed to trying to enroll five people. And so far, I'm at zero. *Enroll her in the life you envision.* I start the conversation by asking her what she wants in her own life. And as if I'm a skunk, she can sniff me out. This is at least the third time I've talked to her about World Works. "Jessi, are you alone right now?" she asks me. "Is someone on the line with you, making you do this?"

It's a reasonable question. In the end, I fail in my enrollment goals. I convince only one person that transformation is possible. Katje is living with me that summer between her junior and senior year of college. The day she decides that World Works is for her, we are sitting on the hill in San Francisco's Dolores Park. It's sunny, and the city sweeps down beneath us until it runs into the bay. Her junior year has been a monumental one. She spent a semester in Austria. The evening before, she had dinner with her boyfriend and his bosses at the radio station where he works. They got through the entire meal before one of them asked her, "What's your name again?" She wants to be more than "Jake's girlfriend." She's thinking about her own future, about what she'll do after she finishes college. She's witnessing how much I've changed, how happy I seem. She signs up.

TWENTY-ONE

What Persists

A week after his knee surgery, Evan spikes a fever. It's June 2000. He's by himself in the Frisbee house, and he's been watching his left knee grow bulbous; the two incisions just above its cap have crusted over with a pussy yellow. The thermometer says 103, and ibuprofen doesn't help. He's cold and hot at the same time. He keeps his eyes at a squint so the light doesn't get all the way in. Exams have finished, and now all the students are leaving. Jamie keeps watch over him until the dorms start to close and he keeps getting sicker. She drops him off at the hospital on her way home to her family, and he's alone.

He calls Mom from the hospital but can't reach her. He calls Dad, who says he doesn't know where Mom is. "I'm back at the hospital," Evan says.

"Is it serious?" Dad asks.

"I'm not sure," he says. He has lost all sense of what serious means.

"Call me if it's serious," Dad says.

Evan figures out it's serious, because he hears the doctors outside his room say the word "amputation." Later, he'll wonder whether this word is intended for him. Are they aware he can hear them? Right now, he feels as though he's on the outside of his body, observing. The infection has gone septic, and rather than wait until morning, the doctor tells Evan the team will need to perform surgery that evening.

Then Mom arrives. He's not expecting this. He doesn't know the hospital has called both of our parents. She tells him she's on a road trip with her best friend, Alan, the boy who lived next door when she was growing up. Grandpa died earlier in the year, and they're driving to the Grand Canyon to spread his ashes. When Evan's doctor reached her, she was only a few hours away, driving west. So she took a detour to stop in on him.

Evan doesn't know where Alan is and doesn't ask. He doesn't know if Mom's staying a day or a week. He'll be going into surgery in an hour, and seeing her is stressful. He's always so worried about her, and he doesn't know how to be anything other than worried about her—even when he's the one who's sick. But also he's relieved to see a familiar face. The kind of relieved you are when you're sick and you really want an idealized version of a maternal presence to wrap you up and assure you that things will turn out fine.

The nurse comes in with a couple of techs to push Evan's bed to the operating room. The last thing he sees is Mom, who assures him that she'll be there when he wakes up. He counts backward from five, four, three . . .

THIS IS THE SEASON WE all learn that as much as we seek transformation, some things are persistent. We may hope to be different versions of ourselves, to break out of the patterns that we have been cementing for as long as we've been alive. But hoping isn't a path to freedom. Our relationships are dictated by histories we can't change or ignore. We must sit with sadness, accept disjuncture, let things unfold.

We all want to change. We're all trying to grow into better versions of ourselves. Mom has started a master's program. Dad has hired an executive coach. Katje flies out to Orange County for World Works' intro session during her spring break. I sign up for the next level of World Works, leadership, which lasts for six weeks. We will all discover that we can endeavor to improve ourselves, but we cannot schedule our revelations. There is a more organic process to healing. Time has its own rhythm, its own beauty. This is how I'll describe it when I have perspective.

Among the five of us, Evan is the only one who hasn't yet asked more of his life. Partly, it's because he's young. But also it's his approach. If he doesn't expect anything different, he's less disappointed. It's the way he protects himself. There's a steadiness to this approach. Evan is holding on.

In the end, he doesn't lose his leg. When he comes to, he's in the post surgical room. He notices the way his tongue feels in his mouth. Heavy, cotton-like. Then his head starts to pulse. He looks down and sees his elbows, the soft rise of his stomach beneath the hospital gown, and the bandage that encases his left knee. And there's Mom. She sits beside him, and she smiles at him. He's going in and out and in and out, and then he is conscious.

"How're you doing?" Evan remembers her asking. He kind of nods.

"Okay," he says. "I'm okay."

Is he okay? Yes, he thinks, he seems to be. And then she starts to lobby him for his summer plans. This is the first year that she and Dad live in separate houses, and she wants to know where he'll go when he's ready to leave Ohio. He can't think straight yet. Is he in Ohio? Oh, yes, he's in a hospital in Ohio. She wants him to come to her house, to commit to being there. Is she really asking him this right now? He doesn't know where to go. He doesn't want to be anywhere. He's scared he'll be in a hospital in Ohio forever. He closes his eyes, and he's sleeping again.

I DON'T LEARN THAT EVAN is hospitalized until much later because, despite all of the personal transformation I've done in my World Works courses, I forget to call him. There's so much else going on. Katje is staying with me for the summer. I help her get an internship at a nonprofit called Children of Lesbians and Gays Everywhere, or COLAGE, that I learn about through friends. COLAGE is a grassroots organization run by and for people with queer parents. Once a year, it coordinates the tween and teen programming for a week of activities in Provincetown, Massachusetts, called Family Week. And it advocates for queer families by working with the media. Katje and I are both obsessed with COLAGE. It's among the first places we meet other people with gay parents. It's a pathway to a new community, a place where we feel a sense of belonging and recognition.

COLAGE's offices are in a tiny room in the Women's Building in San Francisco's Mission District, and sometimes after work I meet Katje there and we hang out. The building is adorned with the mural images of iconic women like Audre Lorde and Georgia O'Keeffe. Inside, the rooms are populated by other small nonprofits working on behalf of the underrepresented. It's the same sense of belonging that I had when I hung out in the basement kitchen of Mount Olivet as a child: *I am of this place. It's mine.*

The final weekend in June is Gay Pride. The city is so geographically small, the LGBT community so outsize within it, that Pride feels like a neighborhood block party. On Sunday morning, Katje and I gather downtown for the annual parade. This is before Pride parades are populated by gaudy floats sponsored by multinational corporations, when the march is still a reasonable size and the point is the people. I bring my new girlfriend, a long-haired folk singer I met while training for the AIDS Ride from San Francisco to Los Angeles. We all have signs. I've painted two pink rings on a yellow posterboard, and in all caps, I've written "Like Father, Like Daughter." So many COLAGErs turn out for the parade. There are maybe a dozen people my age, people who will become my friends. And there are so many kids: middle schoolers walking with their parents, younger children being pushed along in strollers. There's a name I learn for what I am: Second Gen. I'm a second-generation queerspawn, a queer child of a queer. It's like a double pass into this community, a deeper gradation of belonging.

I spent so much of the past decade hiding my family, being angry about and ashamed of the ways they weren't like everyone else. But now I have a new way to understand them. Maybe my parents were so unhappy with each other—and me—because Dad was gay and closeted.

What if my family had looked like these families? What if my parents had separated when we were young enough that we could be raised by a self-accepting dad and maybe even a stepdad? As we march along, I can feel the gaze of people watching me, cheering. What do they think I represent? Here, today, more than three thousand miles from the bungalow on Main Street in Shrewsbury, I pretend I've lived a different life. I imagine that I belong in the company of these out families. This feels great.

But as our youthful wave of signs and strollers rolls down Market Street, I feel like a poser, too. I've landed a late-in-life pass to this club. This narrative isn't the full story. These families that I see around me don't have the straight beginnings that my own family had. They appear to be more united—the children, especially. Many of these children were adopted, or they were created and brought into the world through artificial means. That's not my family. We were just a nuclear family, heteronormative, until Katje discovered Dad's infidelity. And truth be told, he's not exactly out, still. While Katje and I march in public to celebrate his identity, he still hasn't told our church friends, at least not directly. My father in 2000 would never have marched in this parade. And Mom. Where does Mom belong in the Pride parade? I want to be part of this other group, these COLAGE families, and for my family to be special enough to be celebrated. But I don't yet perceive our queerness to be the center of our family's identity, which is punctuated by dysfunction and an impending divorce. I don't really believe I belong here.

THIS IS FALSE THINKING, THOUGH I don't know it at the time. As I work on The Project, I start to wonder about the composition of other queer families. I discover they are no more nuclear or intact than any other family. Lots of kids are born to heterosexual couples in which a parent comes out. This leads me to a bigger question: How many queer families are there exactly? Marching in that Pride parade in 2000, I still sensed that I was part of a tiny community, people who'd remained hidden or who'd chosen to live in certain places, such as San Francisco or Northampton, Massachusetts, to help ensure their safety. But twenty years later, everything is different. Culture has changed, as more and more prominent people have come out. The law has followed. In 2015, same-sex marriage became legal in the United States. In New York, my name is on my son's birth certificate even though I'm not genetically related to him. The state recognizes that I'm his parent. According to research conducted by the Williams Institute at the UCLA School of Law, there are more than 11.3 million LGBT people in the United States right now, including 1.4 million people who, like my brother, identify as trans. That's 4.5 percent of the United States adult population. Of that group, 29 percent are parents. There are millions of children being raised in queer households.

So how many of these households have multiple queer members? Parents and children, or brothers and sisters? This turns out to be a much tougher question to answer. I finally call Abbie Goldberg, who is a psychology professor at Clark University. Abbie has been conducting research on LGBT families since I marched in that San Francisco parade, and she has published some of the only work I could find on adult children of LGBT parents. When I tell her I'm trying to learn more about families with multiple queer members, the conversation immediately turns to genetics. "Well, there's that old research, right?" she says, and we both know what she's talking about. There's research papers from the late 1980s and early 1990s that look at sets of male twins. In short, in most of these studies, if a man is gay, his twin is more likely to be gay. "It just shows that, okay, it runs in families," she says.

More recently, the gay gene theory has been debunked. The largest genetic research on sexuality was published in the journal *Science* in 2019. It's a study of nearly half a million people. Its finding aligns with what I've always intuited: DNA is a bad predictor of sexuality. Yes, it's possible some aspects of our genetic code contribute to whether we are queer, but sexuality seems to be more fluid. It's decided by an ever-changing mix of biology, psychology and life experiences. It's impossible to separate one factor from the others.

The conversation about genetics has always left me feeling fragile and defensive. It suggests there's something to fix about me, if science can only identify the cause of the issue. Sure, I joke about this with other queer friends. I tell them we're a walking, talking argument for the gay gene theory. But if other people ask me about this question, I deflect. I tell Abbie this, and she says she's heard it before. It's almost as though I can hear her nodding over the phone. For queerspawn, there's an implicit criticism of our parents: Did they make us gay?

"I remember I did media training for COLAGE when I was younger," I tell her. I learned that when a reporter asked if I was gay, I shouldn't answer directly. Instead, I should reframe: *I think you're asking if I turned out okay, and I did! I'm happy and healthy!*

"I know, it's so tricky," she responds. Queer families often, but not always, cultivate environments in which children have exposure to more different types of families, so maybe they have more role models. And they're not as afraid of being rejected by their own parents when they come out. Then again, Abbie points out, in her research on second-generation kids, she heard from many young people who felt their parents were constantly being judged, and they were protective, careful not to share anything at all that painted their family as anything but perfectly perfect—which translated to mostly heterosexual. "Many kids don't want to show the difficult parts of their families to the world," she says.

AT THAT PRIDE PARADE IN 2000, I'm not yet thinking about any of this. After the march, while Katje and the rest of the COLAGE staff gather the signs and return them to the office, my girlfriend and I bring the sandwiches we've packed to Yerba Buena Park. It's packed. A Village People song is blasting from some nearby speakers: "YMCA." We lie on our backs in the freshly cut green grass, looking straight up at the sky. Having just recently finished our 580-mile bike ride, we're as strong and free in our bodies as we'll ever be. I already suspect we won't last past the summer, but this feeling that I have—of being young still, and in the context of this community, desirable—is an elixir. I stretch out my arm until it rests on her shoulder. "I love you," I tell her.

"I love hanging out with you," she responds.

It doesn't even feel like rejection, more like truth. I pull it back. "That's what I mean."

Over the summer, I take a break from World Works. I'm busy with bike rides, and going out with the biker, and hanging with my sister. These things lend a sense of purpose to my days. But by autumn, I feel adrift again. The AIDS Ride is over. The biker breaks up with me. Kat goes back to school. Heather is in love and has no time to hang out. One by one, my college friends begin to depart for graduate schools of various sorts—med school, business school, law school. What am I doing exactly? Bottoming out in my administrative assistant job, at which I'm terrible. I fill journals with poem fragments and make plans to write a novel that I don't ever seem to start. I begin to believe that if I truly want to experience personal transformation, to step out of the calcified belief system that has held me prisoner to my unhappiness, I need to sign up for the six-week World Works leadership course.

This course requires a full commitment.

As part of the leadership course, I'll spend several weekends with a small group. We'll participate in a ropes course. We will take on challenges individualized to help us grow in the areas we are weakest, where our world views are most stagnant. The core of the leadership course is a contract in which we spell out a half dozen goals we expect to achieve during the three months that we train together. These goals are, by design, audacious. They fit into a bunch of categories like "family relationships" and "professional life" and "health." The contract requires a check-in call with a volunteer coach at the start and end of each day.

This course is consuming. Just to reach my health goal, which is to lose twelve pounds, I sign up for a cleanse. I drink a green drink every day, swallow a teaspoon of raw garlic, and take an Epsom salt bath in which I scrub every last inch of my body with a loofah. I give up all sugar and, then, all cooked foods. I eat only raw fruits, nuts, and vegetables.

During this time, I start dating someone new, a woman who won a national orienteering event in college and therefore has an exceptional sense of direction. She introduces me to riot grrrl bands such as Sleater-Kinney and Le Tigre. We both discover Magnetic Fields' *69 Love Songs*. Like my last girlfriend, this woman is an intellect and a great listener, and she cares about me. She's tolerant of, and even amused by, my allegiance to World Works, up to a point. There are only so many times I can leave her sitting at a restaurant table—a vegan restaurant where I have ordered a raw dish because I'm basically only eating kale and nuts—to take my nightly call with my coach before she grows impatient and concerned. And she's not interested in doing the program. When I cannot enroll her successfully, it becomes clear that I must choose: her or World Works. I choose World Works.

TWO-THIRDS OF THE WAY THROUGH the leadership program, I'm standing outside a salad restaurant in a strip mall when I realize that maybe things have gone too far. I'm about to embark on a personal challenge that has been designed for me.

Along with a few other people in the program, I continue to struggle with enrollment. It's the one part of my contract at which I am failing. To challenge me and a few others struggling with this, our trainer has developed an exercise in which I can hone my ability to win others to my cause. We'll raise money for a charity, she tells us. Let's assume it's a real charity. I only remember that I'm not familiar with the charity, that the cause means nothing to me. We have two hours to mingle through this strip mall, identify and connect with strangers, and raise five hundred dollars. This is a true test of everything we have learned. I head into a salad restaurant and look around. It's one of those places where you work your way down an assembly line of fresh ingredients, selecting a mix of things that never taste quite right together. The clock is ticking, and I feel the pressure to perform, on the salad and the task. I notice a family, a mom and a dad, a girl of about five, a boy who looks about two. I get behind them in the line, working up courage as I tell the guy behind the counter that I want red onions and avocado. As the family pays, I see where they sit, in a long booth. The dad pulls over a high chair for their son. I clutch my tray so hard the salad jostles. I flash a smile and walk to their table with confidence. *Enroll them in the life you envision*, I tell myself.

"Excuse me, I'm in town for work and have no one to sit with," I say. "May I sit with you?"

Who does this at a fast-food restaurant? No one. They look uncomfortable but I have learned that one trick to navigating these moments is not to indulge the discomfort. What do I lose if they refuse me? Nothing. I continue to smile. "Sure," the mother says. Before long, we're chatting away, and now I follow the next step in successful enrollment. I get them talking about the things that matter most to them. "What do you want for your daughter?" I ask, and the question feels deep, but not inappropriate. "Like, what do you *dream* for her?"

"Well," says the guy. He'll bite. "I suppose I want her to be fulfilled."

"Yes," says the woman. She's smiling at her daughter, who is shy with me. "Happy, too, but mostly fulfilled. Also, I hope she can do that *and* have a nice car." Now we are all laughing. We're sharing a joke. We've just had a moment. Now is when I go in for the close.

"You know, I'm in town because I work for a charity," I say. "We're raising money. I'm trying to raise five hundred dollars by two p.m. Will you help?"

The energy changes. Smiles disappear. The background sounds in the room fall away. I'm failing. The family that has been so welcoming to me is not so sure that sending me off with a check, even a smaller check, is a good idea. They're too polite to turn me away entirely. Instead, they ask for more information. I write down a web address for them. They promise to look into it. We both know they won't look, and I'm relieved. It's a fake address.

I've lied. I think about this on the flight back to San Francisco from Orange County. I've lied to support the lie. I've misrepresented in the name of achieving the one goal I cannot achieve, the goal that is holding me back from personal transformation. Standing on this sidewalk, processing this truth, thinking about the nice people who agreed to have lunch with me, I realize I'm done with World Works. I've gotten so much out of it, but now it's time for me to graduate, move on, call it quits.

The problem is that this is not a program that is designed to end. After the leadership program, there's one in which you spend a year mentoring future leaders. Transformation work is never done, it would seem.

And even if I think it is, there's the small matter of my sister, who has completed the introduction and advanced courses. Having just graduated from college, she has moved to Orange County, where she lives with a housemate from World Works. Her best friend there, a woman who will remain an ally for life, is from the program. If I leave, what will happen to Katje?

When I screw up the courage to tell the trainer I don't want to participate anymore, that I've had enough, she says I need special attention. She sets up one-on-one coaching sessions with me. When I stand firm in my insistence that I've learned what I can learn, she has my sister call me. Then, the trainer gets dirty. She makes it clear that for my sister's own transformation, Kat should take distance from me.

I don't know what to do. The thought of losing touch with Katje is terrifying. So finally, I take this problem to Heather's parents. Like everyone in my life, Karen and Tom have grown concerned about my frequent trips to SoCal. They assure me that even if Katje takes space from me for a little while, she'll come around. I need to be done with World Works. They volunteer to write a letter. Karen types it up on letterhead from her pathology office. In the letter, she tells the trainer to stop contacting me or I'll be forced to retain legal counsel. I don't hear from the trainer again.

WORLD WORKS TEACHES ME THAT I can change my relationship to my past, that I can reconsider history through a lens that empowers me toward a better future. But it also teaches me that I can't wish my past away.

Not long after I leave the program, I call Evan. We've been talking a little bit more often. A year has passed, and still I think about his journal and my transgression almost every day. He's in a good mood when he picks up the phone. He's in the early consuming phase of his first real love. He never comes *out* to me, just tells me about Hallie. His knee is better, and he is playing Frisbee again. We've taken to sharing music, sending cassette tapes. Evan makes the best mixtapes. As we talk, I'm walking down the long central hallway of the old Victorian flat in which I rent a room in San Francisco's Mission District. I let myself into my bedroom and close the door. I tell him that when I came out for his surgery, I read his journals. "I want you to know this," I say. "I love you. I'll never bring it up again. But I want you to know that I've done this."

"Thanks for telling me," he says. His easy mood has changed. His words are measured, forced. We never discuss it again.

KATJE AND I REMAIN DISTANT for a while. After looking at MFA programs, I start an application for the journalism master's program at Cal, mostly because I need a writing career that will pay the bills. If I get in, I'll finish in two years with no loans. Katje gets a job in Orange County with support from a World Works friend, buys a royal blue Honda Civic right off the lot, settles in. We have short awkward visits in which we don't discuss World Works. During one of these, she's in San Francisco, driving me around as we look for a parking spot in the Mission. It's 2001, now, and San Francisco is empty, the first wave of internet startups having recently crashed. Still, we can't find anywhere to put the car. We give up and decide to head directly to Karen and Tom's, where we're having dinner. Kat is single now, and this is her first trip up to San Francisco in which she won't call her ex, who is still a radio DJ. We're talking about Evan. "You think he'll ever come out to us?" I ask. "Like, really come out? We all know he's gay." It's an assumption I'll later remember and regret.

But then Kat says it: "You know, I'm pretty sure that I'm bisexual."

"Really?" I say, and I don't say it kindly. She says it's something that's on her mind, that she has always liked girls and boys. I take this in, and I don't have a mental model for how to place it. Part of me thinks this is cool. This is a thing we have in common. But also I've only ever known her to like guys without question. One thing I don't know, because she never told me, is that she used to make out with one of her friends in middle school. Although it was a secret, this never felt like a transgression to her. The desire never felt defining.

The following summer, the COLAGE staff invites us to volunteer for Family Week. This is the week that queer parents and their children descend on Provincetown, Massachusetts. There's family programming—babysitting for the littlest kids, evening stuff for the parents. In exchange for acting as day camp directors, we'll stay in donated housing. And, if we're feeling up to it, we'll be able to hit the bars and have our own social life at night. We both agree to come, and neither of us confides it to the other, but we're excited to have the time together.

Family Week planning has been haphazard, and the whole event feels as though it might come apart at any point, but we also have a camaraderie with the other adult kids of queers, many of whom we know by now. The comedian Margaret Cho—who, with her saucy mouth, has long been a friend to gays—is performing in P-Town this week, and she gives COLAGE a dozen free tickets. Kat and I use the tickets to bring a group of kids to the show. Once we are wedged onto a bench in the town hall between a bunch of twelve- and thirteen-year-olds, we realize the raunchy humor is confusing for our younger friends, and we attempt to decode it. Beside me, a little boy leans over to his older brother: "What's a dildo?"

"You know," he replies. "Mom has one." I elbow Kat to listen.

"She does? What does she do with it?" his brother responds. Kat suppresses a laugh.

"She puts it in a blender and mashes it all up and eats it with a spoon."

"Oh. Oh, okay," he says, as though he remembers, and I never figure out what they're talking about, but I am relieved that I don't have to explain "dildo."

There is one more thing I remember from Family Week. That's the nature of teen romances, the rumors that would fly about this camper and that camper going down to the beach to make out. This is supposed to happen at camp. It's almost a requirement of camp—that young teens, given an ounce of freedom, will explore the emergence of their sexuality—except that at our camp, there is another joke that is funny only in this context. Only when you are around other kids of queers, when you feel completely safe in who you are, when you know your own birth story and you know you are among other kids who use the words "birth story" to describe where they came from. Many of our friends here have been conceived through sperm donors. Many of their parents used the same banks, and the taunt often comes up—as an inside joke, a reason to laugh with, rather than be laughed at—when you heard of two people hooking up: "He could be your brother!!" *No, seriously. He really could.*

This is the largest group of kids with LGBT parents that either of us have ever been a part of. In the final snapshot, taken the evening of the talent show, there are thirty-seven of us campers and counselors. It's a grainy black-and-white photo in which I can barely recognize my sister and myself, squatting in the third row. But then I see the two of us, leaning in together. Katje's long hair is woven into two braids that are tucked up in back of her head. I have shaggy hair and those quirky green glasses; all week I wear a sleeveless black shirt with a butterfly on the stomach, red board shorts, and a baseball cap turned backward.

On our last morning, just before we zip up our bags and head for the ferry back to Boston, Katje cuts my hair. I haven't had time to go to a salon. It's in that awkward phase, growing back after it has been shaved, and it needs shaping. I've come to rely on Katje for my haircuts. She used to do the shaves, but next week I'll start at Cal. I'm ready for something different, to see what happens when I let it grow. As I pull out the scissors and drag a chair onto the deck, I ask her whether she's still doing World Works. We haven't said that name out loud since we've been together. "I'm still involved," she replies.

"So do you think it's too much yet?" I ask her.

"Let's just agree to disagree," she says. This is hard for me because I don't want to disagree. I want to be right. But I want to be close to her even more. I let it drop. I have this photograph of the two of us from that afternoon, sitting on a balcony at the COLAGE condo. My head is thrown back, my hair blonde and thick, and I am laughing. Katje has clippers that she is using to clean up the back of my neck, which seems impossible to reach with the angle of my head, and she is laughing too. We are both laughing so hard.

TWENTY-TWO

Tattoos

Dad's flight lands at the Baltimore airport sometime before breakfast on March 24, 2001. He remembers the date because it is his wedding anniversary; it's also just a week after the courts have granted his divorce. He's as fit as he has ever been, but he feels full-body exhausted. He stops for a coffee, which he takes black, and he seizes these few minutes to sit with it, to review the local paper. He's about to see his father, Ed. Dad's flight home will leave at eight thirty p.m. It's going to be a long day, and he's not looking forward to it.

Ed knows about the divorce, but Dad hasn't decided whether to tell his own father that he's gay. Dad is still assimilating this information for himself. Sometimes he has trouble separating his sexuality, which he now views as healthy, from his infidelity, of which he is ashamed. He worries about his ex-wife. He shields himself from having to feel any of this consistently by throwing himself into his career. There are just a few moments in which his context changes, in which he is alone with himself, face-to-face with the full weight of his life and his choices. That's what these trips to visit his father have become for Dad. He rests a minute longer, flips to the business section of the paper. Then he pulls himself up and heads for the rental car facility.

Ed lives in the same small southern Pennsylvania town that I visited as a child, two hours northwest of BWI airport. His home is a two-bedroom ranch, dropped onto a flat half-acre plot out in the middle of a field, as if a farmer running low on cash had sold a half dozen acres for one row of homes to be developed.

By the time Dad comes to terms with who he is, Ed is at the very end of his life. He has Parkinson's, and his health is failing. His wife has been gone for a decade, and he's remarried to a woman who had been the secretary of a church he'd run in the early 1970s. Ed is frail in body only; in mind, he hasn't faltered, and his unwavering, evangelical faith in God has remained intact. He has finally stopped preaching, after retiring formally, then being pulled back into a new church assignment, and then retiring again. These church communities have left him with dozens of friends who look in on him and Ruth, stopping by with casseroles to visit and pray together.

When Dad arrives, there are a half dozen people packed into Ed's tiny living room, which smells like ham casserole. They're sandwiched onto the sofa. They've flipped dining chairs around and pulled up the piano bench. They've been praying. Dad had called over the weekend to say he planned a visit, but Ed seems genuinely surprised to see him. "Oh, my son has come to see me," Ed says to the group. People greet Dad warmly. He hasn't met these people before. He fights an impulse to take a step back. The old man continues. "It's a really big day for Paul because it's his wedding anniversary, and he has come to see me anyway," Ed says to his group of friends.

Dad remembers this now, the words like acid poured onto an open wound. This is not the senility of old age speaking; Ed knows that his son has divorced. Ed has simply chosen not to accept the fact. "Dad, we're not together anymore," Dad says. "We're already divorced."

"Yes, but today is still an important date," Ed says. "It's the date you *were* married." And now the people sitting around are picking up on tension they don't expect. They're uncomfortable.

"I'm thirsty," Dad mutters. He walks across the living room and lets himself into the kitchen to pour a tall glass of water. This is his moment for a power self-talk. What would his therapist tell him right now? He reminds himself that he has not come all this way to fight with Ed, that his time with this man is limited. He can be a good son to his father without giving up on himself. Outside the kitchen window, the yard is covered in a soft snow as far as Dad can see. With no children around to tramp it down, it has been lying there, undisturbed, since it fell. Everything beneath the snow is dead now—the grass and the gardens. Ed plants the most beautiful gardens; a green thumb is one thing Dad has inherited from his father for which he is grateful. Dad steers himself back into the living room to join Ed and his friends. They're praying again and make no move to leave. Dad doesn't really want them to, because what might he have to talk to his own father about? He's trying to make these day trips to visit more frequently, but since he can't talk to Ed about almost anything in his life, conversation is often tough.

People leave, and then more people come. Whenever anyone new enters the house, Ed introduces Dad again, with the same refrain: "It is a big day for Paul, and he chose to be here," Ed says. With each repetition, he adds a bit more edge. He's telegraphing all of the ways in which he judges my father for the dissolution of his marriage. Something could have been different, Ed implies without directly suggesting. If you had been there. If you were there.

After two hours, Dad can't take it. He announces he must leave in order to catch his flight. It's only three p.m. The flight is at eight thirty, but no one knows that. If he stays, the image his father has of him—weak, unfaithful, immoral—will subsume him. Dad leans over his father, whose arm is trembling as he lifts it to his son's shoulder. "Love you, Dad," he says.

"I'll pray for you, Son," Ed says, which is how he tells his son he loves him.

WITH TIME TO KILL, Dad drives into the nearest town, Chambersburg. He has always been intrigued by a building that he passes on the way to and from Ed's house. The whole thing is decorated in tattoo art. On an impulse,

Dad pulls his car into the parking lot and walks into the store to check it out. There's a glass case filled with piercing jewelry: earrings and nose rings, but also barbells and bone-like pieces. Behind the case, pictures of tattoos line the wall. The gentle odor of weed hangs in the air. Dad feels out of place at first. He stands in the door, eyeballing the young man working the tattoo gun in a chair behind the counter. The guy is scruffy, wearing a tank top to show off the black-and-white sleeves on his own arms. He's finishing up a small moon on a client's arm, and he looks up.

"How long does it take to do one of these?" Dad asks.

"Depends how complicated it is," the guy says. He nods to a binder on top of the case. "About an hour if you see one you like."

Dad flips through the drawings, and he can't find anything he likes. He explains what he's looking for—something that blazes with anxiety and also hints at the inner peace that's trying to balance it out. "I can do that," the guy says, and with very little description, Dad trusts him. After the woman has paid her bill, her small moon covered in gauze to soak up the drops of blood, Dad steps behind the counter and settles into the tattoo chair. While the artist works, they discuss another idea, a symbol to represent the Leo nature of my dad, born in the month of August. The artist agrees to mock it up and fax it to Dad, a second tattoo in the works before the first one is finished.

A while later, Dad leaves the store with a blazing sun the size of an orange in the center of his right calf. In the middle of the sun are a yin and a yang, fused together as if they are holding each other. The outside is a mess, his leg says, but the inside is finding its peace.

Now it's six p.m., and Dad realizes he must hurry to catch his flight.

THIS IS THE YEAR THAT Dad draws up a mission statement for his life. Things have been going better and better for him professionally as he has come out. For the first time, he's comfortable financially. He can afford to travel. As he transitions into a large new role at work, he begins working with an executive coach he meets in Los Angeles. She asks him to put together a plan for what he hopes to achieve, goals, and how he plans to achieve them, strategies. During our conversations for The Project, he digs up this document for me. We're on Zoom again; he's got a small bit of time for me while he waits for his corned beef stew to finish cooking, so this is only meant to be a short chat, but it grows long. He zaps me the document over email, but I can't open the attachment. He messes around with the settings on his computer and sends it again. I'm glad I waited because the document is a treasure. It's entitled "Paul Hempel: Mission Statement and Goals & Objectives." This document lays out a plan for him "to live in a way which integrates my work, my spiritual development and my physical pleasure" so that he can assist clients and friends with their problems, provide for his family and himself, and enjoy his life. This statement is four pages long, and it is very specific. For example, he plans to set aside six hours per week for hobbies that he will develop. These hobbies will include one "around-the house" hobby, one sport to do regularly, and one vacation sport.

One of Dad's goals—listed second after "hobbies"—is "relationships." He really wants to be good at showing up for people in his life. But people are confusing to him. Take us, his kids. We have all fled. We've moved to the Bay Area or gone to college. On school breaks, our center of gravity becomes California, where I live and Katje eventually moves. He can tell that we don't want anything to do with him. Thinking back on it now, he remembers how baffling this is. "I mean, at first I thought, 'Well, geez, all these kids are, you know, two of them are *gay*,'" he says. He's talking about me and Evan, who had his first girlfriend at Oberlin at that point. "So why are they angry at me?"

It takes Dad time and a lot of therapy to figure out the dynamics of this. We don't care that Dad is gay, nor do we feel similar to him. We care that he has failed to father us the way we needed to be fathered. In light of his absence, we've each found our way forward, but none of us is invested in learning to trust him again.

Dad's mission statement lays out a strategy for rebuilding his relationships with us. It's methodical and requires consistency. He will call each of us once a week. He'll write short emails twice a week. He'll visit each of us for a long weekend twice a year, regardless of whether we agree to see him. He'll go to where we are, make himself available, and wait.

The first time he comes to Berkeley, he spends two nights at the Golden Bear Motel, which is kitty-corner from my house. I test him. I don't agree to see him the first night he is there, because he can't just show up and expect me to shift my plans. The next morning, he suggests we drive up to Napa and go wine tasting. I'll go only if my girlfriend can come, I tell him. At the time, I'm dating someone from work who had to leave West Point for being gay. It's not a serious relationship, but I spend the afternoon making out with her in front of Dad and generally ignoring him. He doesn't say anything about this. He just suggests cabernets for us to try. It's a great day. I'm not accustomed to great days with Dad, and I don't want to become accustomed to them. One great day after ten hard years is merely an anomaly. In my journal, I write: "Saw Dad. It was fine."

FOUR MONTHS AFTER DAD'S WEDDING anniversary, Ed dies. Dad is on his way out to California to visit me, and he doesn't cancel the trip. He calls my cell from the airport to tell me. "You don't have to come," I say, even though just saying it makes me feel like I'm inviting rejection.

"Oh, I'm coming," he says. "There's nothing for me to do right away anyhow." I get the sense that he wants to come, because who else does he have to be with?

By now, Dad's trips have become routine, and over time, I have started to look forward to them. My involvement with COLAGE has made me curious about him. I'm living in the heart of the Mission, two blocks from Osento, the lesbian-owned bathhouse. It's just after the internet crash, so rents are cheap. One of my two housemates is a member of the Sisters of Perpetual Indulgence, a group of drag queens. She's a woman who identifies as a gay man who dresses in drag. I still work part-time at the nonprofit, but all I want to do is write. I've just found out that I've gotten into Cal's journalism program for the fall, and now I have time on my hands. Nearly every day, I cart my heavy laptop around the corner to a café on

Guerrero where the barista is a friend from college, and I write. I've decided to write a novel, not because I believe it'll ever publish, but because I relish the daily escape into an imaginary world in which I've created the rules. My book is about a family in which the mother moves to the Mission and gets involved in an insular leadership training program that I am careful to name something other than World Works.

Dad stays at a gay-owned bed-and-breakfast called the Parker Guest House. It sits up on a hill between the Mission and the Castro, a block from Dolores Park. I arrive at the yellow Victorian in the midafternoon, and Dad and I sit in the parlor. There are tea biscuits on a porcelain plate. Dad is expressionless. We're supposed to meet some friends at a piano bar called Martuni's, but now that seems wrong. "When's the funeral?" I ask.

"You don't need to come back for it," he says.

"But it's Grandpa's funeral!"

"Your life is busy here," he tells me.

I let it go. We head to Martuni's, and Dad buys everyone a round of mixed drinks.

I'm sad that my grandfather has passed, but I don't have much of a relationship with him any longer. Too much has happened to my own family of origin, and everything feels as though it is always coming apart. My siblings will not be going to the funeral. My mom will not go. I won't go.

AFTER A LUXURIOUS LONG WEEKEND in which we eat at The French Laundry and hang at A Different Light, my favorite gay bookstore in the Castro, Dad reroutes his flight home to go to Baltimore instead. The funeral will be Wednesday in Chambersville.

Dad never told his own father that he was gay. It's something I ask him about a number of times when we're working on The Project. At first, I just don't understand Dad's answer. Finally, he consents to explore the point further. "I actually spent a lot of time working through that with my therapist," he says. Dad knew his father was not just close-minded on this subject—he was antigay. When Ed's illness hadn't yet confined him to his home, he'd regularly held religious signs in front of the local bookstore because it was thought to be a gay hangout. He was also sick by the time Dad came out. In addition to the Parkinson's, Ed had prostate cancer. "And so the question for me was, what, what's more ethical here?" Dad remembers. What would the impact of this information be? Why does he want to tell his father? Dad says, "Is it so that I can feel good that I came out to him but make him miserable in the last year of his life? What was the point of this misery?" Dad kept his silence. "In my view, it was the right thing to do."

In the end, his peace won't come from Ed anyhow. Dad's acknowledging that. He will find it on his own. The funeral is a small morning affair, and there's a catered lunch afterward. Dad sits with his sisters, each of whom has brought their families. He is by himself. He has no regrets. By two p.m., he hops in his rental car to get back to Baltimore's airport. On the way home, he stops at the tattoo parlor in Chambersburg. The tattoo artist there inks a Leo, bold and perfect, on Dad's other calf.

TWENTY-THREE

Transitions

I'm walking fast across campus, and my phone stops ringing before I can fish it out of my backpack. It's probably my latest ex, Daphne, and I shouldn't answer it anyhow. I'll graduate from Berkeley's Graduate School of Journalism in a week, and the campus is as beautiful as it ever gets, dressed up for spring and the collective rush of tuition-paying parents who will soon assemble to watch their progeny accept diplomas. Northgate Hall is a particularly sweet building, academic home to just one hundred journalism master's students at a time, with a library and a couple of computer rooms and classrooms around a courtyard. I've just arrived, and I begin mingling with professors at an end-of-year mixer, when my backpack starts vibrating a second time. Ugh. Daphne and I have been in an eighteen-month emotional tug-of-war but can't seem to quit each other fully; the more she pushes me away, the more I pine for her. It's as if I enjoy the rejection. But when I tell her I can't be friends, she doubles back to me. I've used up all my minutes processing this relationship with her in these last few weeks of school, and here we are. But when I finally get to my flip phone, it's not her. It's Evan. I click "answer."

"Is everything okay?" I ask. I sling my backpack over my shoulder and head out the back entrance of the J-School for a walk across campus to the studio where I've been living. His voice sounds different, a little crackly. Is he sick? "Hey," he says. "I wanted to tell you I'm going by

Evan now." I slow down my pace. *Huh?* He explains that he's transgender, that he has only just started taking hormones. When he comes out
for my graduation, he may look a little different.

"Cool," I say, because it is cool. I'm cool with transgender people. I
have trans friends. But I'm also scanning back over the past year. Evan
and I have seen a lot of each other. I've visited him this year, and he's
visited me. For Christmas, we both went to Los Angeles, where he wore
a dress—a long floral sundress with lace lining the bottom of a very full
skirt, his shoulder-length blond curls pulled back in a rubber band. Did
I miss something?

He explains that he'd like us to call him Evan at my graduation. His
pronouns are either "him" and "he" or "ze," but, he says, it's okay if I get
them wrong at first. "Cool," I say again. It's a short conversation.

THIS IS THE SPRING OF 2003. In the next two weeks, three of us will graduate.
Mom is getting her master's in art therapy from Springfield College. I'm
set to receive my master's from Cal. And Evan will finish up his under-
graduate degree at Oberlin.

Mom's ceremony is the same day as mine, so she skips it. The party
was never the point for her. Her life has assumed a new, consistent
rhythm. Her boyfriend helps with the horses, which she takes joy in
feeding and cleaning up after twice daily. She rides Bandit as often as
she can. She is already practicing therapy, working several days a week
at a local hospital, where she mostly sees children who are on the autism
spectrum. She's drawn to these clients, able to see in them what others
miss and connect to them in ways others can't. The coursework brought
her to this threshold, but mostly she has developed her approach herself.
When her diploma arrives in the mail later that summer, she'll leave it on
the kitchen counter to gather dust.

I plan to move back to New York City. I tell myself that I'm definitely
not following Daphne, who is also moving there. Most of my classmates
are searching out newspaper jobs, but I want to work in magazines. I've
been told this is a long shot. A journalist friend has said I can sleep on her

couch while I get established. When I arrive, I'll hit up a bookstore, work my way down the magazine stand, and cold-call the names listed on mastheads. I'll also email everyone I've ever met who might know someone in magazines. This is a plan that will work out. The writer for whom I babysat in college will introduce me to a friend who will know a former student who needs an intern at *BusinessWeek*.

And Evan. His graduation comes last—and it will result in the biggest party. In addition to our parents, our aunt, uncle, and cousins plan to come. He hasn't told any of us what he plans to do afterward just yet. He is more comfortable than the rest of us with being in the middle of transitions.

TO THE PEOPLE IN OUR family, Evan's orientation has always been an enigma. He has valued this air of mystery. He has thought of it as a way he maintains a certain power. During his teenage years, up until Hallie, he never tells any of us whether he is dating anyone, male or female. As he grows, he dates lots of people of both genders, sometimes at the same time. He's polyamorous. He doesn't believe we should commit to any one person. There's too much of life to experience.

Evan keeps these thoughts to himself. He's a vault. If I work out stuff by talking to people, Evan works it out in his journals or on his runs. He doesn't feel the need to share a lot of things about himself. It doesn't even occur to him to come out to our parents, because he hardly ever talks to them. And besides, he says now, "I don't think that anybody ever really thought that I was all that straight."

There's also a certain kind of family pressure by this point. There's Dad and me. There's Mom and Katje. (And sure, Katje has told me and Evan she's bisexual, but we still don't take her seriously.) Evan is the tiebreaker. "Basically, I felt sort of like, Mom had a lot of dice in the game for me to be straight. And Dad had some dice in the game for me not to be. So I was like, I'm not telling you anything."

Then during his sophomore year at Oberlin, Evan falls in love, hard, with Hallie. She's a New Englander with long blonde hair and the most inviting smile. He's dating someone else, and so is she. But it's Oberlin, the place where the newest iterations of liberal ideas are first hatched and explored, and so they are both polyamorous, which is fine at first. Before long, though, they've fallen into each other so that all other people, and all other inputs, fall away. They are Brad and Angelina. They're John and Yoko. They are Johnny and June.

One evening, he's talking with Hallie in the off-campus apartment they share. It's toward the end of his sophomore year. He's going through his journals, and he's joking. He tells her that if anything ever happens to him, she should burn them.

"Yeah, and after I burn your journals, I'll make myself disappear," she says. He snickers, but then turns to look at her and sees she is not joking. That's when he realizes that his choice not tell our parents that he's queer has come at a cost to her. She wants to be known. This is the first reason Evan decides to come out. He loves her. He wants her to feel the power that comes with being publicly known.

Evan telephones our parents. Then he calls our aunt and uncle. He tells them he has fallen in love with Hallie. The conversations are brief and unexceptional, because the information sounds correct to Mom and Dad, to Aunt Rosie and Uncle Bob. It's Evan who feels most awkward about the whole thing.

"So you're a lesbian?" they ask, each in their own way.

"Yeah," he says. The word "lesbian" rolls around in his mouth, and he pushes it out in a declaratory statement. "I'm a lesbian." But he doesn't *feel* like a lesbian. He thinks it's internalized homophobia, and probably it is, but there's something more. Picking an identity at all is not something he feels ready to do. Why should he have to? He's Evan. He loves Hallie. Isn't this enough?

WHEN EVAN FIRST LEARNS WHAT it means to cross gender boundaries, it's an academic conversation. He's a junior. He's taking a women's studies course, and in his class there's a trans feminine classmate, someone who was assigned male at birth but identifies as female. She challenges the way that Evan thinks about feminism. Doesn't it belong to her, too? In this course, Evan learns about systemic oppression, the way we internalize the messages of our culture and repeat them without realizing it. We are aiming weapons at ourselves. We are holding ourselves back. What happens when he stops conforming to, or believing in, notions of what is masculine and what is feminine? What happens when he just loves whom he loves, lives as he lives?

Evan begins to read trans authors. Kate Bornstein. Leslie Feinberg. He becomes mildly obsessed with the iconic transwoman actress of the 1960s, Christine Jorgensen, a male stage actor who went to Germany, had a sex change, and came back. Then Evan begins looking at any scrap of historical evidence he can find about someone who transgressed gender. There was a jazz musician in the 1920s, Billy Tipton. There was an intersex woman in South Carolina, Dawn Langley Simmons, who had gotten pregnant and carried a baby.

At Oberlin, Evan becomes involved in organizing to get the women's resource center turned into the women and transgender resource center. He wants to bust open feminism and make room for everyone. Only later does he realize that he's trying to make room for a new version of himself.

It begins with a name.

This is when he starts to let go of the name he was given at birth. He tries this out, first, with a few friends, asking them to use the "he" and "him" pronouns. As his junior year wears on, the name begins to catch on in his social circle. He meets his first friends who don't know his earlier name; they only ever call him Evan.

Evan's experience of gender doesn't match the mainstream, to the extent that there is a "mainstream" in 2003. He's not a person who spent his earliest years alienated from the gender he is perceived to be. For Evan, this has never been about wanting to play baseball when the other children danced ballet. He did dance ballet. He danced ballet in high school, and he really loved it. For Evan, being transgender is simply getting closer to his truest expressions of himself.

It doesn't take long for his gender shift to catch up with him in unpleasant ways. At Oberlin, he lives in a bubble, a joyful progressive dream for a future that does not exist, not even really at Oberlin. Before long, members of the women's Frisbee team tell him that he's no longer on the team. It's a women's team. He discovers that he can't effectively live between genders. He has to choose. And if he chooses in favor of something that he is feeling out, that is beginning to feel right, there are no take-backsies. He'll opt out of many of the things he has come to love—such as Frisbee.

Looking back on our correspondence, I can see that Evan and I are in touch a lot during that year, our final year at our respective schools. In September, Evan writes in an email to me that he is depressed. He's down, really struggling. He's considering meds. I remember this about my brother, that his bouts of depression, of downness, are different from mine and Katje's. They descend, hold on, last. They don't seem situational in the same way that mine do. Rather, they appear more like a weather front that is moving slowly through. They can be incapacitating. Only later do I put it together that maybe this state can be traced to his grand internal reorganization, his process of finding his way to himself.

IN THE SPRING OF EVAN'S senior year, he and Hallie take part in the drag ball, and they win. The annual drag ball is a big deal at Oberlin; everyone goes. Evan and Hallie perform at the student center, on the big central stage. He doesn't remember the song, but he does remember they are dressed as a sailor and a soldier, and they dance with flags turned upside down. They strip off their uniforms toward the end of the routine, and they're wearing anti-war clothing underneath. Hallie's white shirt reads "Make Love" in red letters. Evan's reads "Not War" in black marker. He has used an eyeliner to pencil in a mustache and has affixed a faux goatee to his chin. He has a buzz cut. His chest is bound tightly in an ACE bandage wrap, and he holds the crown he has just won over his crotch.

Evan has never felt more himself than he does right then. The other students are cheering him and Hallie on. She looks sweetly feminine in her sailor's outfit, transgressive, but he doesn't look transgressive in his soldier's uniform, and he knows this. He looks like a guy. He feels confident and alive, the opposite of depressed. This outfit doesn't feel like drag. It feels like home.

EVAN HAS BEEN TAKING HORMONES for less than a month when he arrives in Berkeley for my graduation. My parents are meeting at the Rose Garden Inn, a bed-and-breakfast about a mile from my house. This is where I first see him. He's wearing a Boston Red Sox cap over his shaved head. He looks like a teenager, his skin broken out, his weight shifting around on his frame. His voice still retains a high pitch that confuses the mind and might cause you to stop and listen a little longer: *Is that a boy or a girl?*

It's late, and even later for everyone who has just arrived from the East Coast, and we're snacking on pizza since we all missed dinner. Mom is there, and Dad is, too, even though he's staying across the bay in the city. Right then, I realize that Evan has phoned me and Kat about his gender change, but he hasn't yet spoken to our parents. The first time Mom hears her child's chosen name is when I introduce him to a friend in this hotel's small garden. I notice her surprised expression, which evaporates as quickly as it appears. Despite Evan's changed appearance, both Mom and Dad throttle any surprise or concern. I'm distracted by the awkwardness of being in the same place with Dad, Mom, and Mom's boyfriend, who is just meeting Dad for the first time. Everyone is out of sorts, and no one is weirded out. By this time in our family, nothing is off limits. Everyone else has come apart so completely that any sort of further path to knowing oneself is met only with a timid acceptance. This is the first time we begin to say my brother's name out loud. "It's Evan?" Mom asks.

"Yeah, Evan Reese," he says. "The middle name is a nod to the one you gave me originally, with the *R*."

Later that evening, Evan, Kat, and I get time together at my tiny apartment, where they're both sleeping on the couch that, when pulled out, runs up against my bed and takes up the full floor space of the studio. We're wearing matching goofy pajama pants that Mom sent all of us for

Christmas. We're all in the midst of physical transitions. I'll fly across the country in a week. Kat has decided to go traveling in New Zealand. Evan has no idea what he'll do once he has his diploma. Probably stick around Oberlin, where Hallie has another semester of school. He's thinking about taking some premed courses. But, he explains, this transition—the one he has just undertaken—clouds everything for a while. Imagine going through puberty a second time but speeding it up, so that instead of five years, it takes five months. All the feelings. The rush of hormones. It's all so new. And he tells us about anger. It's a different, new feeling for him, a physical sensation that pulses through his body and makes him want to hit things. "It's not like I would," he says. "It's just that before the hormones, I never understood what this felt like."

Evan and I have always been doppelgängers, identicals, nearly six years apart and still practically replicas of each other. Watching his physical body change is surreal, a bit like losing a version of myself that I have come to know and depend on. The muscles in his jaw drop and begin to fill out. The fat gently shifts from his hips, which narrow out, to his belly. Peach fuzz fills in around his chin, while his thin wispy hair recedes back. Eventually, he'll buzz it.

After a while, the crackle in his voice will disappear, and it'll settle into a lower octave. I won't be able to remember what he sounded like before the T.

THE GRADUATION CEREMONY IS ON Sunday afternoon, and I'm one of the graduation speakers. That morning, we gather for the buffet brunch at the bed-and-breakfast. Mom has brought both Evan and me graduation gifts that she has made. She pulls wrapped boxes from beneath the table. She has made each of us framed shadow box collages of childhood photos and other assorted memorabilia from our childhood. She has culled through our picture books to find the sweetest and most feminine representations to include. There I am with my French horn, barely able to hold it up as a middle schooler. There's my brother in pink dresses and ballet tutus. When we were little, we had wooden puzzle pieces that spelled out our names on our dressers, and Mom has included these. There is his name, which is now his dead name. We all look at the gift. My mother smiles in anticipation, and then as she sees our reactions, her face falls. My brother mutters "thanks." As if to compensate for his lack of enthusiasm, Katje and I begin to clap with delight.

The shadow boxes really are beautiful.

Then we head over to the courtyard in Northgate Hall, which has been lined with folding chairs. I sit along the side of the stage, and when my name is called to speak, I clamber up to the podium. There, in the seventh row, I can see my family, looking at me: Mom, Katje, Evan, Dad. Evan has taken his baseball hat off for the ceremony. It's the first time we've been together, as a group, in years, and despite myself, I really like it. It gives me a sense that I'm from somewhere, I guess. We have all been through so many transitions, and we're in the midst of transitions. We've gotten a lot of things wrong, but I can't help feeling just now that we're getting a lot of things right, too.

TWENTY-FOUR

Surfing

In 2002, Dad offers to fly Katje to London for Thanksgiving. He's work-ing there and will be alone over the holiday. She's living in Long Beach, with friends she met in World Works. She's been done with the program for a year, and with these friends' support, she's got a good life set up for herself. She's got an entry-level job in human resources, and a new bright blue Honda Civic. But she's a bit adrift. Although I'm just a short flight north in the Bay Area, our relationship continues to be strained. After a lot of stop-and-go with her college boyfriend, she's completely single. She figures Dad's holiday invitation is the best one she's got.

She arrives the Wednesday before Thanksgiving. Dad has booked them into a design-y hotel next to the portrait gallery in Trafalgar Square, where she sleeps most of the day. When Dad finishes at his office, he swings by to fetch her, and they see a play. As they return to the hotel after dinner, Dad grabs his wallet. This new version of our Dad takes some getting used to. "Have a nice evening," he tells Kat, and then he heads out again.

Kat's wired. It's three p.m. in Los Angeles. She hasn't been to London before, and doesn't know where she is or what's around her. She would smoke if she was a smoker. She'd get high if she had any pot. All she has is a novel in which she's not that interested and a cell phone that doesn't work abroad. What person would she call anyhow? She's not even sure.

Even now, this evening singes a hole in my sister's memory. "I had no idea what I was doing with my life," she says. She's alone, with no purpose and no perspective. The only person she speaks with daily is Mom, and those calls remain freighted. Kat still worries every time she sees Mom's number that Mom is calling because she's not okay. Katje sinks into the plush velvet chair by the window and looks out over the street. Just outside her window, crowding out every other sign, is a billboard with an advertisement for New Zealand's airline. "Air New Zealand," the sign reads, the words spread across a beachscape: "The World's Warmest Welcome."

New Zealand.

The country's chief feature is that it's as far away as anything she has ever imagined. What happens in New Zealand? She's unsure. What are the people like? Probably nice enough. Where is it? In a place so far away the water drains counterclockwise in the toilets and snow falls during our summer. The flight from Los Angeles takes twenty-one hours. New Zealand is a place from which Katje cannot just return if there's a family crisis. It's a place where Katje can effectively disappear. Sometimes signs present themselves in subtle and unexpected ways. Sometimes they are just signs—literal billboards outside hotel windows.

BACK IN CALIFORNIA, KATJE STARTS picking up a bit of photography work on the weekends. Headshots mostly, as well as assisting jobs at weddings. She has always had an eye for colors, for the reflection of the sun off objects. She wants to be a photographer, but she doesn't feel she's good enough to make a go of it professionally. Art's commercialization is 99 percent a confidence game, and she has none. A friend introduces her to a couple who plan to marry in Florida. He's British, and she's Brazilian. After their marriage, they will move to Auckland.

Auckland, Katje thinks. *New Zealand.* She remembers the sign.

As new friends, these people hit it off with her. Katje strikes up a barter with them: She'll shoot their wedding. In return, they'll cover her flight and expenses to New Zealand and put her up for three months. That winter, Katje puts in her notice at work. She pauses payments on her student loans for one year. She sells most of her furniture. She packs what's left into the Civic, which she drives across the country in four long days. She parks the car in Mom's driveway in Massachusetts. Then, Katje packs a few belongings and her camera equipment into a backpack and heads to Clearwater, Florida. This wedding will change her in ways she doesn't know yet. For the first time, she'll experience the sweet allure of exchanging economic value for artistic judgment. Her skills will be in demand, her professional path set on its course. But this will be a small insight compared to her larger discovery.

CLEARWATER BEACH IS A THREE-MILE stretch of white sand on a barrier island abutting the Gulf of Mexico. Injured dolphins and sea turtles are often rehabilitated there. The bride and groom have rented a house on the ocean. A half dozen of their friends are staying at it, including my sister. It's at the rehearsal for the ceremony, which takes place in a nearby garden, that Kat notices a tall goofy woman with a shock of brown hair: Lucy. She's the groom's best man, his go-to for everything from emotional advice to a new bow tie after a spill.

Katje finds herself watching this willowy British surfer, noticing how she moves around the edge of the rose bushes with her awkward Gumby-like features, completely comfortable with herself. As photographer, Katje attempts to go unnoticed. It's part of the job. She dresses in black and sidles around the back of the room, looking for just the right angles to capture the rehearsal without appearing to be part of it. But the gathering is tiny, and before long she can feel Lucy watching her back.

"Oh, hello!" Lucy finally says, and that's all that it takes. They strike up a conversation about music and surfing and traveling. Kat has always wanted to surf. Lucy tells her the surfing is amazing in Australia. There's no end to their words. They stay up very late, and the next morning, they're the first two people nursing coffees on the porch, watching the birds swoop and dive in the morning light. They don't have a name for this thing they are doing. They're not so much flirting as falling into each other. Neither has dated a woman before.

Over the next five days, through the wedding, the reception, and the cleanup, they both stay in the house with the couple. The two of them talk all the time, and it means nothing except that they have a lot to say to each other. On the final day, Katje is preparing to go to the airport when she discovers that Lucy's flight back to Britain is at the same time. They share a car, talking all the way, and then pass through security together before heading in different directions. "I didn't realize why, but I knew I couldn't wait to talk with her again," Kat remembers now.

Just like that, New Zealand is no longer the star of my sister's trip to New Zealand. Now there's Lucy. They talk on the phone. They write long emails. My sister rearranges her trip so that she stops in Australia for six weeks before going on to Auckland. They meet in Melbourne and rent an old black hatchback. With the Indigo Girls blasting, they drive the Great Ocean Road from Melbourne to Sydney, camping and surfing. By now, they aren't calling this anything else. They spend this elongated summer and autumn falling in love.

WHEN KATJE FINALLY ARRIVES IN Auckland, she's already a different person. She unpacks her backpack in her friends' spare room, and she picks up a temporary job in a closet factory. The irony of working in closets isn't lost on her. She buys a beater car and begins getting to know other travelers through the hostel she's moved to. Lucy takes leave from her job and joins Katje in New Zealand, and they travel together for another two months. Katje shoots photos for coffee-table books. They both spend some time WWOOF-ing, working on remote organic farms in exchange for room and board.

At Thanksgiving, Katje finds herself in London again, passing through on the way to see Lucy, who is back in Britain. This time, Katje's life feels impossibly full. She stays with Lucy for six weeks and spends Christmas with her family. Then Katje returns to New Zealand, where my dad has planned to meet her for two weeks of traveling. Dad has remained committed to his twice-a-year visits, and he pledges to go on a longer trip with each of us. He and Katje hike on a glacier and even try a tandem skydive. It's the start to a thaw in their relationship.

This longer New Zealand sojourn is remarkable for all that my sister figures out, not about Lucy or about photography, but about herself: She's a person who can make things happen. She can trust her artistic judgment and trust that other people will compensate her for it. She can surf! She can love a woman. If everyone else misses the important things about her, that's okay, because she can see herself clearly. She can trust herself.

WHEN KATJE LEAVES NEW ZEALAND, she can't figure out where to go. After a half-year of the giddy honeymoon phase, her relationship with Lucy begins to fall apart. They don't know how to manage a life together while balancing their own goals and ambitions. Lucy wants Katje to follow her, and Katje wants to do that! But she also intuits that she needs to figure out what she wants to do, where she wants to live, who she is on her own. Lucy is a decade older than her, established in a career, grounded in a community in London. Are these things right for Katje? How would she even begin to know? The future looms, and their love fades. It's dramatic because drama makes all of us kids feel loved. Katje is drawn into the cycle of that drama but also repulsed by it. She knows drama doesn't total a life; somehow, ahead of all of us, there's an opportunity to have a different kind of love.

Now it's the summer of 2004, and I'm living with a housemate in a third-floor walk-up in Park Slope, putting in long hours as a permanent intern at *BusinessWeek*. I make fifteen dollars an hour, and I sell my French horn, which I haven't played since college, to cover my rent. Within a year, my role will turn into a full-time job with benefits. My home becomes Katje's landing place: together, we sort out where she'll live, and how. She'll stay at my apartment, and I will sublet a room from a friend down the street. She plans to get a temp job in human resources and pursue a career in photography.

Evan comes to visit us that summer, and we are a powerful trio. He has spent a lot of the last year in Ohio, hanging around with Hallie. He's also seen a doctor who has kept him supplied with biweekly testosterone shots.

Evan stays with me, and that night we make plans to go to a bar with a bunch of friends. Most of them are queer, too. "Wait, so you're all gay?" one guy asks. This is a question that comes up now and then, and when the friends who bring it up are a bunch of queers, we have a good chuckle about it. "It must have been something in the water when we were growing up," I say. We're all laughing, a little drunk. I like being grown with my sister and brother, being independent and also part of something.

I know this, can feel the power of it, feel grateful for it. It's half past ten, and we're walking across Brooklyn to a bar to grab a beer, and a friend jokes that she's going to make us a family T-shirt. "It's going to say 'Hempel Muffdiver'!" she says, and I'm disgusted, but also amused. Then in a nod to Katje's bisexuality, she adds: "Except Katje's. Katje's shirt is going to say 'Hempel Muffdiver—Part-Time'."

TWENTY-FIVE

Oscillations

After a year in Ohio, Evan decides to settle in Boston. He and Hallie have started to grow apart. It's hard for him to put the why into words, but Evan senses that it has something to do with the way that coming out as trans has changed him. The hormones have altered who he is, physically and emotionally. He is more centered in himself, something that makes him a better partner to Hallie. But he's finding his mascu-linity just as she is embracing her appreciation for femininity. They'll remain very close even as their lives move in different directions, but just now his life is in expansion mode. He rents a studio apartment on the top floor of an old house about two miles from Dad's condo in the South End. Evan gets a black Lab mix puppy and starts casually dating a genderqueer artist. And he brokers a sweet relationship with Dad, who is also new to Boston and has two besties, both named Paul like him. Dad and Evan are finding their way to an adult friendship. Evan becomes active in the slam poetry scene. His poems are raw and talk about sex and queerness and coming out. Sometimes he looks up to find the three Pauls sitting at a table among the androgynous twenty-somethings, cheering him on.

Not long after he arrives, Evan needs a refill on his hormones. Dad suggests he check out Fenway, a health clinic for the LGBT community. Evan makes an appointment to see a doctor there who treats people with gender identity disorder. That's the diagnosis Evan has had to claim in order to qualify for medical intervention. He doesn't like thinking about his gender identity as a disorder. It's ridiculous. His gender identity is the quality that brings order to his life. But if this is what it takes for him to get the drugs he needs, he'll comply.

On the day of the appointment, Evan is a few minutes late. He apologizes, and the woman behind the counter checks him in and gestures him to the waiting area. Evan looks around. There are three other people, all gay men. He sits in the chair closest to the door, his knee jiggling.

After a few minutes that feel like an hour, a middle-aged woman beckons my brother into her office. Evan explains that he has been living as a man for more than a year, and he'd like to continue the process of transitioning. The doctor appears skeptical. She asks Evan a series of questions. Evan doesn't realize this at first, but these questions have correct and incorrect answers. This is a pass-fail test. "Are you attracted to men or women?" the doctor asks.

"Well, mostly women but sometimes men," Evan replies. He's not really sure why this is relevant. His gender is different from his sexual preference. Couldn't he be a gay man?

And then there is the second issue, the much larger issue. Evan wants to be a parent. In fact, he wants the option to carry a child. It's one reason he opts not to have chest reduction surgery; he may one day want to feed that child. Keep in mind that it's 2004. At this point, most doctors, including this primary care physician at Fenway, are still likely working off the standards established in the 1970s by German American sexologist Harry Benjamin. This framework held that in order to access hormones, a patient had to prove that they had been irrevocably misclassified. As Evan explains it to me when we talk it through, "You had to say, 'I am a boy. I have always been a boy. I feel lonely, but I've never felt like a girl. I like trucks. I never liked dolls.'" Even the idea that Evan would have an instinct to parent, let alone carry a child, is inane to this doctor, who tells my brother she doubts very much that Evan is actually transgender. The doctor won't prescribe the hormones. Evan leaves the office feeling angry, wanting to put his fist through a wall. Only what purpose would that serve? In the face of this medical establishment, he is powerless.

IN MAY, DAD IS DIAGNOSED with melanoma. It comes as a surprise to all of us. It's not good. Dad has a tiny mole at the base of his spine, squarely in the middle of his back, that is cancerous. He has the mole removed, and we all wait for the blood results. His doctor informs Dad that the cancer is in lymph nodes on both sides of his body. It has metastasized. There are nodes in his lungs that need to be tested. There will be surgery and then chemo. The next round of tests will tell us whether the cancer has moved into his bloodstream and is settling into other parts of his body.

Katje and I go to Boston to visit because we don't know what else to do. The doctors have told Dad the cancer is stage 4, and melanoma is tricky. Even if you manage to get rid of it, it creeps back and then it kills. I google it, and what I learn is not to google it. I tell people that my dad has melanoma, and more often than not, they reply, "Oh, so-and-so had melanoma!" and then tell me a gruesome story about someone they loved or knew . . . who died. It's hard to imagine this, though, because Dad looks so healthy! Healthier than he's ever looked. He looks like the kind of guy who wrote "take up a sport" on his life plan and then never deviated.

Evan is at the house when we arrive. Dad has made a frittata. We all pull up to the kitchen table and talk about the cancer—only there's nothing to talk about. We make jokes about what he might say to the people at Soleil, the tanning salon where he just renewed his membership with a ten-visit pass in April. He's only used one credit. We all try to persuade him to go back to the salon and inquire, quite casually, about the expiration date. Evan pretends to be Dad: "Because I've just been diagnosed with skin cancer, but chemo should be done by December . . ."

We're belly-laughing, falling on each other. Even Dad is snickering. Evan keeps going: "Actually, do you give refunds for skin cancer?"

THIS IS THE YEAR THAT both Dad and Evan must navigate the medical establishment. They both have a set view of what they want for their futures. Evan imagines a future in which he can be masculine and preserve the ability to birth a child. The hormones make him truly who he is, and he needs to establish medical care to support this. Dad imagines a future in which he survives. The doctors are preparing him for another outcome, but he is not willing to accept it. Dad and Evan both accomplish their goals in different ways. In doing so, they establish their relationship with each other.

From his experience at Fenway, Evan figures out that he must lie about who he is in order to get what he needs. He doesn't tell Dad about the doctor and doesn't go back to Fenway. Instead, Evan goes to another doctor, and this time, he claims severe gender dysphoria. The doctor isn't a partner in Evan's health so much as a gatekeeper for his drugs.

This time, Evan gets refills of his meds. But he's still trying to figure out how he can preserve his ability to have children. So, he modulates the dosage himself, cycling on and off the testosterone. He stays on the meds for nine months or so, then slowly weans his body off them. The testosterone is a weekly intramuscular injection. When he goes off it, his body takes anywhere from two weeks to a month to clear the testosterone and then another month to start to cycle again. Once he is clear that his body can do this, he goes back on the testosterone. He's the first to say this isn't wise. Every time he comes off the meds, his crash is worse. He has mood swings. He's depressed. But it's okay with him because he has proved to himself once more that one day, he can have a child.

DAD HAS SURGERY. THEN HE undergoes an experimental chemotherapy treatment. It involves being checked into the hospital for a heavy dose of interferon every third week for three cycles. The interferon makes him very sick and kills the melanoma. Since Dad is without a partner, the three of us kids all pitch in to help out. Katje and I take turns being present when he comes home from the hospital. I get permission from *BusinessWeek* to work from home, and I take the train from Boston to spend time with Dad. These are awkward moments for us. Dad needs care that I'm un-comfortable providing. He needs help getting to the bathroom. He can't really get out of bed. I'm in his private space, and neither of us enjoy this. Every morning, I make him an egg-white omelet. He dictates the instructions precisely. I slice up a shallot. I brown it without burning it. I throw two slices of Canadian bacon on the skillet. From Dad, I learn what a shallot is, the gentle onion-garlic taste. I also learn something about the power of focusing attention on making something nice for oneself.

Evan takes the hardest shifts with Dad. He becomes the hospital liaison. I can't do this. Hospitals weird me out. I don't remember instruc-tions or names of drugs, and I think this is on purpose—as in "I don't want to." I can't handle the bodies, the bodily functions. I really can't handle long days of sitting next to someone I love who is out of it.

None of this bothers Evan. He sits at the hospital with Dad and mon-itors his medications. Evan is working a nine-to-five job doing intake as a clinical research coordinator at Dana-Farber, the hospital just across the street from where Dad is being treated. In conversations for The Project, I ask Evan whether he ever considered letting Dad sit in the hospital alone when he was so sick. Evan is in the car, on the way to pick up his own son from kindergarten, and he's in a hurry. "I mean, Evan, it hadn't been that long since you'd been in the hospital in Ohio," I remind him. His bluetooth disconnects, so he puts his phone on speaker. I have to strain to hear him over the noise of the road.

"Oh," says Evan. "Oh, I see what you're getting at." Why does Evan feel compelled to show up for Dad, when Dad didn't show up for him just a few years earlier? But the misunderstanding, explains Evan, is mine. Life isn't fair that way. It's not equal. We don't do things for people we love in exchange for the expectation that they will do the same things for us. That's just not how it works.

In fact, Evan explains, the melanoma year is a turning point for him. He realizes that he has a choice to make. He can reciprocate in kind and let the Pauls handle it. People manage hospitals alone all the time. Or he can stop being angry at the father he had and start focusing on the son he wants to be. Evan wants to be the son who shows up for his father, without subjugating his own needs in the process. This is the only thing that matters.

IN AUGUST, EVAN PUBLISHES A chapbook of his poetry. It's called *Oscillations*. Katje and I help sew the bindings for this chapbook one Saturday afternoon, while we all visit in Dad's hospital room. Evan's opening reading will be that night at the Gender Crash Reading at a community hall called Spontaneous Celebrations in Jamacia Plain. Evan is already dressed for it, and he's so handsome. He looks like a sixteen-year-old boy, his blond hair buzzed, a green plaid button-down over his white T-shirt. Katje and I sit in the third row while he reads, and she whistles through her teeth when he's done. I take a close-up photo of Evan autographing his collection that evening. He has brought his puppy, whose outsize paws are splayed on the table beside Evan's pen.

Two days later, the three of us escort Dad home from the hospital. It's his birthday. He's wearing his New Zealand T-shirt. He has a pink plastic container with six bottles of pills. We pose for a photo with him on his sofa, and we all feel so old. Katje is on his left and Evan on his right, and I'm squeezed in beside Evan. The photos feel staged this year, as though any photo might be the last, the people in it gone. The crazy thing about this particular bout of melanoma, the thing we don't predict, is that it passes. Once it's gone, it never comes back.

TWENTY-SIX

Marriage, Round One

On Thanksgiving Day in 2006, Evan calls to tell me he's getting married. To whom? I spend every Thanksgiving in Berkeley with Karen and Tom Rowley and their family, even now that I'm back on the East Coast. I'm finishing up key lime pie in the living room, and I take the phone out on the front porch where I have just one bar of service. Evan's voice sounds far away and keeps cutting out. He's been dating Kristi since August, he explains, and he's sure I'll like her. The wedding is set to happen three weeks later at a Buddhist monastery in Wappingers Falls, a small river town in New York's Hudson Valley.

And *click*. We lose our connection. Have I heard him right? I pace to a different corner of the porch and punch redial. "Tell me more," I say, which is what I have often said to him to keep him talking. At twenty-six, Evan can be hard to pin down. He sometimes doesn't answer his phone or return a call for weeks.

This won't be a *wedding* wedding, Evan explains. He and Kristi are polyamorous. They each plan to have multiple partners, though they consider each other "primary." They've gotten to know each other because both want babies.

And *click*. Redial. I'm processing this. Evan wants to be a parent.

Early on, he explains, they realized they should just have children together. A marriage contract will give them legal and financial protections.

Here, Evan pauses. I'm supposed to say something. Congratulations? This doesn't feel right. "What's the hurry?" I ask, to which he answers, "Why wait?"

AT FIRST, NO ONE IS invited to this wedding. Both of Kristi's parents have died, her mom very recently. Gathering our families might only remind her of her loss. But you try to tell my mother that she's not invited to her son's ceremony. She can accept that her child is gay. She can accept that he is, in fact, a different gender than she'd believed him to be. She can accept that he has fallen for someone quickly and that he's opted for a wedding as a legal vehicle, not a traditional union. But denying her the opportunity to watch her child walk down an aisle? That is too much. She isn't really able to explain it to Evan because she's crying so hard over the phone. My brother acquiesces. She can come.

After that, everyone is invited. Evan gives us notice of this turn in a group email, in the same breezy manner that you might let people know you're having a last-minute Super Bowl party. We can all come, he writes, *if we want*. No need to cancel existing plans in order to make it. The wedding is set for a Sunday morning in December; an invitation arrives by Evite. It doesn't specify a time—just "morning."

I never consider *not* attending this wedding. But it feels like a lot. The whole thing seems rushed. My brother has made a lot of announcements that seem abrupt in the moment, dating back to that phone call he'd made three years earlier to tell me he was trans. In retrospect, it isn't that his proclamations are sudden; it's that I've missed seeing him for who he is all along, so that when he finally tells me, I'm caught by surprise.

Mostly, the reason is that I'm so preoccupied with myself. Everyone is doing marriage this year. Of the five of us, three are now engaged, each to someone that they've known less than six months. Earlier this summer, my dad meets Ron, a charismatic HIV-positive man with a fish tattoo down his back. I haven't met him in person yet, but he'd won everyone over when he sang "What the World Needs Now Is Love [Sweet Love]" a cappella spontaneously at my great-aunt's funeral. Then in September, my sister announces her engagement to a woman I'll call Jenna. She is heavyset with dark hair, and she wears expensive jewelry and crisp Thomas Pink button-down shirts with cuff links. She holds herself in such a way that she always comes off as the director of any event. I like Jenna quite a bit, but this is during a period when my sister and I don't talk much, so I don't know her well.

I take these weddings personally, as though each member of my family is casting off from the shipwreck that our fivesome has become, leaving me behind. I am thirty-one and very single. Not recently-broken-up-with single or I-know-they're-out-there single. I am the kind of single person who hasn't been in a successful relationship in years and wonders whether some mechanism within me—the one that pairs well with others—is broken.

In fact, I'm fairly certain I will always be single. It is a belief I've harbored since childhood, and I remember exactly when it crystallized. I was grocery shopping with my mom and siblings at the BI-LO in Greenville, South Carolina. The cashier complimented my mom on her kids' matching outfits and the way our hair was tied in high pigtails. "Three girls!" the cashier said, perceiving us exactly as we exhibited. She'd been reading one of those checkout-line magazines at the register, and the headline piece was about marriage: "Only two out of three girls will find husbands," she told Mom. I have no memory of Mom's response, whether she even heard the woman at all. But at that time, my stomach seized with fear. *I am the one who will not*, I thought right then in the third grade, and I believe this from then on. I didn't share this belief with other people, though. Instead, it took seed in my gut, and everything I have become seems to have grown from that seed.

That summer as the announcements arrive, I shrug them off, as if to suggest I am not bothered. An email update I send to a friend at that time reads: "family news: katje is getting married. evan is getting married. dad is getting married. i am so boring. Lol." In reality, I believe a wedding, even one that is merely a contract designed to afford legal protections, is the event that signifies you've found someone to put you first, to take care of you, to love you. Privately, inwardly, I think myself to be deeply unlovable.

That year, I attempt to prevent myself from ever having to face this truth. My writing career is in overdrive as I report on the founders of social media companies, who are mostly my age and younger, for *BusinessWeek*. I start traveling out to the Bay Area constantly to meet with them. I structure my life so that I'm never alone, my time never unplanned. On the December morning that Evan gets married, I recruit a friend to stand in as my plus-one. I borrow a car from another friend to drive to the ceremony, picking up bagels and two coffees for the road. We aim to arrive by ten. The time is a total guess.

THE KAGYU THUBTEN CHOLING MONASTERY sits on a cliff overlooking the Hudson River, an hour and a half north of New York City by car. The quiet here has a ring to it, especially in December when the birds aren't around and there are no leaves to rustle in the trees. I inch down the long drive and park in a crescent-shaped lot, just as Kat and her fiancée are getting out of their car. No one has told us what to wear, but Kat and I look more or less the same: She wears a sheer black blouse tucked smartly into black dress pants, her hair falling in loose curls to her shoulders. I wear black leather boots, a black skirt that falls to my knees with a white antique lace accent, and a simple, solid-color button-down sweater. We look as though we might be attending a funeral. Or an art opening. Or, really, any event at all in Manhattan.

We are the first ones there, and we can't figure out exactly where to go. There are no other people in sight. I let myself into the main building, where there's a summer-camp-style dining hall and an empty kitchen. Just beyond, a sign is pinned on the closed door of an office: "Today is December 10, and we are observing a day of silence."

"Wait, so no one here can talk to us?" Jenna asks. Her deep voice makes her sound authoritative even when she doesn't know what's going on.

"Doesn't look like it," I say.

We stumble back out into the parking lot and open the back of Jenna's Bronco. I sit on the edge of it, dangling my legs off the side. Kat leans against it. I watch her eyebrows frown as she tries to think through what we should do if Evan and Kristi don't show up. Despite our interpersonal challenges, my sister and I are often capable of leaning in together to challenging family situations, knowing through a sisterly telepathy what needs to be done and doing it.

By then, other people have started to assemble. My aunt and uncle have driven down from Boston, with my two cousins who are just younger than us. My mom shows up with her boyfriend, Ted.

Dad is the last of the big five to arrive. A tall man I haven't met unfolds from the passenger seat. He lopes across the parking lot toward us, lumbering and delicate at the same time, and engulfs me in a squeeze without asking first. He steps back and smiles. "I've been waiting to meet you," he says, as if he has in fact been waiting all of these many weeks since he and Dad hooked up at the tea dance in Provincetown just to meet *me*. I take a step back, aware that I don't know this man, aware that I'm not a hugger by nature, aware that my mom is watching her ex-husband's new fiancé hug me. Despite myself, I love Ron immediately.

Then come the people we don't recognize. Kristi's aunt and uncle have driven up from Washington, DC, to stand in as her parents. They're a deeply Christian African American family, and her aunt has worn a full fur coat for the occasion. They pop the trunk, which is loaded with pies and a casserole. It hadn't even occurred to me to bring food.

STILL NO SIGN OF MY brother, but since people are clearly unloading, my mother opens the back of her Jeep, which is completely taken up by an enormous art project. My sweet mom. Stuck at home, having not yet met her son's bride, having no assigned role for the event, she has come up with an idea to celebrate my brother. She has gathered all of her favorite images from his childhood on a poster. Evan in a pink leotard with tap shoes. Evan in an Easter dress, hair pulled back in tight pigtails. Evan in a Brownie Girls Scouts uniform, hawking Thin Mints. A childhood drawing of his, signed in his imperfect first-grade handwriting. These are the images of the child she birthed and raised, but as much as they remind her of tender early times, they evoke someone he is not.

Katje and I see this happen at the same time, and we sweep in from each side, rolling the poster in on itself. Because there is something Mom doesn't understand: this is hurtful. For many trans men, a birth name is a curse. My brother has chosen never to speak the name he was given at birth. By now, I wouldn't utter it to anyone either, even if he weren't there, even while drunk among close friends. Its existence is a reminder of everything he has worked to overcome.

There is another, even more pressing reason to hide my mom's project. It's the one I whisper to her to try to explain things while Katje slips an elastic band around Mom's rejected poster. Evan has told me only one thing about Kristi's family: they don't know he is transgender.

JUST WHEN I START TO wish I'd brought snacks, Evan and Kristi pull into the parking lot. It is ten minutes after one. By now, the sun has risen high over the river, the temperature hovering around forty degrees. We're all shivering—except for Kristi's aunt, who is wrapped in fur.

Evan emerges in his new suit, smiling in that way people do when they've just found Jesus and nothing bad really matters anymore. I step over to embrace him, and he slips me his wallet to hold. Evan has been on hormones for three years by now, but they haven't yet shifted his appearance completely. He still has a mop of blond hair, and his jaw muscle hasn't dropped in the way that it does as boys grow into men. Kristi's uncle leans over to his niece, muttering in a stage whisper so we can all hear him, "Is he eighteen yet?" She nods. He cocks his head to the side and doubles back, looking alarmed, then says to her, "Are you pregnant?" No one says anything.

KRISTI WEARS A MAROON GOWN, bold and elegant. Her hair is pulled back and fastened at her neck. She is two inches shorter than my brother and leans into him, squeezing his hand. This day is the only time I ever remember seeing her happy.

The monastery is obviously a familiar place for Evan and Kristi; it's clear they've spent time here before. Once they arrive, a grinning man appears wearing a maroon monk's robe and, pulled over it, a frayed sweatshirt that says "Mississippi State" in maroon letters. This is Lama Norhla Rinpoche. He, at least, is not observing the vow of silence. The trio huddle briefly to greet one another, and then the lama gestures for us all to go inside so the wedding can commence.

Just inside the main building, we climb a narrow wooden staircase to a light-filled sanctuary. I have been in places like this before, while traveling in Nepal. I hadn't realized they also existed in New York State. Rows of small red pillows. The elaborate ornamentation around a gold statue of a Buddha, his thumb and pointer fingers touching as his hands rest lightly on his knees.

Katje and I drop cross-legged onto pillows in the room's center, flanked by our plus-ones. My skirt keeps riding up my thighs as my knees drop open until I finally drape my jacket over my lap. The older adults file into two rows of benches along the back wall, Ron and Dad sitting behind Mom and as far away from her as the bench will allow.

Nothing happens for a long time. Then, the monks file in. Maybe two dozen of them. Young Tibetan men and a few older ones, heads shaved, wearing maroon robes, chanting in Tibetan. My brother and Kristi follow. They sit cross-legged, right in front of the Buddha statue, facing an ornate chair. Then, as if on cue, everyone stands up—and so we do, too. The lama walks in. He's laughing, as if he is in on a joke with himself. He speaks for a few minutes in a quiet monotone. A translator announces that we will begin the ceremony with a silent meditation.

This is the longest meditation I've ever experienced, drawn out both because we aren't told its length from the outset and because we are so anxious about what will follow. In reality, it's somewhere close to twenty minutes, which is basically an eternity when you are hungry and at your brother's last-minute wedding. My mind drifts into a loop of questions: *Aren't you supposed to dress nicer for a wedding? Why are the monks chanting if they've taken a vow of silence? Who makes the rules? What is a wedding in Buddhism anyhow? Aren't Buddhists all about detachment? Wedding is attachment, no?*

A bell brings us back into the room, and as I shake out my knees, the lama welcomes us. He speaks for a long while about things I don't remember now, while Kristi and Evan sit on a pillow in front of him, never once turning back to check on the rest of us. I start daydreaming again and feel completely put on the spot when, a few minutes later, the translator explains that the lama wants to know whether any of us would like to speak.

We sit there, mute. But the lama is a patient man. He smiles and waits, and then he smiles and waits. So, I stand up. My voice cracks, and my hands are clammy. "Evan and Kristi, look around," I say. "We're all here. We got here quickly, because we believe in you." Then I roll into my marriage toast. It is a pro forma speech I pull out a lot in my late twenties and early thirties, all about how marriage is hard and worthy, and we're all here to witness it and to support the couple. And I'll be honest, I think I got the speech from the movie *Wedding Crashers*. I certainly haven't lived its wisdom yet. Nevertheless, I remind Evan and Kristi that we love them. Then I sit down.

"Very good," the translator says, replicating the lama's words. "Next?"

I nudge my sister, who stands up and salutes the couple. It's an odd gesture, but feels appropriate. "We want you to be happy," she says, and it is exactly what she means, what we all mean.

But somehow these speeches aren't enough for the lama. We wait, and we wait. And then Ron rises and begins to sing. He starts softly, as if maybe the act of starting will encourage the rest of us to join: "What the world needs now," he sings, "is love, sweet love." When no one joins, he begins singing louder. Then he adds hand motions, crossing his arms over his chest to denote "love" the way we did as children in summer Bible school. And as he finishes up and sits down, the lama begins to clap. So we all begin to clap.

Then the translator says that the lama says, "I know a song, too! A drinking song!"

The lama begins to sing in English, "Take me out to the ball game." The monks join in, the words jagged and rendered slightly off in the way that you pronounce words of a language you don't speak. "Then it's one, two, three strikes you're out at the oooold baaalllll gaaammmmme!"

There is more talking after this. The lama speaks. Kristi and Evan each speak. At some point, the lama announces that they are married. The monks drape dozens of white, loosely woven silk scarves, or *khatas*, around the couple's necks to wish them a long, happy life together.

AFTER A DRAWN-OUT LASAGNA LUNCH, we pose for a few photos against the backdrop of the Hudson, and everyone heads home. On the drive back to Brooklyn, I stop at a gas station to fill the tank. I reach for my wallet and find my brother's instead. Tucked inside is a five-dollar bill, a driver's license that still has his birth name, and a copy of a poem entitled "Crossing the Line" by the poet Brian Andreas. The poem is a conversation between two people in which one laments there is too much to be lost if she crosses the line. The other asks, "Like what?" I'd emailed it to Evan earlier that fall, and he'd printed the email and folded it into eighths. The poem ends: "There's always another / line somewhere."

Now, I understand how much my brother and I love each other and how little we can do to save each other. He will go on to be married happily for six more months. They'll move to Washington, DC, where he'll be married unhappily for another four years. The weekend that he turns thirty, Katje and I will drive down to their house while Kristi is away, rent a U-Haul, and take his belongings to a storage unit while he sits on a step, rocking gently back and forth. This is all in the future, but I can already guess that things won't work out. So why don't I stand up at that wedding and tell the lama that this whole thing is a bad idea? Why don't I explain more clearly to Evan that the legal document he is signing will be hard to undo and will throw him into debt for a decade?

These are not rhetorical questions. I am too busy thinking about my own sorry state of aloneness to think too much about Evan's future. But even if I were more aware of our future, what might I have said? Most of the advice that people offer up goes unheeded. We all have to learn our own lessons. And in the process, showing up is the only thing we can actually do for each other.

The next day I FedEx Evan his wallet. I keep the poem.

TWENTY-SEVEN

H-1-Fucking-V

Two weeks after Evan's wedding, I go up to Boston for Christmas. Evan and Kristi plan to host, but they live with housemates in a crowded apartment, so I opt to stay overnight with Dad and Ron. As I straddle a chair in Dad's kitchen on Christmas Eve, I watch Ron arrange white roses in a crystal vase. I notice how tall he is, a lumbering bear of a man with almond-shaped eyes and fuzzy hair. Dad's not there. I think he's at the office finishing something up, but I don't remember. This is only the second time I've met Ron, but he's the kind of person with whom familiarity is easy. Katje explains it the best. In a family where she often felt unnoticed, he made her feel seen every time they were together. Somehow, he manages to do that for all of us, often at the same time.

Still, it takes me a while to give in to his familiarity. I'm thirty-one years old, and I still feel that this guy doesn't belong in our kitchen yet. I mean, he and Dad are engaged, and it all feels too quick. I tell Ron this. It's a rude, entitled statement, at least the way that I deliver it. My words are curt. Without looking up from the roses, he gives a short laugh. "My life has taught me not to wait for the good things," he says.

RON HAS HIV. HE WAS diagnosed in 1984, when the disease was a death sentence. It was taking his friends down, one by one. He expected he'd die, but instead he lived. He lived long enough to take part in the gay rights march on the capital that happened in October 1987. It's a story he tells me one afternoon later that year while we're splayed out on the deck in the backyard of the house he and dad have bought in Provincetown. He was one of three hundred thousand people who swarmed the National Mall in Washington, DC, with posters demanding rights for everyone. The Great March. This was the first time ACT UP, the AIDS activist group, received national press attention. It was followed by a day of mass civil disobedience actions in which people were arrested in front of the US Supreme Court. Ron gets up and tells me to follow him to the attic, where he has boxes of clippings and photos. He's a keeper. If his collections—of everything from Virgin Mary statues to JFK magazine covers—weren't so neatly organized, one might call him a hoarder. He rifles through a box and produces a photograph of a much younger version of himself in cuffs.

A clinical psychologist, Ron lived in San Francisco back then. He was a Shanti counselor on ward 5A, the original AIDS ward at San Francisco General Hospital. This was grim work that mostly involved being present with people as they died from the disease that hadn't killed him yet. He lived long enough to help develop the protocol for telling people and in particular, children, that they were HIV-positive.

Ron kept living. He lived long enough that he began to take the cocktail when it became commercially available in 1995. Suddenly, his disease was not one from which all people died. It became one with which many people lived, and he became a survivor, a man for whom life no longer had a known and expected expiration date.

In 2001, Ron moved to Washington, DC, to start Pulp, a gift store that specialized in rubber duckies, greeting cards, and all things rainbow. Rainbow towels. Rainbow candles. Those wedding cake toppers in which two men in suits with rainbow pins are holding hands. (The whole store is a throwback to Dad's earliest days as a queer.) Ron was ready for a lighter life, a path to daily joy. Pulp DC took off. It became a

center of the local community, and a few years later, he decided to bring
it to P-Town. "Can you believe it?" he says. "I thought I was coming to
P-Town to open a store, but then I met your dad!"

I've gravitated to the far side of the attic, where Ron's collection of
antique ashtrays is wrapped in newspaper in an open box. They're mostly
from the 1960s, designed to be the visual anchor in a midcentury modern living room. "Look at this!" I say, lifting up an ashtray shaped like a
ceramic teal amoeba with gold flecks and spots for six cigarettes.

"Imagine that, darling!" he says, plopping himself dramatically into a
wicker chair, imitating a frustrated housewife taking a drag.

"Did you ever smoke?" I ask.

"Nah," he replies. "Not me. I did other things." He winks at me.

IN THE TIME JUST BEFORE Ron enters our lives, love has a feeling of scarcity
to it. No one has enough to go around. None of us gets along that
well. Katje and I have moments of closeness, punctuated by weeks and
months of coldness. We live less than a mile from each other, but we
don't get together that often. From our emails at the time, I can see
that we're wrapped up in a constant cycle of freezing and thawing, but
I can't tell anything about where our conflict starts or why it has flared
up so aggressively now that we are young adults. I know I'm jealous of
her. I'm lonely. It doesn't occur to me that she might be lonely, too. She
and Jenna are planning an outdoor wedding near the Berkshires. Katje
has left her full-time job to photograph weddings. They have a dog,
and they've settled in a residential part of Brooklyn with leafy trees
that frame wide streets. Meanwhile, Evan is making a life with Kristi.
The closer he grows to her, the farther he feels from us. Dad is hard to
reach. He continues to schedule twice-a-year visits, but his attention is
scattered on these visits, and I've come to believe things can't improve
much more in our relationship.

When Ron shows up, he finds everything about my dad delightful,
especially his children. Ron wants us around all the time. He takes us to
be his own at once. Ron loves Dad, for sure, but we are the humongous

bonus. Ron has a great and warm and fuzzy life, but his own sense of family is laced with loss. He himself was adopted, and he nurtures a desire to be a parent that has not been fulfilled. Ever since he came out as a very young man, ever since he was diagnosed, also as a young man, he believed he'd never have children. This is part of what it meant to be a gay man in the 1980s and '90s, to have survived AIDS.

Then he meets Dad and inherits three strong-willed adult children who are just beginning to lean toward their father again—and Ron loves us. It's an unqualified love. He writes us letters. When I'm offered a big writing job at *Fortune*, he sends me an antique pennant flag that reads "Good Writers' Club." He thinks about us all the time and then calls us to tell us he's thinking about us.

Ron draws us together. He's a unicorn. He's the dad and the mom we all wished we'd had, wrapped up in one sparkles-and-glitter package. Everything runs together in my mind now, but when I think of my earliest times with Ron, I think about sitting in a café with him and Dad on Commercial Street that first summer that Pulp Provincetown is open. He's asking me personal questions about myself: Do I have a girlfriend? Have I ever been in love? What kinds of people am I attracted to? I try to explain myself to him, knowing that my dad is listening, too, and Ron asks deeper and more discerning questions, never taking his gaze off me.

Ron doesn't change my dad. If he tried, he couldn't, but he doesn't even try. The guy is still my dad, his attention pulled sideways and inward. I remember this one time I am visiting Ron and Dad in their 1970s Cape home in Provincetown. It's August, and it's sunny and hot. Dad has purchased a lobster from the fishermen in town. It's straight off the boat and as big as a cat. We're in the driveway, examining the lobster, which is swimming in a pot of water balanced on a small table. Dad tells Ron to hold the lobster up, and he does. The lobster is as long as Ron's arm, from shoulder to wrist, and Dad pulls out his camera and starts taking pictures of Ron and the lobster. "Hold it up!" Dad says. "Okay, now smile!" He has taken maybe ten photos of Ron and the lobster, and I stand there, just out of the frame.

"Here," says Ron. "Come get in the photo." And he pulls me into the frame. Ron is always pulling me into the frame.

It's as if, by the transitive property, Ron helps us feel how much our dad loves us. Dad showers Ron with affection and attention, and Ron showers us with the same, and so we feel that our dad loves us, that our family is a family.

Times are easy with Ron. We've been waiting forever for times to be easy, and now they are.

RON AND DAD HAVE BEEN dating for only seven months when Ron is diagnosed with liver cancer, and we're all like, "Shit, what?" Dad has just beaten his melanoma. Ron is set to open Pulp Provincetown for the first time this spring. They've just gotten a new pup, a poorly trained Lab mix named Merry who can't be trusted to return when Dad throws balls for her on the beach. She'll swim straight out into the winter waves and tread water until the moment they think she's a goner, and then she'll come back without the ball and sleep the rest of the day in the store as Ron and his friend Bev set up the displays for a soft opening in May. This is the life Dad imagined when he sat with Martha on her porch and contemplated the future. We're all feeling invincible—and then this.

It's a straightforward cancer, a cancer that happens to a lot of gay men who initially manage to survive HIV. That early cocktail is toxic. It builds up in the system, all those chemicals over time, and eventually the system breaks down. Ron has become sick from the drugs that saved his life.

That spring, Ron is hospitalized four times. We believe he will lick this. We do that in our family: we lick cancer. They find a surgeon who believes he can remove it. Evan's wife drives Ron to his doctor's appointments; I set up a blog for him so that he can update us on his developments.

Dad and Ron are going back and forth between their home in Provincetown and the duplex in Boston. But now that Ron has so many medical appointments, they're spending more time in the city. After the first hospitalization, they decide to marry immediately so Ron can be insured. Ron calls to tell me they're tying the knot that Saturday in the living room. It all feels like too much to digest—that the best thing has happened and Ron has showed up, and that the worst thing may happen and we may lose him. I hitch a ride to Boston with Jenna and Kat, and Evan and Kristi join us to watch Dad and Ron recite vows in the living room. They wear Hawaiian leis made of white and light green orchids. The minister reads a Buddhist prayer and a Native American blessing.

Whenever they can, Dad and Ron get out to P-Town. That April, the weather on the Cape is severe. Big waves, driving wind, sand blowing way up into town. It's very cold. Ron stays until the afternoon before he is admitted for his liver resection. The surgeon removes Ron's gall bladder and about 40 percent of his liver. It's a nine-hour surgery from which the recovery is long and hard. Ron just wants to get back to the beach as quickly as he can.

Way before his doctors suggest it's a good idea, Ron makes his way down to Commercial Street, where he throws open Pulp's doors. Merry settles in to sleep at his feet all day. She has stopped chasing the ball and doesn't want to go to the beach anymore. She won't leave him.

RON HAS A SIMPLE APPROACH to life: lead with the heart. It never steers him wrong. He gets better for a while, and we celebrate. He's healthy for Katje's wedding party the following summer, and he wears a blue pinstripe dress shirt with a screaming lime green tie. Then in 2008, he gets sick again, and we visit all the time. Just after Labor Day, when the tourists finally start to recede, I'm in P-Town, sitting at the breakfast bar in the newly completed kitchen, when Mom calls to tell me her oldest sister has died. Mom's been crying, and when she starts to talk, she can't get the words out. She's crying again. Mary has been her best friend and closest confidant for her entire life.

In the wake of our parents' divorce and our family outing, our relationship with Mary's family grew strained. Mom often felt forced to choose between the conservative and consistent values embodied by Mary's family, and her own erratic and unpredictable ex-husband and children. As frustrating as this was for us kids, it was excruciating for Mom. Again and again, she had to pick between her sister and her kids, when there was no right answer, only love and messiness. Then, in a development no one saw coming, Mary developed early onset dementia, and now we have lost her before we were able to make peace with her.

Now I don't know what to do. The funeral is the following Wednesday. Neither Katje nor Evan plans to go. I'm not sure I have the vacation days. The plane ticket to Chicago and on to Peoria, Illinois, is five hundred dollars, which will drain my savings. I don't keep in touch with that family, and it's not clear where I would stay. Do I go? I'm worrying over all of this with Dad when Ron interjects: "Oh, it's clear what you do," he says.

"It is?"

"Yes. You sit next to your mother at her sister's funeral."

I get on the plane because Ron tells me to. I never regret this. In trying to make decisions about other hard moments in the future, I will embrace Ron's words as my mantra. *You sit next to your mother at her sister's funeral.* Another way of saying it: *You show up.*

RON IS GETTING SICKER. We all deny this. That Christmas, he and Dad invite us to the Cape. Provincetown in the winter is crisp and empty, the beaches soft white, the waves large and frothy. Kat is there with Jenna. Evan and Kristi come. They've just moved to Washington, DC, and make the nine-hour drive back. We've come to see Ron, but Ron is already living in a different dimension. He's there, but he's not. That's when we understand that he is getting close to dying. He has stopped concerning himself with the living. His body is present, but his presence is missing him. We quiet down when he comes into a room. We try to make life more comfortable for him. He is in hospice now, nurses visiting daily. He has chosen to live out his life in Provincetown, and we live it with him.

The last time I see Ron is at a Japanese restaurant in the lobby of a hotel in Columbus Circle. It's late January, and he has come to New York City to walk the gift fair at the Javits Center, to visit with his vendors and purchase the summer season's stock for Pulp. It's a strong faith in a future that he knows he will not live out, but even so. If he can just get the season's gift orders in, he knows the store will continue. Dad rents a motorized wheelchair for Ron so that he can make it to every booth.

He's in so much pain, and he looks it. His skin is yellow, his belly distended. He, my dad, and Ron's friend Bev join us for dinner in the hotel's restaurant, but partway through the meal, Ron needs to go upstairs again. The pain of sitting is too great. We get the bill without eating the food, and I assist Dad in helping Ron up to their room. I watch Dad brace his arms under Ron's shoulders, facing him as Dad lowers him onto the bed. It's awkward and uncomfortable. I know this will be the last time that I see Ron, and I cannot process this. I'm crazy with wild feelings that will evolve into grief but are, for now, writhing within my body.

TWO WEEKS LATER, I'M IN California about to pull an all-nighter when I get the call. I'm working on my first cover story assignment for *Fortune*, and I'm sitting in my rental car in a parking lot near University Avenue in Palo Alto. Dad puts Ron on the line. He tells me that he's getting very near the end. He tells me that he wants me to stay and finish my big story, that he's worried about my father. "We've said our goodbyes," he tells me. "I love you. Promise you'll come as soon as I pass to be there for your dad." Then he's too tired to talk.

The story I'm writing is a last-minute profile of Facebook, and I'm heading into my interviews with the founder, Mark Zuckerberg. He explains to me that Facebook is going to be a utility that everyone in the world will be on, and I'm listening to him, but I'm also thinking, *Ron is dying. Ron is dying. Ron is dying.* I accompany Mark to his photo shoot where, since he has decided to wear ties every day in 2009, he's dressed like a banker. He appears annoyed to be there. He doesn't like photos. I only sort of care. Ron is dying.

I take the interview tape back and start writing. In the morning, I send a draft of a story to my editors. The next three days are a scramble. I almost do not sleep. I fly back to New York and return to the imposing Time-Life Building in midtown, where a reporter and an editor are already at work on my prose. I'm a green feature writer, still honing my skills in story structure and barely cognizant of basic business rules, and the team does a nearly full rewrite. I don't have time to eat, really, or talk to my friends, or check in with anyone. Somewhere Ron is dying, and I'm writing, and it's going to be a cover story. On the night we put the story to bed, I leave the office after one a.m.

That Saturday is Valentine's Day. I am spent, and I don't have a Valentine. I go out to eat with a friend, and I leave my cell phone in a cab on the way home. I sleep hard and long, and I wake up sometime after eight a.m. It's the first time I feel rested in a week. Then I realize my phone is gone. *How is Ron?* I open my laptop to check my messages through Google Voice, which spits them out in audiograms. It's Katje. Just as the sun came up that morning, Ron died.

WITHIN AN HOUR, I'M ON my way to P-Town. I fly to Boston, then take the thirty-minute Cape Air hopper to the airport there. Katje and Jenna pick me up, and we don't talk on the drive home, because there's nothing to say.

My father is a wild animal. His grief is leaking out of his body in every direction. People bring food. More people bring more food. Six days later, there's a memorial service. Dad's sisters come. Mom's remaining sister, Rosie, comes, along with her family. On the day of the service, we pile into two cars for the five-minute drive over to the funeral home. We file into a small viewing room, where the first row has been reserved for us. It's packed with people I know but also people I don't. Ron had so many friends. For everything that the service lacks in traditional prayers, it makes up in the testimonies of people who have loved him. My dad's talk is uncharacteristically short, because he can barely get words out.

Then it's wrapping up. Katje, Evan, and I close the program. We come up to the front of the small funeral home chapel, and we start off very quietly. None of us can carry a tune. "What the world needs now," our voices warble. Then my cousin Laura, who is a perfect soprano, comes up out of the crowd to join us: "is love, sweet love." Other people start to sing. Now we have added hand motions, and we're belting out the words. Everyone claps and snaps and sings along, until we hit the second repeat of the final refrain: "It's the only thing that there's just too little of."

TWENTY-EIGHT

The Duckling in Her Bra

A few months later, Mom comes for a long weekend. I've gotten Saturday evening tickets to see a chamber music program in a small concert venue on a barge in Brooklyn Heights. She'll spend the night with me and then we'll go to Katje's the next morning for brunch.

Mom's driving the three hours from the farm. She's still living there, with Ted and all of the animals. Mom promises to arrive early on Saturday morning, but I'm not holding my breath. Sure enough, at ten a.m., she calls to say she's just getting on the road. Her GPS was being finicky, so she had to print out directions, and then it took some time to feed the horses. She expects she'll arrive in Park Slope in the early afternoon. In the background, I hear a small peeping sound, like a text message coming through. "Mom, do you have another phone on you?" I ask.

"What?" she says. "Oh, that. I've got a duckling in my bra."

"Huh?" I say.

I kind of don't believe this, but also, I do. This is such a Mom thing to happen. She explains that a couple of days ago, her mama duck's eggs had hatched. She'd woken up that morning to discover that a fox had gotten into the duck's nest. It had killed all of the ducklings except this one, which the mother had subsequently abandoned. She scooped it up and put it in her bra to keep it safe and warm, and she has been feeding it every couple of hours with an eyedropper. Mom is smitten with this orphan duckling. She feels she must protect it, love it into adulthood. "I've decided to name her Annie if she's a girl," Mom tells me. "Oliver if it's a boy."

SOMETIMES IN LIFE EVERYTHING HAPPENS at once. This becomes the weekend that many people I love converge in Brooklyn. My cousin Charlie emails to say he'll also be in town. Can he stay with either me or Katje? Yes, of course he can—he'll stay with Katje and Jenna. I pick up an extra ticket for the concert. Then, at the start of May, Heather sends along her itinerary. She's moving to New York to start graduate school. She and her dog, a blue heeler named Pablo, are driving across the country. And I knew about this trip, but I don't expect that they'll be arriving very late on that same Saturday night. Of course, without any question beyond the shadow of a doubt, they will stay with me. And Mom.

I live with my surly geriatric one-eared cat, Ruby, in a 480-square-foot first-floor apartment in Park Slope. Everything is miniature. The couch is short, and the dining room table is tiny. The bedroom is just larger than my queen-size bed. I've mapped out every square inch of my hosting abilities and timing for the weekend. It's a choreographed dance. Mom and I will spend the afternoon shopping in the boutiques along Brooklyn's indie Fifth Avenue. Maybe we can catch a coffee with Charlie, then go see music. Heather will arrive late, likely after the music. Ruby can sleep with Mom in the bedroom, and I'll sleep on the couch with Heather and the dog. See? It all works.

But now there's a duckling.

MOM FINDS A PARKING SPOT on my block, which is a miracle. I lug her pink plastic suitcase into my bedroom and come back to give her a hug. I lean in, and she pulls back a bit so as not to squish Ollie. That's what we're calling him. In lieu of more information, we've decided he's a boy. On Mom's outbreath, I hear *pheep-pheep-pheep-pheep-pheep*. Mom reaches into the V of her shirt and scoops out the tiniest little duckling, a start of a bird. "He's hungry," she says.

Charlie has stopped by, and we sit at the round white Ikea table in my kitchen-living-dining room and coo at Ollie. Mom pulls out an eyedropper, and she drips sugar water into his beak. *Pheep-pheep-pheep-pheep-pheep,* he peeps. After a few minutes, Ruby slinks out from beneath the bed and stalks around the side of the room, taking in our new visitor.

There we sit, catching up. Mom's therapy practice has recently grown, and she's just started running social groups for autistic kids. This is immensely satisfying work. As we all watch Ollie, she tells us about the young children who are learning how basic greetings work and what it means to take interest in one another's hobbies. This is an amazing thing about my mom—her growing ability to recognize possibility and potential in people (and ducklings) who struggle.

These types of conversations are also the common ground that Mom and I have discovered: our devotion to our professional lives. In different ways, each of us has become an expert on how people get along with one another, the ways in which we are social beings. At *Fortune,* I write about Facebook and Twitter. I study the technologies involved in how we exchange information. Mom is also obsessed with communication, the actual logistics of it.

Once Ollie is satiated, we all head out to wander through the stores, Ollie wedged in his cozy bra nest near his mom, who is my mom. We walk into a gift shop, and we're sampling candle scents when I notice the proprietor looks at Mom funny. There's the sound. *Pheep-pheep-pheep.* The proprietor's squinting her eyes. I feel protective of Mom. Is the woman going to laugh, or tell us to leave? "It's a duckling," I say, without being asked. There is a confrontational undertone to my voice. The woman backs off.

THE EVENING PRESENTS A PROBLEM. We can't bring the duckling to a chamber music concert. We can't even bring our cell phones to the show, and the duckling is louder than our phones. But we can't leave Ollie at home with Ruby, who has taken on a menacing countenance as she slinks around the corners of the room. Just before we absolutely have to leave if we're going to make it, Heather rings the bell. "Can you baby-duck-sit?" I ask. I don't think I even take the time to pour her a glass of water or bring in her suitcase before I transfer Ollie to her bra. I leave her there with the duckling. And my cat. And her dog.

There's a great photo of Charlie, Mom, and me standing on the pier, outside the barge where we are about to listen to chamber music. Charlie is tall, six feet three inches, a gentle giant, a queer anarchist. He has a shock of thick blond hair and a goatee, and he's wearing pink women's skinny jeans that show off his muffin top, of which he is unabashedly proud. Mom is smiling. She looks young, younger than she has looked in a decade, and so much like me.

After the show, Charlie heads to Kat's house to sleep; Mom and I take a taxi home. Heather is sitting on the couch with Pablo, keeping Ollie warm. Ruby meows loudly from inside the bathroom. "She's been doing that all evening," Heather says, raising her eyebrows. I feel awful to have left Heather on her first East Coast night. I leave Mom and Ollie to get ready for bed and take Heather around the corner to a narrow bar with great live music, Barbès, and buy her a glass of the most expensive Scotch in the house to celebrate her arrival (and thank her for baby-duck-sitting). We knock it back quickly.

When we get home, it's past midnight. Ruby is still shut in the bathroom with her food and her litter box, but she has stopped crying. Heather stretches out on the couch with Pablo at her feet. I unroll a sleeping bag on the floor, but I can't sleep. On the other side of my bedroom door, Mom is snoring. She sucks air in like a train, and when she breathes out, the duckling nestled on her chest sings *pheep-pheep-pheep-pheep-pheep.*

THIS IS ONE OF MY favorite visits with Mom. I like it when things are happening all around us, when the time we spend together is in the company of other people. It's easier. Because at this point in our lives, now that we have come through the storm, it's not hard to love my mom. She's bubbly and kind. Some people become more ornery as they age, but not Mom. She gets nicer. She thinks everything is amazing. I've never given her a present she hasn't *loved*. She believes everything's for the best, and if things don't go right, she shrugs them off.

When we're alone, she sometimes wants to process the past. She still has questions. I always shut these conversations down. She begins each one with an apology, and she rarely understands what she's apologizing for. I'm afraid to go there with her. I've only recently come to a gentle peace around the past for myself. I fear that if I really tell my mom what I think happened to me, and to all of us, in our childhood, she'll never get over it. It'll break her. Or worse: I fear that if I tell her, she'll deny it. And that'll break me.

Instead, we keep conversation light. We talk about her growing career and mine. We discuss art and animals. We have so very many conversations about animals. This isn't avoidance. It's a different kind of building. We're building something new, a relationship we're opting into. My mom has become someone with whom I want to spend time.

THE NEXT WEEKEND, I CALL her to see how Ollie's doing. The phone rings five times before she answers. She sounds out of breath. There's talking in the background. "I can't chat right now," she says. "The Jehovah's Witness people are here." *Why does she answer the phone when she can't talk?*

"Okay," I say. "Who?"

"The Jehovah's Witnesses! They're so nice. They stop by sometimes. We're having coffee," she says. I consider asking more about this, but maybe I don't want to know more.

"I was just calling to see how Ollie was," I say.

"Who?" she says.

"Ollie," I repeat. "The *duckling*. You brought him to Brooklyn last weekend?"

"Oh, sorry, I didn't hear you at first," she says. "He died." I feel crushed.

"What happened?" I say. But Mom is feeling rushed. A man and a woman are sitting on her sofa, sipping coffee she's made, waiting for her.

"Oh, a fox probably got him. Listen, I'll call you back?" It's a comment that strikes me as heartless but is more a product of Mom's effort to get off quickly. She hangs up before I can answer.

A FEW HOURS LATER, Mom calls back. She's elated. She explains that the Jehovah's Witnesses arrived just as she was emerging from the crawl space beneath her barn. She'd been looking for Ollie all morning. She thought maybe he got caught down there and couldn't get out, but the only thing down there was a mouse. Mom says that she'd been praying that Oliver was safe when these people pulled in the driveway.

Mom invited them in, they'd had a good long conversation. As always, she politely declined to attend church with them. When Dad left her, Mom signed off organized religion entirely. She wants nothing to do with churches, nothing to do with the busybody people who join churches and who expect things of her. But she's a woman of faith. She doesn't push it down anyone's throat, but she is a believer. God provides for her. She knows it. Her pink leather Bible is dog-eared from personal study. She's not the least bit surprised that the religious people have arrived just as she's discovering her duckling is lost. She doesn't mention the duckling to them, but she's very happy to have the people in to pray with her.

These folks come over regularly. They like Mom, and Mom likes them. Today, they actually have a bit of an agenda. Someone in their community has given them a duck, and they can't keep it. The woman is carrying it in a cat carrier. They know Mom keeps animals, so they ask whether they can leave it with her. Mom is filled with the light of possibility and promise. Of course they can, she says. She feels a little less sad. Then as they're leaving, the woman turns around to tell Mom that her granddaughter has named this duck. It's called Oliver.

"See, Jessi?" Mom tells me on the phone. "God provided. I got my Oliver!"

TWENTY-NINE

Everything Falls Apart

Ron's death marks the year that everything falls apart. Dad's P-Town house begins to smell like cat piss. He doesn't touch any of Ron's things but instead hires someone to caretake the place and spends most of his time at the Boston condo or working. When he's not at work, he's not present. He engages in risky behavior of all sorts because who-cares-Ron-is-dead, and by April, Dad has thrush and fatigue and shingles. HIV. He waits until he has started meds to call us. "Now that I've got it under control, my viral load is barely detectable," he says. "I'm going to start doing yoga and eating better." He sounds tired when he says this. I worry about it, and I'm angry at him. How could he have done this to himself? I vow to call him more often, and then I forget. It's a deliberate amnesia. The weight of his grief and illness feels like too much to carry.

Since we lost Ron, Katje and I have become much closer. The small stuff doesn't matter as much to us. That spring, we make summer plans to take Mom to hear James Taylor play at Tanglewood, an outdoor concert venue in the Berkshires. Every year, he plays an end-of-summer benefit concert with the Boston Pops. James Taylor is Mom's favorite artist, his music constantly on her CD player. We figure we'll make a fun time of it, maybe stay nearby and have a special weekend. It's a spot of sunshine, a fun event for all of us to anticipate.

To plan, we chat during the day in the corner of our Gmail screens.

"Mom's so excited!" Kat taps out. "And so am I." We'll bring a picnic. She has lawn chairs. But then the Thursday before the concert, Katje pops up in my Google Chat to say there's an extra ticket. Her wife isn't coming. "Things are hard," she writes. "I don't want to talk about it." I'm curious, but I don't push it. We've only recently started hanging out more, and digging into her personal life seems invasive.

Also, I'm distracted. By the time the concert comes around, my circumstances have changed. I've fallen head over heels for a British lawyer named Susannah whom I've been dating for six weeks. She's slightly reserved and mysterious, and she sends me a poem from a different poet every day. From the first night that she sleeps over, we are never not together unless we are at our respective offices. I'm drunk on the feeling of infatuation, barely able to think of anyone else. I've been single for years, watching my family pair up and sinking into my certainty that there will be no one for me. Then along comes Susannah. I'm still in the earliest innings of this pairing, which I'm certain will last the rest of time, and I'm in a very good mood.

Susannah has a friend with a house near Tanglewood, and on the James Taylor weekend, we decide to stay with him. Mom and Katje find a room at a nearby hotel. Mom picks me up in the Jeep, which smells like hay. Susannah pops out to the car to say hello. "Are you sure you don't want to come?" Kat asks one more time. "We have that extra ticket." But Susannah is having dinner with our host, so it's just us Hempels. We get to the lawn early and spread our blanket on the hill behind the stage. Mom sits in a low lawn chair behind us. It's warm, but breezy. Mostly, that evening, I enjoy the music. I enjoy being young, feeling loved, and having nothing to strive for because it's all happening exactly as I've wanted for all of this time. I love watching Mom watch James Taylor. It's a joy to see her love something, simply and completely. She's somehow become the least critical person I know, and this constant gratitude is among her best qualities. I think about this a lot, how Mom is easy this way. With her depression now treated, her career taking off, she's satisfied. Mom squeals when James starts singing "How Sweet It Is." Katje and I lean back on our elbows on the picnic blanket, and I swipe Kat's phone and start redialing the last numbers she called and then hanging up after one ring. I've always done this to her, a childish prank reserved only for her. For the next hour, various friends will call her back, "You called?" But she's on to my intentions by this point, and she grabs the phone back. We're both laughing. We share a humor and a perspective, born of genetics and experience, that is unavailable to everyone else, even our partners. This laughter fuses us until we feel like one being, and this is the best feeling I know.

Even so, I can tell that something is sitting heavy with her. We don't really have the space to discuss it without including Mom, but at some point, we excuse ourselves to go find the bathroom. As we walk across the lawn, Katje breathes out heavily. Her eyes are bloodshot. "Things are hard; something's wrong," she says. "I can't figure out what, and I don't know how to fix it."

"It's going to be okay," I say, because I don't know what else to say.

THE NEXT DAY, KATJE DRIVES back to Brooklyn to discover that her marriage is over. While she was away, her wife left her for someone else. It's a complete surprise. Jenna has left instructions for what's going to happen next and made plans for where my sister can stay. Just as in their marriage, in their separation she has tried to control everything.

The life Katje knows has just vomited her out on the sidewalk. She has only her cameras and Molly, the puppy that she and Jenna have just adopted. She's not sure whose life she's living, what alternate dimension she exists in. She's left to sleep on other people's sofas. But her friends are *their* shared friends, and those sofas offer no comfort.

That week, Katje and Molly come stay with me. Molly is just six months old, and she's spastic. She's a hound mix with long ears and the kind of puppy teeth that find every leather shoe in a house and destroy it. She reminds me of a rubber band that someone keeps stretching too tightly and snapping. All week, Katje sits on my couch and surfs Craigslist for rental listings. Once an hour, she takes Molly out to pee. She isn't really sleeping, and one morning as I head out to catch the subway to the office, she and Molly amble down the steps with me. Molly slips out of her collar and dashes up the sidewalk, spinning a quick figure eight. Katje lunges for her and begins to scream. Molly thinks it's a game! She's prancing about, evading Katje's reach. I stand there, unsure how to help, my reflexes frozen as Katje dives for the dog. It's as though she is about to lose the only thing left that belongs to her, the one living being for whom she is responsible. At last, she slips the collar on Molly, sits down on the step, and begins to cry. I sit next to her, but she doesn't want me there. "Go to work," she hisses quietly. She wants to put herself back together.

BIT BY BIT, KATJE FIGURES out what to do. She signs a lease on a sunny, slightly run-down apartment in South Slope. It's not close to any trains, but the light is beautiful, and she can grow an herb garden in the window. Susannah and I show up at her old place to help her pack. We pick through her nuptial belongings, which include so many expensive wedding presents barely unboxed, and take everything we think she would want. It's not that much in the end. A leather chair. Glass candleholders. As we work, we start to brainstorm what will happen next for her. Running a wedding photography business is less fun when your own marriage implodes. She'd really like to work in human resources . . . Maybe she should apply for HR jobs?

At the bottom of an underwear drawer, I find a four-hundred-dollar gift certificate to The River Café, an elegant waterfront restaurant that boasts a perfect view of the Brooklyn Bridge. "Shall we all go out to eat?" I ask her, but when I turn to look at her, her eyes are spitting tears. She tells me to keep it. It's odd to be the one with a partner for once, while Katje suffers from a heartsickness that threatens to consume her life force. "You sure?" I say.

"I never want to go to a fancy restaurant again," she says. I slip the gift certificate into my pocket and throw an arm around her shoulder.

Later that fall, Susannah and I dress up and go out for filet mignon. By this time, we have nearly burned the oxygen out of our own relationship. We still spend every night together, but it has begun to feel to me as though Susannah isn't there. Shortly after we met, on an impulse, we flew to Paris for a weekend. We walked through the flower market and lingered at Musée d'Orsay. She told me she was in love with me. Now she doesn't say that anymore. I'm looking for ways to hear her say it again—such as a four-hundred-dollar dinner at an elegant, stuffy restaurant. We sit at a table by the window, sharing the tiramisu with the chocolate topper of the Brooklyn Bridge while we watch the lights twinkle on the actual bridge. We aren't looking at each other, but really, she's not looking at me. Is this true, or am I imagining this?

Just after Thanksgiving, Susannah leaves me. She says it's not my fault, and looking back I can see that it's not her fault, either. We've dated only a few months, and they've been turbulent and confusing, hot and cold, but still, I'm wrecked. I can't eat, and I can't sleep. I can't imagine a time when I'll feel better. Susannah has been the only person in my adulthood to offer me something of which I don't believe I'm capable or worthy: a promise of a future together as a pair, a family. It's something she said from day one, something I always wanted but did not even voice.

Now I'm single again.

I mourn this relationship in an outsize way. I can't come up for air at times; I can't breathe. This is when I learn that the grief we carry isn't always attached directly to the events that unlock it. This is the grief of my childhood, the pain of being left every time that I've ever been left. I have spent my adulthood alone, dating and playing out the trauma of my earliest years endlessly in search of a feeling that felt familiar, a feeling I called love. That moment when I fear everything might go away? That's the moment I *feel* loved. Finally getting close to something approximating the family I see around me, and then losing it, dredges up every feeling I've ever had about losing family, every fear I've ever entertained about being stained by that loss and incapable of sustaining anything else.

For three months, I weep. I hardly work. I cry every day. Most nights, I wake sometime in the three a.m. hour and never go back to sleep. I walk through social engagements like the living dead. I write mean emails to Susannah that I erase. I write some that I send. All the sad comes rushing out, endlessly.

The weeks, at least, have the structure of work to distract, the professional demands of colleagues to pull me from my haze. The weekends crawl by. That winter is rough. The gods dump snow on Brooklyn endlessly, the kind of snow that stops the subways and causes buses to get lodged in the streets. Snow makes things quiet. It sucks in all the sounds of a city, leaving me stuck in a vacuum. Does anyone else in Brooklyn feel this alone? One January weekend, a friend calls to see whether I'll go to a bar in Red Hook for a literary reading. I've been by myself in my apartment for days. We agree to take the bus. I pull pants on over long underwear, adjust my scarf around the edge of my hat, and then trudge three blocks through the crusty, icy snow. We meet on the corner of Seventh Avenue and Ninth Street and wait an impossibly long time. We're the only people outside. And maybe we're dumb to go, but I need to see someone, at least.

The only thing that makes this post-breakup living better is my sister. She's also coming back from heartbreak, just fifteen blocks away. On her first wedding anniversary that she doesn't celebrate, I invite her on a "date." Anniversaries can suck, and it occurs to me that we could in fact decide to celebrate it, as if it were the holiday we'd been waiting for all year. It's a Thursday night, and we dress up. I make her a mix CD with a dozen songs: the first six are angry breakup songs, and the final six are I'm-all-better songs. We go out to eat and to a movie. "Congratulations!" I tell her. "You've got your life back!" We really are celebrating. Life has taken us all this way, and here we are, somehow finding fun in close proximity.

AFTER THINGS FALL APART, THERE'S freedom. All of the expectations that have constrained us have been demolished. The concentration of the psychic pain will dissipate, and in its place will be time and autonomy, if you can recognize it. That spring, I turn thirty-five. I treat Katje and Heather to dinner in the neighborhood. All three of us live within a few blocks of one another. Heather's a year into her graduate program. Katje has just accepted a full-time human resources job at an ad agency. We're all nominally single, open.

During this time of despair and depression, friends begin a joy email

chain with me—just before we fall asleep each night, we email one another five things we have appreciated during the day. We do this for a full
year. This is how, a decade later, I know exactly how I spend that time.
I run in the park. I make chana masala for friends. I host a young cousin
on the couch in my living room for a month. I go to concerts and plays. I
work long hours reporting and writing about technology at *Fortune;* it's a
job that proves so satisfying it makes a mention on my joy list repeatedly.
Even as I work, Katje, Heather, and I text and chat virtually all day about
ex run-ins, weekend plans, our parents. I am waiting for my life to begin,
and I don't notice at first that I'm living my life and it's wonderful.

We all have a sense that this period is limited, and this is one of the
reasons we love it. We all want things for our lives. Katje is planning to
one day move to Portland, Oregon, a place she has only visited but hopes
will hold nature and mild weather. Heather will soon finish school, and she
wants to have a child. What do I want? After decades of false starts with
relationships, I decide not to want anything that I consider conventional—
especially kids. I have reached the age when people I work with or report
on sometimes ask me what my plan is. I've seen other women struggle with
how to have kids when they don't have partners. No biological imperative
ever prompts me to feel that I want kids, but more than that, I'm scared.
Wouldn't kids just test me in every way? On the recommendation of a
friend, I consult a medium who tells me that it isn't written in my karma to
be a parent. In the moment these words are delivered, they are a kindness.
They give me permission not to exist in a state of *wanting* children. But as
the years go by, I repeat this belief to myself until it becomes my truth. It's
easier not to want something than to consider whether I want it and cannot
have it.

IN THIS UNENCUMBERED YOUNG ADULT existence, only Evan is missing. He's gone silent again. I haven't seen him and Kristi since Ron's funeral. He doesn't
return emails. His voicemail box is full. He's living in the Maryland suburbs, just outside of Washington, DC, where his wife has inherited the
tiny ranch home in which she grew up. I've never seen it. I call and ask

to visit, but it's never a good time. He says Kristi has decided that Mom is inappropriate. He says she's decided that Dad isn't a good influence. He says she doesn't feel welcome in our family. I volunteer to come and stay nearby with friends, and we can just go to dinner, but he says he can't get away.

Then one day he calls. It's a Friday. He doesn't sound like himself. His voice is scratchy and tired, and he tells me he has no money and nowhere to go. His wife has drained his bank account and locked him out of their home. She's cheating on him, or has left him, and she also might have a substance problem. Things have been deteriorating for so long that he doesn't know how bad they are. Then one day, it comes to him: *I'm locked out, and I shouldn't go back. I need to leave.*

Now he's on a street corner, calling on his cell phone, and he doesn't know where to go. I tell him to come to Brooklyn. I go online and buy him a train ticket that he can access by flashing his license at the station. He has that, at least. I lend him a little money. He tells me he'll pay me back before the year is up, and he does.

Evan retreats to my couch. In the evenings, I come home from work to find him there, sitting cross-legged, working from his laptop. He teaches me to make spaghetti squash in the microwave, and we watch TV together.

Evan isn't ready then for his marriage to be over. He's attached to Kristi in a way that I recognize. It's as if, the worse she behaves and the more he has to become invisible in order to survive in his relationship, the more he leans into the commitment he has made to her. They are married. They took vows. While he's staying with me, she sometimes calls. Every time they talk, he breaks down. One day, I find him sitting on the floor in the bathroom in the spot where I sometimes end up when I have the emotional flu. It happens much less frequently now, but I remember and recognize the experience of it. His face is tearstained, but he's not crying. He's rocking gently.

All three of us have done this, in our own ways. We've opted into relationships in which we've had to change who we are to survive. We've found ways to become smaller and less noticeable until one day, we weren't there at all. But now, this year, we're finding our way out—all at the same time, with help from one another.

BY LABOR DAY OF 2010, Evan is looking for a new apartment back near his Maryland place, in Washington, DC. He comes up to Brooklyn every weekend. When he isn't in my living room, he's in Katje's. He likes his job running clinical trials for a drug development company, or he'd just move. He's not ready to leave the area yet. So he finds a small studio to sublet. It's a basement apartment with a hot plate instead of a full kitchen. Katje and I drive down to help him retrieve his things. We all rent a U-Haul and head out to his old house in the Maryland 'burbs. It's a 1940s ranch with white vinyl siding. It's run-down, a physical manifestation of their marriage. The appliances are broken, and the kitchen is moldy. Kristi is gone. We pack up everything he says is his and then go check out the new place. Then we all go out to eat at a local Olive Garden. A cousin meets us, and we sink into a deep booth with a tall back and order an onion blossom and beers. The next day is Evan's thirtieth birthday.

THESE ARE GOOD TIMES. None of us has relationships figured out. We are all solo. We are all in search of something, and it's less lonely because we've got one another. I date. I go online, on OkCupid, which I come to call OkStupid, and post photos and descriptions of what I'm looking for. These first dates don't amount to much, because I'm not *really* looking for anything. Life feels so full, so rich. For once, I'm not lonely. I have my siblings and Heather to keep me company. I dissect these dates with them in chats that run down the side of my Gmail all day. They read like this:

> *me:* i don't remember anymore why i didn't dislike her
> *Evan:* did she annoy you?
> *Evan:* is she boring or creepie?
> *me:* no and no and no
> *me:* it's just that there are so many normal fine people in the world and so few people i grow to love

Evan: have you read All about Love
Evan: by bell hooks?
me: yes you gave it to me
Evan: she's all about it being some big cultural myth that love just happens
Evan: and it really being a choice

In her book on love, written in 2000, bell hooks argues that in our culture, we expect love to function like a drug, leading to an immediate, sustained high. "Genuine love is rarely an emotional space where needs are instantly gratified," she writes. To know love, we must invest time and commitment, but that is not in fact what we do: "Relationships are treated like Dixie cups. They are the same. They are disposable," she writes. "If it does not work, drop it, throw it away, get another."

Around now is when I begin to think that maybe I've been looking at romantic love the wrong way, searching for the wrong thing. I've spun through person after person, coffee date, evening concert, long walk. So many first dates, I could fill a year of my life with only these events. In each, I've been feeling around for something. A feeling, a moment of immediate recognition, an instinctive prod to the gut to alert me: This is The One. This is the Person who makes me feel different, alive, as though I want to inhabit the sum of us. Every few months, there is a One. I find The One, again and again. Only what I don't realize is that I have been pattern-matching, gravitating toward women who have, for their own reasons in the moments we've matched, been unable to meet me. The relationships end in one of two ways. Either these women reveal themselves to be unavailable, and the more this becomes true, the more I pine for them, re-creating the patterns of my childhood. Or they turn toward me, exposing their own vulnerability, and I'm uncomfortable. I don't have a playbook for this. It's unfamiliar. They don't make me feel the way I believe I'm meant to feel. In every situation, things end. I throw away my Dixie cup. I hit up OkStupid and look for a replacement.

THIRTY

Falling

Now I'm nearly thirty-seven. As I've become more senior at *Fortune*, the job has grown more demanding. I'm in Silicon Valley constantly, interviewing tech founders, and I co-chair *Fortune*'s annual technology conference in Aspen, Colorado. Back in Brooklyn, I'm close with my siblings, and I've found common ground with my parents. The emotional flu has stopped coming on; the panic attacks are receding. Is this what it means to be satisfied with your life? I've cultivated numerous single friends, each figuring out how to navigate this chapter of life—just before midlife but well after youth.

One overcast Sunday morning, I'm Skyping with a friend who lives abroad. He works on country rebuilding efforts, and it can be a solitary job. He's had to become skilled at spending time alone. Sunday mornings can be a little wistful for me; Saturdays involve decompressing from the grind of the week, but Sundays stretch out empty in front of me until I fill them. I can't shake that feeling that other people are busy with fuller lives, taking children to soccer practice or reading the paper over brunch, while I sit here on this couch, legs pulled up beneath me, waiting for the week to start again. Waiting. "I like being single," I tell him, "only I get lonely."

Lonely is a condition he knows well, a feeling he has had to strategize around. "Do you think that when you're not with people who love you, they're not loving you?" he asks.

"No, of course not," I say.

"Exactly," he says. And he tells me that whenever I feel lonely, I need to close my eyes and meditate on this. He suggests that I imagine each person who loves me putting a chair down in front of me and standing up on it, until the chairs crowd the room. Now, when I feel loneliness coming on, I sit on the couch, close my eyes, and begin to meditate until I can see all the people standing on chairs, all the love around me, and then I can feel it, too.

And still. Still there is this one area of my life that has atrophied, that remains gray. I don't have a partner. I haven't managed to maintain a relationship longer than three months in well over a decade. I don't really believe I ever will. It's as if that part of life is closed off and unavailable to me. Can I *have* a wife or kids? Do I *want* those things? I don't know the difference between these two questions, one expressing possibility and the other, desire. What is queer liberation if it's not a pathway to step outside the boundaries of heteronormative culture, to choose any partner, or partners, or to choose no partner at all? To define family on my own terms? I remember the freedom I felt when marching with COLAGE in the Gay Pride parade, tucked in among so many different constellations of kids and adults, claiming one another. I can claim anyone. But I've claimed no one.

At this point, the brief window in which all of us were single and available is shifting. Everyone is traveling in different directions. Katje is ensconced in a new relationship with a short, tattooed woman who is pragmatic and present in equal measure and never tries to control her. Evan is dating again and also planning a move to Boston so that he can be near our cousins. He wants to start a family and plans to do it on his own. He knows he needs to line up support. Having ended things with her boyfriend, Mom is planning a move to North Carolina. She's loved the South ever since we were little kids there, and this is her moment to test her independence. By the time she is there a year, she'll learn just how independent she can be and also that she's a northeasterner. She'll return. Dad meets Bruce on a brief layover at the Denver Airport; they strike up a correspondence and then start visiting each other. Within a year, Dad moves to Oregon to make a home with Bruce, and they plan a wedding.

And me. I'm being left again. Meditating on each one of them, standing on a chair in my living room. No one comes for me. Nothing changes for me—until it does.

THE FIRST TIME I SEE Frances, she's wearing cowboy boots, blue jeans, a thick tan belt, and a white V-neck T-shirt. She has long brown hair and bangs cut straight across her forehead. It's a cold Saturday afternoon in early January. She's gotten to the Museum of Modern Art before me, and she's standing there in the lobby, trying to figure out who I am. I don't know beforehand what she looks like, but I know immediately that she's who I'm looking for. It's the way she scans the crowd, also looking for a stranger. I pull off my hat, my long hair jumping up from the static so that I'm certain I look disheveled. Once I see her, I'm sure that this will be the only afternoon that we spend together. She's not my type. She's pretty in an easy sort of way, comfortable with herself in places I don't perceive myself to be.

Oh, well. Maybe we can still have fun.

We've been set up. A month earlier, I'd been having brunch with my friend Kate when, toward the end, she mentioned Frances. "She's really funny," Kate told me. "She's a social worker from Mississippi. I think she wants kids pretty soon."

"What makes you think we have anything in common?" I ask Kate. She knows that I'm uncertain about the South and certain about kids—or, rather, certain about not having them. When anyone asks me, I explain, "It's not my path in this lifetime." It sounds regal, as if I have it on a higher authority.

"Well," says Kate—and she demurs until I finally get it.

"This is the *other* gay person you know," I say. "Right?"

But then I agree to go out with Frances anyhow, because why not? I've decided to take a new approach to dating. What I've been doing for the past twenty years hasn't worked, so I'm going to do the opposite of whatever I *feel* like doing, as an experiment, to stress-test this new strategy.

It takes a month for me and Frances to sort out a time to meet up. It's the holidays, and Frances returns to Mississippi for a couple weeks. In Brooklyn, Heather and I host a Christmas Eve dinner for friends. On Christmas Day, I fly to Massachusetts for the day and have lunch with Mom. Just before the new year, Dad and Bruce get married in the back room of a French restaurant in Park Slope. We don't really know Bruce yet, but we like him. He's sensitive and genuinely interested in getting to know us. He was raised Mormon and came out when his own kids were tiny. They're a decade younger and appear to be very close to their father. Katje, Evan, and I host these new stepsiblings for New Year's Eve. It's so much family and company and celebration and a whole mix of feelings. I forget, in the midst of this, that I've made a plan to see Frances at all.

Then I get a calendar alert the following weekend: "Email Kate's friend." I drop Frances a note to see if she wants to go to the Degas exhibit. It's a low-stakes daytime date, a chance to see some art. I can always take in some French Impressionist work.

Now here we are, folding into throngs of people who are passing a frigid weekend among paintings. My heart flies into my chest as Frances begins to talk. Her voice is melodious, thick with a drawl that is particularly strong since she has just been back to see her family. The word "hey" has three syllables (he-AY-ee). Frances is mysterious to me. As we ride the escalators up to the sixth floor, she confesses to having been part of a sorority and to having *enjoyed* being part of that sorority. We walk so quickly through the rooms that I don't pause to look at the paintings. I'm self-conscious. I've worn a teal sweater that keeps riding up on my hips. Does she notice? She tells me about a secret society she was part of in college at the University of Virginia and then mentions that she was actually elected "king" of it. And this is when I'm certain that we won't see each other again. Because she's not just the kind of person who slides into social situations easily, but in fact the kind of person whom others like *best*.

But, still, it's fun to talk to her. I don't know a lot of people like her.

When we're done looking at the art, we want to keep hanging out. We cross the street and head down a block to a characterless steakhouse. Over a glass of rosé, she tells me about her massive family—brothers, cousins, aunts, uncles, and an older gentleman whom she calls Grandaddy. Almost all of them live in the small town where she grew up and to which she'll likely move back. This is how I know for sure that we won't be a match. Can you imagine me in Mississippi? But her questions are as insightful as her stories. I really do love talking to this woman. It's not like that breathless kind of OMG-love, just a sense that she's solid.

As we finish our wine, Frances tells me she needs to get her puppy home. I walk her to her car, and in the back is the cutest shepherd-collie mix with a pink stripe on her nose: Zoe. Zoe jumps up and licks my cheek, and I scratch her belly. But inside I'm thinking, now I know for triple sure that we won't go out again. A dog is a lot of responsibility in a city, and I'm not up for it. Frances gives me a hug and steps back. "I had a great time," she says.

"Me, too," I say. And since I'm now certain we have no long-term potential as a couple, I'm not even nervous when I drop her an email the next day. Absent the pressure of defining whether she might one day be The One, I am free to get to know her. If she's up for it, that is. Katje has gotten me a couple of tickets to a concert. Does she want to go?

FRANCES AND I BEGIN GOING out regularly. I don't want to get too attached, to move too quickly, to lose myself in the process. I don't want to let myself like her too much, to grow to depend on her. So I make lots of plans with lots of people and take good care of these other friendships. I insist Frances and I only see each other every other week or so. And I don't want to be exclusive. Also, my work travel schedule is grueling. I get out to the Bay Area at least twice a month, and I'm writing a story about the Utah tech scene. But this cadence seems just fine with Frances. Her stepdad is sick that spring, and she is also traveling a lot to visit him.

When we do hang out, we have consistent fun. We see movies, go to restaurants, plan adventures. She gets tickets to the Philharmonic and takes me to Lincoln Center. I ask if she wants to accompany me to the Tony Awards, where I've gotten tickets through work. But anytime I think beyond the spring, I can only see this relationship ending. Eventually we won't agree on where to live. Eventually she'll want to have those kids.

Am I falling in love with Frances? No, I'm not. I'm pretty sure I'm not. I write to my friend living abroad and tell him I like her okay, but I don't know where things are going. I don't feel starved for oxygen when I'm with her or as though I'm going to dry up without her. I don't worry about her changing her mind about us. Also, we never fight. There's nothing to fight about. Frances is easy about things. She's willing to entertain my whims, to shift plans. She's reliable, predictable.

This doesn't feel like anything I know to be love. We are layering shared experiences on top of each other. We are starting to be willing to be known by each other. But love?

EARLY IN OUR RELATIONSHIP, I attempt to break up with Frances. I know how special she is. My sister is her biggest champion. Heather also approves. Frances is sweet and pretty and so compassionate. If I don't feel by now that I'm consumed with her, I reason that I'm letting her down. She deserves someone who feels that way. She deserves someone to love her better than I'm doing, to think about her every minute. That's not me. I plan out how to tell her all week. I'm just not falling for her.

That weekend, Frances has planned to come to Brooklyn, and she's bringing Zoe. (I've grown to love this dog. She is a tight emotive ball of wiggle and slobber. Maybe I can offer to watch Zoe for Frances regularly afterward?) I decide to end things right when she arrives, but when I see her, I lose my nerve. I'll upset her. Maybe she'll get angry at me. Worse, maybe she'll tell me she doesn't like *me* all that much. We have plans to go to a friend's fortieth birthday party; why ruin a perfectly good weekend? I hold off.

The next day, we go to brunch with a couple of her friends. They're lovely, a lawyer and a theater director, and I wonder whether I can be friends with them even after Frances and I break up. When we get back to my place, she gathers her things to head home, and I can see my window closing. I launch into my breakup speech. I explain that Frances deserves to be loved, worshipped, adored, and I'm not sure how I feel. She listens. She doesn't cry or even look upset. When I'm done speaking, she's quiet for a long time before she says, "You go this way." She draws a squiggle in the air, up and down and up and down. "And you're used to choosing people who do that, too." She continues, "I go this way," and she draws a straight line that moves gradually up and to the right. "Right now, you're bored. You're looking to stir things up. But if you stick around, you're going to learn something new here."

This logic appeals to me. When she leaves, we're not broken up. We don't break up again.

THIRTY-ONE

Magic Penny

"Have you looked at Instagram?" Frances asks. Her question comes on a Tuesday evening as I let myself into the prewar apartment we share on the Upper West Side. The whole place smells like rosemary. Afternoon light filters through the tops of the trees that graze the windows in the living room. Frances is in the white galley kitchen, baking chicken for dinner. She's the director of a residential program for adolescents, and she's still dressed in her work clothes: a conservative maroon cotton skirt that falls to her ankles and a button-down sweater. I can tell she's being selective with her words. "Your father's been on it."

I pull out my phone and scroll through the images. My father has shared a set of portraits. The photos are taken in Joshua Tree, just outside Palm Springs, where he and Bruce are vacationing. Dad is maybe sixty-six, but he looks fifty-five. These days, he shaves his head to mask a bald spot. He has tattoo sleeves that hug his shoulder blades and travel down to his wrists, and a paunch of a belly that protrudes despite his best efforts to suppress it. In the photo, he stands behind my stepdad, who is thinner and slightly shorter, and who has the body of a man who does five hundred sit-ups every morning. They are photographed in the buff, from the waist up, Dad's finger suggestively resting inside Bruce's belly button. I scroll to the next photo, and my father is solo, shot from behind, crouched on a rock like a cat readying for a pounce. He is naked, except for a pair of gray Teva sandals (it's rocky in the desert). He glances back over his shoulder at the photographer with a come-hither expression.

If Dad wants to be naked on the internet, that's fine by me. He's a guy who didn't come out until he was fifty years old. For most of his life he felt he had had to lie about who he was, to himself and to everyone else. What I want most for my dad is his complete freedom to be who he is, to represent himself the way he wants to.

But this is where it gets complicated. In practice, I'm uncomfortable. My dad is a social media devotee. He documents his extravagant vacations and his gardening victories. When he wins a dollar at gay bingo, he posts a smiling selfie. And he's an aggressive friender, making the digital connection to nearly everyone—and certainly every guy—I've ever introduced him to. We have sixty-eight friends in common on Facebook. They include the guy I babysat for in college, a massage therapist we've both briefly seen, Frances's childhood friend Justin, and my mother-in-law.

Which is to say that *everyone else* I know can also see these photos.

These moments happen often enough in my family that Katje, Evan, and I have a standard protocol: When an issue comes up with either of our parents, we jump on the phone to hash it out. I text our group chat, a closed trio of phone numbers that carries the title "Magic Penny": "Have you seen the photos?" When neither Katje nor Evan knows what I'm talking about, I flop on my stomach on our bed and initiate a siblings' conference call. Frances pops into the room and paces the length of the window. I patch Katje and Evan both in, along with their spouses, and we put our phones on speaker, so that all six of us can weigh in. But Katje can't see the photos, and neither can Evan. It has to do with their settings or something.

I have replayed the three minutes that follow in my head so many times, hoping that if I can scrutinize it enough, I can somehow undo it. The facts are these: I ask Frances to please screenshot the photos and send them to Katje and Evan. Frances captures the images, thumbs my siblings' names into the "to" line on her iPhone, and then hits send. But

Apple's autocorrect is too good. It senses she is sending a message to my family and suspects she has forgotten to include everyone. Just as the loud *swoosh* sound indicates the message has been sent, Frances looks down at her phone and realizes she has sent the naked photos of my dad and his husband to everyone in the family, now including my mom. His ex-wife.

Let me just say that again: Frances sent naked photos of Dad to Mom.

"Shit," I say.

"Shit," says Katje, and then Evan, too. "Shit." I hang up on them before we can even articulate what has happened.

Time slows down as Frances begins to scroll through settings on her device in an attempt to retract the message. It's impossible. I call Mom to tell her not to open the text, but it's too late. She is hysterical. "Why is Frances sending me nudie photos of your dad?" she asks.

"That was me, I did it!" I say. "I was using Frances's phone!" It's a weak attempt to cover for Frances, who now looks like she may be sick in the bathroom.

"Why are *you* sending me these photos?!" Mom asks. This is an entirely fair question. I try to explain it was an accident, but she doesn't understand. She doesn't understand why I have them at all. She is certain that Dad has sent us the photos directly.

"Mom," I explain, "he posted them on Instagram. They weren't sent to us privately." As soon as I say it, I can tell that my comment, intended to make her feel better, actually makes things much worse. The man that my mother married in 1973, a son of a preacher with ambitions to become a lawyer and raise children in the Boston suburbs, was not someone who would have flaunted his butt cheeks on social media. The three children they brought into the world were raised in the church and pushed to succeed in school. We were discouraged from watching *Roseanne* as children because my parents felt it didn't represent good family values. Whatever happened to family values?

SOMEONE TALKS TO DAD. He explains that a good friend and neighbor has taken these photos as part of a fine arts project. Dad believes they're tasteful, beautiful. Indeed, the landscape in the background is as much a character in the photos as my father. But he edits the photos.

We all talk to Mom. Over the next few days, we each call her a couple of times. We assure her we're okay, which is the thing she most wants to know. None of us tells Dad what happens with the text message. We've learned that sometimes it's just better to let things lie.

Frances cannot stomach the size of the fireball she has accidentally unleashed in my family. She doesn't sleep that night. She wakes up at four a.m., worrying about it. It's okay, I say, we're okay. By the next day, Katje and Evan are ready to poke fun at her. Evan calls and tells me to put him on speaker. "Hey, guys, I'm going to send over some more photos of Dad, from the holidays last year." He's kidding here. "Frances, do you mind not sending them to Mom?"

Frances breaks into tears. She's crying so hard that Evan pauses and asks, "Too soon?"

MOM GETS OVER THIS, but she is still so angry. We have all found our way in life, even Mom, and still, she tends this anger, vacillating between shoving it down and lashing out. It's an anger she harbors even though in almost every way, she is happy in her life. At the end of our conversations for The Project, I push her to articulate why she is angry at Dad. They have been divorced now for twenty years. "I was just a cover for his inability to come out," she says. And now she is really getting to it. "And I understand the seventies were a difficult time. And he had a pastor for a father and the mother that he had. I get all of that, and I can be compassionate and feel bad for him. But somehow the trump card is in my hand," she says, and now she is crying a little bit. "Because even with my pets, I wish I had a partner to grow old with like my mom and dad had. That's what I wish. It's not the same."

She's right. It's not the same.

We all start off with ideas about our lives. For some people, those ideas are on course with what life delivers. But for most of us, the only path to freedom and happiness is letting go of those ideas. We have to ditch Plan A. We have to go with Plan B. My mom's Plan B is awesome. But there are feelings she wants and ways she can imagine she'd have these feelings if she also had a partner.

Even so, as I talk to her, I don't understand why the burden of these unfulfilled desires should belong only to my dad. It's clear to me that he went into their marriage with the expectation and desire that he would fulfill his obligations as a husband, that he would live a version of life that they had agreed on. "Yeah, but you also married him," I tell her. "He married you in good faith, because he thought he was in love with you." I'm working this over in my mind now. "It's easy to think, coming out, that everything before coming out was a sham, but that's not really how it is," I say. I remind her that they had several years of shared interests and of a happy marriage.

The problem with a "coming out" story as the punctuation to a marriage is that it lets both a husband and a wife off easy. What has happened is clear. The spouse who is coming out was living a lie and must now live a truth, and so they must separate. But people exist on a continuum of truth and self-discovery over the course of their lives. When my parents were young, they liked each other. They had adventures. They had three children, all of whom—despite the conflicts that have arisen here and there—delight them. By the time they divorced, their marriage served neither of them. There was no softness between them. Was it because Dad is gay? Or was it because the things they wanted even then in their lives were too different, and their ways of showing up for each other weren't recognizable to each other?

My mom tells me what she wanted in a husband. She wanted her father, a low-key jokester and high school teacher who was usually home in time for dinner. Instead, she got my father, a flamboyant intellect who came out and left her.

"You don't have to be angry at him for not having the things you want in your life now," I tell her. "Because the truth of it is, you don't want him." Now Mom is saying, somewhat dismissively, "Yup, yup, yup." I don't know why I think I can explain her out of her feelings, but I continue to try.

Mom listens, and then she's quiet for a long time, and I finally shut up, too. When she talks again, she articulates what the real impact of this marriage has been on her: "I don't think I could find anybody at this point. Because I have a substantial distaste for guys, a distrust."

Loss will do that to you. It'll destroy your confidence in world order. It'll break you. I am reminded of the friend who wrote to me after someone I love died. I was trying to figure out how to go on, how to love people who could disappear so quickly and unexpectedly, to allow all of the big feelings around me, both pleasant and uncomfortable, to find their way to my surface. My friend noted that the first major challenge in our lives is learning to feel love. We must strip away so much of what we're taught in order to connect deeply to love. But then just as we figure it out, we reach the middle of our lives, when the challenge shifts: we spend the rest of our time learning to love through loss.

THIRTY-TWO

You Will Make Mistakes

I find the barn on Airbnb. The listing says it's seven miles outside of New Paltz, just more than an hour's drive from the Upper West Side. It's an unseasonably warm September in 2017, and Frances and I have a weekend to kill as we wait for the renovations on our new Upper West Side apartment to be done, so we decide to go hiking. The dog loves to get out of the city.

The barn is in the backyard of a farmhouse, set back from the road on five acres. It has a small woodstove, a well-appointed kitchen, a claw-foot tub, and shabby-chic chandeliers that hang down over white linen bedding. The whole weekend plan qualifies as an experience, rather like upscale glamping. As a bonus, our host offers her services as a healer. She has a practice as an intuitive reader.

This invitation arrives at a time when neither of us is looking to be healed from anything in particular. Things are going well. I'm now writing for *Wired*, and Frances directs an early childhood learning program. We both like our jobs. Sure, we haven't gotten clarity about how much time we'll spend in Mississippi, where Frances always thought she'd settle. Our future goals are no more aligned than they were that first day we took in the Degas exhibit at MoMA. But we've been living in the present for weeks and months, and those months have turned into five years. Our new little one-bedroom apartment has delivered us a thirty-year mortgage, and beyond anything else we've done, it feels like commitment. We are committed.

Still, we take this woman up on her offer. Why not?

The next morning, while Frances sleeps in, I down a coffee, then knock on our host's side screen door. She has long gray-blonde hair and wears a billowy floral skirt. Crystals hang in her kitchen, which smells faintly of apples. Maybe muffins? She shows me back to an atrium with a foldout massage table. I hoist myself up on it and lie down on my back, and she performs a ritual she calls sonic healing. It involves bells, drums, rocks, and her own throaty singing, and I don't know whether I feel so relaxed because of what she's doing or because I don't have to do anything. She runs stones down my body and puts her hands on my head. Then she tells me that she sees a book in my future. I'll write it. It's about women, she says. No, it's *for* women. This feels interesting to me. I'm a technology writer, and most of my readers are men, but okay. I could see this.

Just as we're finishing up, Frances pokes her head in our host's back door. Zoe pushes past her ankles and into the kitchen, and I grab for her leash, flustered, apologizing. The woman's cat hisses. But the woman doesn't seem to mind the intrusion. I take Zoe into the field behind the barn and throw the ball for her while Frances, who is, by her own account, an atypical candidate for an intuitive reading, spends an hour with our host, allowing her auras to be decoded. When Frances emerges, she looks younger. She has a lighter energy. "What did you learn?" I ask her. Her boots crunch through the dry grass toward us.

"It's time for me to get pregnant," she says. *Huh?* My heart drops. Zoe pushes the ball in my direction, nudges me, but I don't pick it up.

"Did she tell you that?" I say.

"Tell me I'm supposed to get pregnant?" says Frances. "No. It's just that I heard myself as I was talking to her. It's something that I've always wanted, and then I just knew, now is the right time."

I'm a person who always looked to others for answers, who sought out religious figures, was susceptible to cults, and trusted adults and mediums and astrologists. Frances has always sought those answers for herself. So of course she reflected on her session and understood what she needed, and it had nothing to do with the sonic healing.

This healer annoys me. I don't care about my future book-writing ambitions anymore, and I'm annoyed that we thought to come to this barn in the first place.

I've always known this moment would come. I've dreaded it. By this point, I've internalized this belief that I won't have kids. It's not even about my own desire. I believe it cannot happen—like, even if I were to tell Frances that we could move forward, things would unfold badly. Either we wouldn't get pregnant, or we would, and the result would be tragic. Or we'd have a kid and I'd be awful at it, a bad resentful parent. This is a belief to which I cling. It's not that I'm choosing whether to have kids, but that I'm not meant to have kids. So now we have to break up.

I don't tell Frances any of this right away. Instead, I become sullen. We load Zoe into the car and head over to a popular hiking path. We follow a dusty fire road down into a dry, rocky creek bottom. There is no wind, not even a breeze, and the still air cloaks us with the smell of oak trees. I've stopped talking, and it doesn't take long for Frances to notice this, but she doesn't respond at first. Zoe is prancing through the backwoods and then circling back to herd the two of us along our trail.

"Are you going to talk?" says Frances.

"We haven't gotten anything figured out," I say.

"I don't think we're going to figure things out more," she says.

"Okay," I say. It's a soft word, almost swallowing itself.

"Okay?" she says. But what she's asking is for me to commit to a future I can't fully control and to agree to something that runs counter to my sense of self. She's asking me to change. Or maybe, more accurately, I can feel myself changing. What if my conviction that I won't have kids, seeded in me by a medium a decade earlier, is wrong? What if it doesn't have to look like what I think it looks like?

"Okay," I say, and I'm not agreeing to be a parent. I'm just agreeing to take the next step.

BY NOW, BOTH EVAN AND Katje have children. Neither of them ever questioned whether they wanted kids, only when and how. This question involved timing and faith in equal measure. For each of them, getting pregnant took many years.

Katje and her wife, Andy, began to try for kids shortly after they were married. They'd just moved to Portland, where they'd bought a house with the perfect room for a nursery. They always figured Katje would carry the baby. Andy was more androgenous in presentation and mindset. But in the process, after too many disappointing pregnancy tests to count, Katje was diagnosed with Graves' disease, an immune system disorder that results in hyperthyroidism. While she was getting it managed, they decided Andy would try to carry. Although they considered themselves lucky that this option was available to them, it caused each of them to question their identities all over again.

For Evan, kids were always the best outcome of his adulthood, the highest possible expression of his humanity. Not long after his marriage ended, he decided he was ready for parenthood. At the time, he was a single trans guy and realistic about the fact that birth moms in search of adoptive parents would be unlikely to pick him. Adoption wasn't going to work out. If he wanted a child, he'd have to make one on his own.

Evan knew this was possible biologically, but he didn't have a lot of examples. In 2013, when he first made an appointment with his primary care physician at Boston's LGBT health center Fenway, Evan was the first prospective birth father the doctor had seen. Evan's best resource for community with other trans birth fathers was a closed Facebook group, "Birthing and Breast or Chestfeeding Trans People and Allies," which had around 1,500 members globally back then. That's where people recommended trans-friendly doctors, discussed chestfeeding challenges, and "liked" one another's belly photos.

Even though there weren't many men getting pregnant in Boston, Evan got great medical care. His doctor referred him to a fertility clinic where, Evan remembers, the medical professionals almost never screwed up his pronouns, even while doing regular intravaginal ultrasounds. He's still impressed by this. "They were managing a huge amount of cognitive dissonance," he says now. Medical insurance was trickier—because he was a man, all reproductive procedures were considered elective, and the expenses added up. He spent too much of his spare time on the phone with his insurer, arguing, until he finally gave up and registered as female with his health insurance. He reasoned that it was most expedient.

With medical supervision, Evan's body cooperated. It took about three months for him to begin cycling once he stopped his T shots. His doctor prescribed medications to help with stimulating egg growth in Evan's ovaries and triggering ovulation, and monitored his body to get the timing right. Evan worked with a donor he'd met through a free sperm donor matching service. The first time his pee stick came up pink, he called all of us immediately. Six weeks later, he miscarried. It was painful but, his doctor assured Evan, ordinary. One in four pregnancies end in miscarriage. He didn't wait long before trying again. This time the pregnancy stuck. He was in a new relationship by then with a kind-hearted woman whom we all loved named Keku'i. He'd been up front that he was trying to get pregnant, and by the time he got this news, they'd decided to coparent. He called her from his office to tell her. What he most remembers is her happy squeal—so loud that he covered the phone with his hand as he thought, *This is really happening.*

WHEN EVAN FIRST TELLS US he's pregnant, Mom starts hugging everyone. We're getting ready for Thanksgiving at a house we've rented in the Berkshires, and he's got morning sickness. He's lost a ton of weight, and he won't eat anything but the popsicles Keku'i supplies for him continuously. Mom has pretty much given up on becoming a grandmother by this point, and just the idea of a baby causes her to start pulling up knitting patterns on Google. "Is it a girl or a boy?" she asks.

"I dunno, Mom," Evan says. "We probably won't know for twelve years or so."

Mom stares at him, trying to figure out how to respond, before I jump in, "Mom, he's *teasing* you."

A few months into the pregnancy, he calls to tell me he wants to share his pregnancy story. He's been contacted by a film crew who want to follow him—also a reporter who wants to interview him. What do I think? "You're in luck because I know a writer," I tell him. "If you want to tell your story, let me help you." Every other week at an appointed time, I turn on the tape recorder, call him, and listen. This is when I learn how powerful it can be to interview the people we think we know best. These interviews become the precursor to The Project.

Evan goes into labor hours before his due date. He and his partner arrive at the hospital just after midnight. He remembers the nurse who passes them as they walk in, how she stares a little bit too long, confused by the two of them. There's the mom, weighted down with a suitcase, a backpack, and their paperwork folder. The dad carries nothing but the purple yoga birthing ball, and every few steps, he pushes it up against the wall, leans over it, and moans. Hours later, a photo of a shriveled, perfect baby face pops up on my phone. "I'm not sure he's mine," Evan texts. "I've never been on time to anything in my life."

His story is published in the September 2016 issue of *TIME*. In it, he poses for a photograph in which he is chestfeeding, his grizzly beard growing out. It's powerful. The response is overwhelming. We're approached by reporters from CNN and BBC, we're cold-called by newspaper journalists, and it all makes both of us nervous. We decline interviews. People can be so unpredictable. But very quickly, supportive notes begin to arrive. Medical school directors invite us to speak. A trans birth father writes to say that normally he hates everything cisgendered people write, but he "really loved this." A few days later, a man in a Red Sox cap approaches Evan in a park. "Aren't you the guy from the magazine?" the man asks, elongating his *a*'s and adding *r*'s in unexpected places the way Bostonians do. My brother pauses, using his arm to shield his son who is tucked into a sling on his chest. He tries to assess the guy's motives. But then the stranger congratulates Evan and suggests they get their kids together. My brother relaxes.

Evan's son is nine months old when Katje's wife gives birth to their daughter. Evan flies to Portland with the baby to spend a week washing bottles, putting together nursery furniture, and holding his tiny niece while her parents sleep. In fact and form, these infants are opposites: His is a bowling ball of a baby boy with chunks for thighs and an unending desire to chestfeed. Hers is miniature girl with old-man arms and legs, and she's possessed of an early FOMO that keeps her from falling asleep, staying asleep, or returning to sleep once she has awakened. Even so, they share something in common: their existence has changed both Katje and Evan. My siblings are no longer the main characters of their lives.

THERE ARE SO MANY STEPS to creating a family, and I expect that it'll take years, as it has for my siblings. But once Frances and I start the process, like a Rube Goldberg machine it begins to run itself. Frances begins to monitor her ovulation cycle. We school up on her health insurance and look into the local fertility clinics. We choose a donor from an online digital catalog. There are so many options, and we're lost in profiles of nice enough men, reviewing their educational backgrounds and medical health histories and whether they played sports or had hobbies as children. Then we pay a little extra so that we can hear short interviews with each man. It's immediately clarifying. Donor after donor sounds like a stranger, until one donor sounds familiar. Why? I still have no idea. We purchase eight vials of his sperm.

The closer we get to our first attempt at insemination, the more un-comfortable I become. I have started to imagine this future for us, to see the towheaded child (always towheaded in my mind) who will look to us to explain infinity. Will I understand what they want? Will I even no-tice? This is the definition of ambivalence—not that I'm lukewarm, but that I am holding contradictory feelings. I want this! At the same time, I'm afraid to want this! Because what if it doesn't happen? Or scarier: What if it does, and it goes badly?

Would I be a good mother?

Then I know how to resolve the ambivalence. I write to Ellen Meyers.

She's retired now and fighting cancer. It's been a long fight, but the disease is starting to get more serious, and that has made her double down on the people she cares about most. Since my nephew was born, we've been in much more frequent touch. Usually we call or email, but the request I have to make of her feels formal. Early one morning in November, I pull out a card and write her a letter. I explain that we're thinking about having a baby, but I'm really not sure. I'm so nervous. I'm sitting with all of this, and I'm realizing it's not that I'm nervous about the pregnancy. It's what happens afterward. All of these years have gone by, and still I carry my own childhood with me. I carry the weight of my struggles with my family, the ways in which their unhappiness was a poison. And it seems safer not to risk losing the homeostasis in which I find myself. Things are fine now! We have this dog we love, this peaceful life. We have new kitchen appliances. "El," I ask her, "am I capable of this?"

Six days later, El's response arrives by mail. "My darling Jessi," she writes, "you are not your family. You are your own person. You will make a wonderful mother, and you will make mistakes along the way. But you have done the work now. This is your story to write."

THERE ARE FEW THINGS LESS sexy or romantic than working with a fertility clinic to create a pregnancy. On a chill-to-the-bone Saturday morning in January, Frances' ovulation test tells us circumstances are right. To be honest, we aren't expecting things to work this early in the process. We are prepared to be patient. So the pressure is off. We show up at the clinic in midtown, and the security guard rings us up to the sixth floor. Our regular doctor isn't in, but an older gentleman with a great sense of humor is on hand to complete the insemination. We sit in the waiting area until we're called back. The procedure takes less than five minutes. Frances doesn't even feel it.

"That's it?" I ask the doctor.

"Pretty much," he says.

"Should we, like, hang out here for a while and stay horizontal?" I ask, and Frances rolls her eyes at me. She knows the answer. It really doesn't matter. The pregnancy will take, or it won't, regardless. We're out on the sidewalk by eight thirty that morning. Does she look any different to me? It's icy out, and there's snow on the ground. We wander up Fifth Avenue toward the twin lions of New York's grand Public Library, stroll through the main reading hall and use the public bathrooms, and then go shopping.

A COUPLE OF WEEKS LATER, I'm at work, sitting in a cavernous office with no furniture on the twenty-sixth floor of One World Trade Center. This room used to be the office of *Wired*'s editor in chief, but now it's empty because the parent company, Condé Nast, is downsizing and will probably sublet this space soon. I drag a chair from my cubicle to hide out here when I'm on deadline and I really need to focus. I'm writing a feature about Uber, and I keep getting lost in my thoughts and looking up and out the window, directly into the windows of the tremendous midcentury skyscraper next door. My cell rings, and I know it's the call for which I've been waiting. I pick up; it's Frances. "Where are you right now?" she asks. "Look around, because you're going to remember it for a long time." She's just received the blood work from the doctor: she's pregnant. I suck in my breath sharply. We go over the details, try to guess at the due date. "Let's not tell anyone yet," she says. *Let's just let this be ours for a minute.*

After I hang up the phone, I look out the window, beyond the neighboring skyscraper, north, to the glass building in Tribeca that looks like a Jenga game, always a minute away from toppling. It appears that it could fall over, but of course it won't. It's architecturally sound. I think regretfully about the one-bedroom apartment we have just bought. I think about how little we know about what's ahead of us, how the only thing we can do is commit to the present, to confronting our truths as they emerge, to each other.

Conclusion

Two decades ago, in the space of five years, everyone in my family came out. All of us. In our own way, we each figured out how to give voice to our truest nature, but that was only the beginning. From there, we figured out how to accept one another. This could come only from accepting ourselves.

Although our sexuality certainly played a role in this, the more I live in the world, the more I come to understand that everyone has a closet. We are born out of sync with external reality as we all perceive it. None of us fits in. My parents were taught that this was their fault. Their differences were reasons for shame, aspects of themselves that must be hidden. Even at eight, Dad understood he needed to remove his sister's petticoat if his own parents walked by his bedroom. Even at eighteen, Mom believed that her crush on a man who turned out to be threatening was her fault, and she needed to hide it. They stuffed these aspects of themselves so deeply away that they didn't understand they were living out of sync with their true natures. They believed they were following the rules. This is what it means to live in the closet.

When I began The Project, I thought I was looking for a way to stitch together a common narrative, one story on which all five of us could agree: this is the story of our family. But what I discovered is that there is no one story. There are only unreliable shadows of memories, hardened by our biases and our emotions. Had we not come out, we would have been lost to one another. Having survived the hardest edges of our early years, we'd likely seek refuge in others. In this way, we'd also be lost to ourselves.

But, yes, a significant way that I came out of a closet and into alignment with myself involved coming to terms with my sexuality. This is true for my siblings and my father as well. Being queer, and reckoning with that queerness, forced us to do the work that many people never get around to doing, to engage deeply in the process of self-actualization. Being queer has given us community beyond our family, a group of people who experienced rejection of varying sorts and leaned into one another as a result. And, in the end, it has given us our family back. We began to find one another when we found ourselves.

What happened to us?

IN THE SUMMER OF 2021, when the adults are all vaccinated against COVID-19 and we finally feel comfortable traveling again, we plan a huge family trip. It's been eighteen months since we were together, and in that time, all three of us siblings have had another child. So many babies we haven't met! With her Graves' under control, Katje finally carried her son. He was born just four weeks before Evan's second son. At just five months old, our daughter is the youngest.

Mom joins our families for a few days near Mount Hood in Oregon. She took advantage of the pandemic to get in shape, walking a mile every day. She's thinner than I remember, and she has a renewed energy reserve. We rent a huge ski-chalet house, well situated for hiking in the off-season, and take the kids out on short adventures every day. As we hike the pine-needle-strewn path to Little Zigzag falls, Mom is up in front with the three eldest grandkids, who are now two, four, and five. At seventy, Mom still hasn't fully gone gray, and her hair hangs in a short braid. She wears a navy T-shirt emblazoned with the slogan "Practice Radical Empathy." I look at her and see myself. I always have. We have the same geometry to our faces, and this similarity grows stronger as we age. She stops to sit on a tree trunk, her legs straddling it, and I feel in my body this warmth, this gratitude. This feeling I never would have expected when I was younger: I hope that at seventy, my life looks like hers in this way. That I am healthy, strong, sitting in a beautiful place in the company of my family.

Later in the week, Evan and I bring our families down to visit Dad and Bruce. We take their dog for a walk on the beach. Bruce helps the kids feed the fish in their koi pond, and Dad teaches Jude how to pick a carrot the size of his arm. After Jude has gone to bed one evening, while Evan puts his kids down, Frances and I are hanging out in the den. Our baby, Camille, isn't a sleeper, and Bruce has her on his shoulder, singing to her as he sways around the room. Dad sinks into the sofa and asks how The Project is going. Is it written yet? "Oh, I'm writing about the Instagram thing," I say.

"What's that?" he asks. And I realize none of us has ever told him.

I look at Frances for permission, and she rolls her eyes and nods. "He's going to read it anyhow," she says. So I tell Dad about the time Frances sent the photos to Mom by accident. Now he's laughing. Bruce is cracking up, too. It's uproarious laughter, and Bruce hands the baby back and sits down next to Dad, pulling his feet up on the couch and collapsing with guffaws.

"I was mortified, horrified," Frances admits, and this makes both of the dads cackle harder, thinking about her slip. And finally, Frances can laugh about it, too. As laughter sometimes does, it expands until we are all in stitches.

TOWARD THE END OF THE Project, I get a text from Evan. He's been reading sections of this story in spurts, waiting in the school carpool line or rocking a baby late at night. "You start by talking about secrets our parents are keeping, and here we are as adults with our own secrets from each other," he writes. We've been talking about how there are many things that don't make it into this story. Plus, it's uniquely my perspective. If any of the others had written it, it would be different. And partly, that's because there are lots of things we don't disclose to one another. But Evan argues that these things are not the same as the secrets of our parents' generation.

His text reads: "They are fundamentally different because they are not secrets from ourselves."

When I was a child, I believed there were things I couldn't reveal about myself, things that made me despicable, unlovable. These were notions I inherited from my own parents, who had embodied these beliefs without understanding where they came from. Deep self-knowledge wasn't a mainstay of our culture. Nobody taught me to listen honestly to others. No one taught me to listen well to myself.

I came of age in a culture that was breaking open. The more freedom of expression was embraced, the more freedom we were given to express.

I call Evan, and he's in the car, commuting to work. We pick up the conversation, and the point he makes is sound. We will have secrets, too. Our secrets will leave their own tracks, but we'll have to leave it to our kids to navigate those tracks as they grow. The gift we give them is to model the searching. "This is evolution," says Evan. "And I think we had a better chance at emotional presence and being true to ourselves than our parents did. Our kids will have a better chance of it than we could ever conceptualize."

My hope is that our children will always be moving closer to the most authentic version of themselves, closer to knowing and loving one another—that they will always be coming out.

Acknowledgments

This book owes its existence to many people who made time, offered help and advice, and cheered these words along. Thanks, first, to Suzanne Gluck at William Morris Endeavor, who saw this story and then waited for me to be ready to see it too. And thanks also to WME's Fiona Baird, Caitlin Mahoney, and Elizabeth Wachtel, all of whom have played a part in its launch. Thanks to Rakesh Satyal at HarperOne, who found it and me. Thanks to everyone at HarperCollins, especially Judith Curr, Laina Adler, Gideon Weil, David Wienir, Paul Olsewski, Sarah Schoof, Aly Mostel, Ann Edwards, Adrian Morgan, Lisa Zuniga, Terri Leonard, Yvonne Chan, Maya Alpert, and Ryan Amato.

Thanks to Stephanie Hitchcock for the lunch and advice. Thanks to the many readers of early proposals, especially Matthew Swanson, Leena Rao, Rocky Miskelly, James Moed, and Andrew Stern. Thanks to Clare Burson, Kyle Ranson-Walsh, Jen Reingold, Sabrina Tom, and Candy Feit for reading early chapters.

Thanks to Sarah Storm, Dan Roth, George Anders, Beth Kutscher, and everyone at LinkedIn who championed my creative exploration. Thanks to Christine Han for gifting your photographs. Thanks to the Hello Monday Office Hours crew for always showing up, for me and for others.

Thanks to David and Pamela Hornik for loaning me the glass house when I needed a writing refuge, and for leaving plenty of food in the fridge.

Thanks to Camille and Crofton Sloan for taking us all in for several months during the pandemic, and helping watch the kids so I could work and write. Thanks, too, to Sheryl Richardson for childcare. Nothing would be possible without you all.

Thanks to Steven Levy for taking me seriously as a writer from the start, and always seeing this. I am a better writer because of your edits, and a better person because of your friendship.

Thanks to Abbie Goldberg, who has spent more than two decades researching LGBTQ families and took the time to talk with me. Thanks to everyone who came out before me, and fought for the legal protections my family now enjoys.

Thanks to Patti Geier for nine years of Thursday mornings.

Thanks to Robin Rice for embodying the magic.

Thanks to Ellen Meyers; your memory is a blessing. Thanks to all of the Rowleys, especially Heather, for expanding my definition of family, and stepping in when I needed you most. I promise to pay your generosity forward.

Mom, Dad, Katje, and Evan: The Project begins and ends with you. I offer you my profound gratitude for being willing to step into my narrative and trust me with your own memories, hopes, and regrets. Keku'i, Andy, and Bruce, thanks for allowing this story, and our lives, to include you too.

Shortly after I began the proposal for this book, Frances and I had twins, Jude and Aster. Aster was stillborn. He isn't mentioned in this story, but he is a part of it. The promise of his life, and the sorrow at his loss, shaped me in ways that allowed me to understand my own parents better. His presence is everywhere.

Finally, thanks to Frances, Jude, and Camille. You three are the light and the inspiration in all things.

About the Author

Jessi Hempel is host of the award-winning podcast *Hello Monday*, and a senior editor-at-large at LinkedIn. For nearly two decades, she has been writing and editing features and cover stories about work, life, and meaning in the digital age. She has appeared on CNN, PBS, MSNBC, Fox, and CNBC, addressing the culture and business of technology. Hempel is a graduate of Brown University and received a master's in journalism from the University of California, Berkeley. She lives in Brooklyn.